THOMAS CHALMERS

THOMAS CHALMERS

BY

ALEXANDER (SANDY) FINLAYSON

EP BOOKS
Pistyll Hall, Pistyll, Holywell, UK, CH8 7SH

www.epbooks.org
sales@epbooks.org

EP BOOKS are distributed in the USA by:
JPL Fulfillment
3741 Linden Avenue Southeast,
Grand Rapids, MI 49548.

E-mail: sales@jplfulfillment.com
Tel: 877.683.6935

First EP Books edition published 2015

ISBN: 978–1–78397–072–8

British Library Cataloguing in Publication Data available

For Linda

TABLE OF CONTENTS

Introduction and Acknowledgements

In 1996, my family and I visited Scotland for the first time. I was there to attend the General Assembly of the Free Church of Scotland. When we arrived in Edinburgh, we decided to take a bus tour of the city so as to orient ourselves to our surroundings. The bus drove past all the important buildings, including St Giles' Cathedral and John Knox's house. As we passed these buildings, the young tour guide seemed quite pleased to be able to tell us that John Knox was the man most responsible in all of Scotland's history for religious intolerance and the subjugation of women. Needless to say, I was a little surprised at her level of historical analysis, but I kept quiet.

When the bus drove along George Street, I spotted the statue of Thomas Chalmers. As someone who had come to faith in the Free Church of Scotland, I knew enough about him to know that he had played a fairly significant role in Scottish church history. Somewhat mischievously, I decided to find out whether our tour guide had an opinion on Chalmers. So I asked her, 'Who was Thomas Chalmers?' To which she replied, 'Oh, just some dead white guy.' This astonishing ignorance of one of Scotland's most influential leaders has stayed with me, and so I hope that this small book will go some way to answering the question: who was Thomas Chalmers and what can we learn from him?

There are a number of people I have to thank who have made this book possible.

I am grateful to the Board of Trustees of Westminster Theological Seminary for their generous allowance of a semester of leave in 2013, when the book was written. I am also very grateful to the staff of the Montgomery Library: Grace Mullen, Marsha Blake, Donna Campbell and Karla Grafton. They have taken a lively interest in the book, have helped me track down elusive historical facts and have kept the Library running very smoothly during my absence.

A number of other people have provided help and encouragement during the writing of this book. The Rev. Dr Iain D. Campbell, minister of Point Free Church of Scotland, the Rev. Angus Howat, moderator of the Free Church of Scotland in 2013 and the Rev. Dr A. Donald Macleod, Research Professor of Church History at Tyndale Seminary in Toronto have read the manuscript and provided helpful insights. My colleague at Westminster and pastor at Cornerstone Presbyterian Church, the Rev. Dr Carl R. Trueman, also provided encouragement as the book took shape. Many friends at Cornerstone have taken a real interest in my Chalmers project and I want to thank each of them for asking me for updates and praying for my writing efforts.

Finally, I would like to express my gratitude to my wife Linda and my colleague Marsha Blake, for reading and editing the manuscript. Their contributions have made the book much better than it otherwise would have been, but I remain wholly responsible for the opinions expressed and for the blemishes that remain.

Thomas Chalmers is affectionately dedicated to my wife Linda. I have been blessed with a loving partner in life who, as well as being my wonderful wife, is also my best friend.

CHRONOLOGY

1603	King James VI of Scotland becomes King of England
1638	National Covenant is drafted
1707	*Act of Union* unites the English and Scottish Parliaments.
June 1723	Economist and philosopher Adam Smith is born
January 1736	Inventor of the steam engine James Watt is born
1746	Battle of Culloden
1754	Seven Years War begins
August 1771	Sir Walter Scott is born
1776	American Declaration of Independence

1776	James Watt invents the steam engine
17 March 1780	Thomas Chalmers is born
1789	French Revolution
1791	Chalmers begins studies at St Andrews University
November 1795	Chalmers begins divinity studies
December 1795	Writer and philosopher Thomas Carlyle is born
31 July 1799	Chalmers is licensed to preach.
25 August 1799	Chalmers preaches his first sermon at Chapel Lane Chapel in Wigan, England
December 1801	Chalmers becomes assistant minister in the parish of Cavers
May 1802	Chalmers secures the Kilmany parish appointment as well as an assistant lectureship in mathematics at St Andrews
18 May 1803	Chalmers is ordained as minister of the parish of Kilmany
December 1807	Chalmers publishes his first book: *Enquiry*

	into the Extent and Stability of National Resources
June 1809	Chalmers is very ill with consumption
Winter 1810	Chalmers undergoes an evangelical conversion
August 1812	Chalmers marries Grace Pratt
25 Nov. 1814	Chalmers is elected minister of St Mary's Tron parish in Glasgow
June 1815	Battle of Waterloo
Summer 1815	Chalmers moves to Glasgow
November 1815	Systematic visitation of the Tron parish begins
November 1815 –October 1816	*Astronomical Discourses* are preached
21 February 1816	Degree of Doctor of Divinity is conferred by the University of Glasgow
December 1816	Parish Sunday school society is established
1817	*The Scotsman* newspaper is launched

December 1817   Hibernian Society sermon calling for greater toleration of Roman Catholics is preached

26 Sept. 1819   Chalmers is installed as minister of the newly-created St John's parish, Glasgow

1820   Chalmers publishes *The Application of Christianity to the Commercial and Ordinary Affairs of Life*

18 January 1823   Chalmers is elected to the Chair of Moral Philosophy at St Andrews University

November 1823   Chalmers moves to St Andrews

6 Nov. 1828   Chalmers moves to Edinburgh and becomes Professor of Divinity at the University of Edinburgh

February 1829   British government announces plans for Roman Catholic emancipation.

1832   *Reform Act* expands the electoral franchise

1832   Chalmers publishes *On Political Economy, in Connexion with the Moral State and Moral Prospects of Society*

May 1832   Chalmers is elected Moderator of the

General Assembly of the Church of
Scotland

23 January 1834   Chalmers suffers a stroke

May 1834   *Chapels Act* and *Veto Act* are passed by
the General Assembly of the Church of
Scotland

May 1834   Chalmers becomes the chairman of the
Church of Scotland's Church Extension
Committee

1835   Chalmers is awarded Doctor of Laws
degree by the University of Oxford

1837   Queen Victoria ascends the throne

1838   Chalmers travels to Paris to receive award
from the Royal Institute of France

1838–1842   Tensions increase between the Church of
Scotland, the British government and the
courts on the issue of patronage and the
spiritual independence of the church

May 1842   At the Church of Scotland's General
Assembly Chalmers moves the adoption
of *The Claim Declaration and Protest
anent the Encroachments of the Court of
Session*

November 1842 A convocation to discuss the future of the
               Church of Scotland opens in Edinburgh

January 1843   Government rejects *The Claim
               Declaration and Protest anent the
               Encroachments of the Court of Session*

18 May 1843   Church of Scotland General Assembly
               opens; a protest against the state's
               encroachments into the affairs of the
               Church is tabled

18 May 1843   Chalmers is elected the first Moderator of
               the Free Church of Scotland

27 July 1844   First meeting of the West Port Society

1845   Beginning of the Irish potato famine

1846   Famine spreads to the Highlands of
               Scotland

February 1847 West Port Territorial Church received into
               the Free Church of Scotland

31 May 1847   Chalmers dies

4 June 1847   Funeral of Chalmers

1

SCOTLAND: A TIME OF CHANGE, 1780–1847

On Thursday 18 May 1843 the Rev. Dr Thomas Chalmers walked out of St Andrew's Church in Edinburgh along with 202 other ministers and elders. These men were leaving the Church of Scotland's General Assembly for the last time. Within a few hours, Chalmers would be appointed as the first Moderator of the newly-constituted Free Church of Scotland. Ultimately, 470 ministers and 192 probationary ministers also aligned themselves with the Free Church. And remarkably, all of the Church of Scotland's overseas missionaries joined the Free Church. At the local parish level it has been estimated that 40% of the Church's lay membership withdrew from the Established Church.

This event, which rocked the Scottish ecclesiastical scene,

was the culmination of many years of struggle for the spiritual independence of the church: a struggle led by the Free Church's new moderator. Thomas Chalmers was certainly not the only leader, but without his vision, his organizational skills and his ability to mobilize opinion, it is probable that the Free Church would never have come into existence.

But, as we shall see, Chalmers was much more than an ecclesiastical leader and politician. He was that rare breed of scholar and pastor. He was someone who not only had great intellectual gifts, but who had a very practical impact on the lives of many people. As we survey his life in this book, we shall see his various gifts put into practice. Despite his giftedness, however, he was a far from perfect man, and so we need to learn from his failures as well as his successes.

The sixty-seven years of Thomas Chalmers's life saw immense economic, social and political change. More importantly for us, this period also saw significant developments within Scotland's churches. All of these developments would mean that Scotland could be said to have undergone revolutionary change during Chalmers's lifetime. To understand Thomas Chalmers properly, it is important that we briefly draw a picture of Scotland in his time. He was a man who would significantly shape events, but he was also a man of his times.

When Chalmers was born in 1780, Scotland's population was approximately 1.5 million people. By the time of his death sixty-seven years later, the population had increased to nearly 2.8 million. To place this population growth in context, during the whole of the eighteenth century, Scotland's population had grown by less than 600,000.

On the world stage, the conflict with the American colonies was still ongoing at the time of Chalmers's birth. And if this was not enough, Great Britain was also at war with France. While the war with the French came to an end in 1783, the French Revolution of 1789 posed a real threat to the stability of Britain. There was genuine fear that the tide of revolution that was sweeping away the old order on the European continent could well cross the English Channel.

To put the political scene in context, we need to remember that the crowns of Scotland and England were united in 1603 when James VI of Scotland inherited the crown of England upon the death of Queen Elizabeth I. While it was a moment of triumph for the Scots to see James Stuart crowned King of England, the next hundred years saw periods of intense drama and conflict. The rise and fall of the fortunes of the Stuart dynasty, which included the English Civil War and the Glorious Revolution of 1688, would have wide-reaching ramifications for English-Scottish relations.

When Queen Anne died without an heir in 1714, England, and eventually Scotland, turned to a German royal house for their next monarch. There was reluctance on the part of some Scots to embrace the House of Hanover in the person of George I. Despite justifiable suspicions regarding the Roman Catholic sympathies of some of the Stuart monarchs and their families, they were nonetheless seen as a Scottish dynasty. As a result, there was considerable sympathy for their ongoing claims to the throne. James II of England, who had been deposed during the Glorious Revolution of 1688, never gave up his claim to the throne, and his heir, Bonnie Prince Charlie, would continue the campaign. Persistent risings were finally suppressed at the decisive and brutal Battle of Culloden in 1746.

The Acts of Union of 1707 which formally united the Scottish and English Parliaments were intended to emphasize the common aspirations of a United Britain. These acts merged the Parliaments of the two nations and established the Kingdom of Great Britain. Scotland now had free trade with England and her colonies. As Britain's empire expanded, the Scots played a great part in its development.

The end of the eighteenth century has been called 'Scotland's most creative period': David Hume won world fame in philosophy and history, Adam Smith in political economy, and Robert Burns in poetry. In the next generation, Sir Walter Scott made the land and history of Scotland known throughout the world and Scottish inventors made discoveries that helped to advance the industrial revolution. Also during this period the Scots played a major role in establishing the British colonies in Canada, Australia and New Zealand.

Without much doubt, the single largest societal change that took place during the lifetime of Thomas Chalmers was the advance of the industrial revolution. The chief form of employment moved from the fields to the factories. With this growth of manufacturing came a major shift in population from rural areas to the cities. Scotland's two largest cities, Glasgow and Edinburgh, saw massive growth. In 1801 the populations of Glasgow and Edinburgh were 77,000 and 83,000. Just fifty years later they were 345,000 and 194,000 respectively.

While this rapid growth was an indication of growing prosperity for some, the news was not all good. Along with increased wealth generated by the manufacturing industries came massive social problems. While factory work could provide decent enough wages for some, this often came at significant social cost. Working conditions were frequently unpleasant and often dangerous. Many people were required to work seventeen hours a day and then lived the rest of the time in cramped, unhygienic and squalid conditions. While the British economy was viewed as being very prosperous, the question was being asked, but at what human cost?

Immigration was another factor that was changing Scottish society in this period. Cheap labour, particularly from Ireland, flocked to the cities looking for work. Families separated from their roots and social structures added to the challenges being faced by Scotland's cities. In the light of all of this it may well be asked, how was the church responding to the rapid change?

At the end of the eighteenth century Britain as a whole, and Scotland in particular, had a largely church-going populace. In England, the Church of England commanded the largest share of those who attended church, although the nonconformist Protestants and Roman Catholic populations were on the increase. In Scotland, the Church of Scotland, which was Presbyterian in polity, commanded the largest share of the populace.

The Church of Scotland had been made the Established Church by the *Act of Settlement* in 1689. This was achieved after significant struggle and at no small loss of life. The Covenanters in particular, had valiantly resisted various attempts on the part of the House of Stuart to have the Episcopalian form of church government and *Book of Common Prayer* imposed upon them. But even though Episcopalian government and worship had been successfully resisted, there were still problems. One of the biggest issues had to do with how parish ministers were appointed. This issue would loom large during the lifetime of Thomas Chalmers.[1]

Even before the Protestant Reformation, some landowners had taken upon themselves the right to appoint the local parish priest. New ideas of church government that emerged after the Reformation included attempts to do away with this system of patronage and replace it with a system whereby parishioners could elect their own pastors. However, landowners, Protestant and Roman Catholic alike, were unwilling to give up their long-standing rights. During the seventeenth and eighteenth centuries a number of pieces of legislation were passed by Parliament in an attempt to settle these issues. The conflicting laws first abolished patronage in 1649, re-established it in 1662, and abolished it again in 1690, only to have it re-established in the Patronage Act of 1712. Thus by the end of the eighteenth and early part of the nineteenth centuries there was both confusion and conflict within the Church of Scotland regarding who had the right to call ministers.

By the end of the eighteenth century the Church of Scotland had suffered from a number of relatively small secessions caused in part by differing views on the church's relation to the state. The secession churches objected to the establishment principle, which held that that there is a link between the church of Christ and the state. In other words, both institutions had been created by God and it is the duty of each to support and further the work of the other. One implication of this view is that it is the duty of the state to provide financial support for the work of the church. At the same time, both the church and the state have their own duties to carry out and should not interfere in the distinct areas belonging to the other. So, for example, the power of the sword to maintain peace and order in society belongs exclusively to the state, while the administration of the sacraments and the carrying out of church discipline is the responsibility of the church.

Despite the victories achieved by those who had fought for religious freedoms after the Reformation and throughout the seventeenth century, it must be conceded that by the time of Chalmers's birth the Church of Scotland was not in the healthiest of conditions. To be sure, the churches were reasonably full of people and the balance sheets were strong, but what of the Church's spiritual health?

The Church of Scotland in this period was divided into two groups. While generalizing about these two groups can lead to over-simplification, a few important characteristics can be noted. On the one side were the 'moderates', for whom the work of the church was almost as much about appearing respectable in the eyes of the leaders of society as it was about preaching the gospel. For the moderates, the church was as much a social entity within the society as it was a spiritual one. Their guiding principle was that the Church of Scotland must accept the idea of patronage and not give in to the increasing demand that individual congregations must have a greater role in the call of their ministers. To be fair, there were those who believed that allowing patrons to select parish ministers was the best guarantee of having a well-educated and better-qualified clergy. They argued that the average man in the pew did not have sufficient education and background to make a wise choice when calling a minister. To modern ears, this sounds paternalistic; but at the end of the eighteenth century it was a view that was at least plausible.

This group was frequently accused of having insufficient zeal for reaching out to the unchurched or for applying the gospel to the increasing social problems that Scotland was facing. This would become particularly evident in the cities, where there was reluctance to set up new parishes and open new churches to provide for the growing population who desperately needed spiritual counsel and support. With respect to the preaching of the moderates, Thomas Chalmers is said to have described their sermons as being '... like a winter's day, short and clear and cold. The brevity is good; the clarity is better; the coldness is fatal. Moonlight preaching ripens no harvest.'[2] While this assessment is probably not entirely fair, it does give a flavour of how the moderates were viewed.

The other group within the Church of Scotland, who came to be known as the 'evangelicals', were passionate about evangelism and outreach both in Scotland and to other parts of the world. They believed that the gospel could make a real difference in the lives of individuals and in the world. They also were committed to the belief that the church must be spiritually independent of the state and that it was the right of each congregation to select their own minister. But at the time of Chalmers's birth there was little evidence that these evangelicals would have much impact. The Church of Scotland needed change and revival if it was going to carry out the Great Commission.

2

Thomas Chalmers: Early Life, Education and First Appointment, 1780–1803

Thomas Chalmers was born on St Patrick's Day, 17 March 1780, in the small shipbuilding and fishing community of Anstruther Easter in Fife. The Chalmers family had been connected with the area since the beginning of the eighteenth century when Thomas' great-grandfather had become the minister in Elie, a small community six miles to the west. Thomas's father John ran the family business, which included ship-owning and the management of the local thread and dye works. By the beginning of the nineteenth century the family business was struggling. The movement of goods between Britain and France was being disrupted by the Napoleonic wars. Instead of managing a diversified business, John Chalmers would finish his days as the proprietor of a small retail wool shop.

John Chalmers married Elizabeth Hall, the daughter of a prosperous local wine merchant, in 1771. Over the course of their forty-seven-year marriage they produced fourteen children, with all but one of them surviving into adulthood. Thomas was the sixth child and the fourth son. Thomas's father was a devout Christian and was particularly concerned that his children should learn and accept for themselves the tenets of the Christian faith. Like almost everyone in the community, the Chalmers family attended the local Church of Scotland parish church. Along with the preaching and teaching received from the parish minister, another formative influence for the Chalmers children was their father's large library of devotional books, which was said to be the finest in the area. Both John and Elizabeth Chalmers were very active in the life of their community. John would become a magistrate in Anstruther and Elizabeth would devote some of her time to working with the poor in the parish. When it is remembered that she gave birth to fourteen children, it is remarkable that she had any time to be involved in poor relief!

At the age of two, Thomas was committed to the care of a nurse. This lady seems to have been a particularly unpleasant person. Rather than nurturing her young charge, she seems to have believed that stringent discipline was the only way to deal with the young boy. She had a lasting impact on Thomas, as her memory would haunt him for the rest of his life.

At the age of three, Thomas was sent to the local parish school, where he was remembered more for his physical strength and warm-heartedness than he was for academic attainment. The headmaster was both nearly blind and extremely authoritarian, and young Thomas spent more time avoiding punishments than he did learning. Despite his less than auspicious formal education, it became clear that when he wanted to, he could be a very able student. Once he could read he began to explore his father's library, where he found one of his favourite books, John Bunyan's *Pilgrim's Progress*. He was also very fortunate that one of his uncles took an interest in him and began to instruct him in mathematics, which would become a lifelong interest for Thomas. According to surviving reports from his youth, Thomas seems to have set his heart on becoming a minister early in his life, although his motivation for this is unclear. Nonetheless, his choice of career was demonstrated by his pretending to be a minister, preaching to his school friends.

In 1791, at the remarkably early age of eleven, Thomas left the parish school and began studies at nearby St Andrews University. Even by the standards of his day, he was very young to begin university. His academic performance was less than spectacular for the first years of his course of studies. These two years were devoted to the study of arts and philosophy. In later life Thomas would lament that he should have paid more attention. He particularly regretted that he had not acquired a better grasp of the classical languages. If he did not acquire great linguistic abilities at this stage, he was captivated by mathematics.

In fact, he seems to have thought that it would be quite possible for him to support himself by being ordained as a minister and serving a parish, while most of his intellectual powers would be devoted to the study and teaching of mathematics.

In November 1795, Thomas Chalmers began divinity studies. He appears to have been liked by his fellow students. He was athletically accomplished and enjoyed the company of his friends and particularly their 'jocular banter'. Some of his friends did note that he could be moody and was subject, at times, to periods of depression.

Although he was not particularly interested in the theological lectures he heard, he became captivated by the writings of the New England Puritan preacher Jonathan Edwards. Edwards's book *The Freedom of the Will* would have a profound impact on the young divinity student. It presented Chalmers with a world view that he could relate to, one in which one could understand both God and man's place in the universe. Chalmers would later write that while he was by no means an evangelical at this stage of his life he spent

> ... *nearly a twelvemonth in a sort of mental Elysium, and the one idea that ministered to my soul and all its rapture was the magnificence of the Godhead, and the universal subordination of all things to the one great purpose for which he evolved and was supporting creation.*[3]

Two other features of his divinity studies are worth

noting. First, he found himself studying in an environment that predominantly reflected the interests of the moderate party within the Church of Scotland. There was not as much emphasis on Biblical studies and systematic theology as one might expect. Instead, natural and moral theology were considered more important. Many of the students who graduated from St Andrews and who then went on to serve in parish ministry viewed the work of the church as making people good and helping to keep society orderly. This was not a vision of the church best suited for passionate evangelical preaching.

Second, Chalmers spent considerable time working on his rhetorical skills during this period. He was so successful at this that he began to attract hearers when it was known that he was going to participate in college prayer meetings. The time he spent on honing his oratorical skills was well spent and would serve him well in later life. While his written work seems somewhat ponderous to modern ears, he would come to be regarded as one of the best preachers and lecturers of his day.

In the spring of 1798, Thomas's father obtained a tutoring position for him with the Stevenson family, who lived near Arbroath. In addition to providing him with a small income as well as a place to live, his father's intention had been to give him some exposure to the lifestyle of the landowners who dominated Scottish ecclesiastical and social life. While he was required to provide tutoring to the children of the family, he would also be continuing his theological education in his spare time. The young tutor seems to have taken a near instant dislike to his employers, and complained regularly to his father about how hard he was made to work and how poorly he was treated. He seems not to have recognized that his father had had his best interests at heart in finding this position for him, and so in November 1798 he left his post and returned to St Andrews to devote himself full time to finishing his theological studies. This episode of his life points to a young man who had a very definite sense of his own importance and someone who expected to be treated with respect and deference that he had not really earned.

Thomas completed his theological studies in 1799 and then turned his attention to becoming a minister of the Church of Scotland. In order to do this he had to find a presbytery that would be willing to license him to preach, and then he would need to find a patron who would be willing to appoint him to a parish. Here he encountered a problem.

The Church of Scotland's regulations for the appointment of ministers required that a man be twenty-one before he could be licensed, ordained and appointed to a parish. There was, however, an escape clause which indicated that if a man was of 'singular and rare qualities' this rule could be overlooked. Thomas, perhaps not surprisingly, felt that he possessed these singular and rare qualities and so applied to be considered for licensure.

While Thomas waited for the Church to make a decision on his case, his father instructed him to take up another tutoring position with a family in the Anstruther area. But Thomas flatly refused on the grounds that the family was not important enough and that he needed a connection to a family who would be able to advance his ministerial prospects. Rather than doing what his father had asked, Thomas departed for Edinburgh, which would become his principal residence for the next two years.

Despite Thomas' uncooperativeness, his father was concerned to see his son settled and began to do what he could to advance his son's career in the Church. John Chalmers was able to enlist the help of his cousin and friend John Adamson, who was the professor of Civil History at St Andrews. With the help of Anderson's intervention, Thomas was allowed to do both his oral exams and preach a trial sermon before the presbytery of St Andrews. The presbytery was satisfied with both his examination and the sermon and, on 31 July 1799, licensed Thomas Chalmers to preach the gospel.

Normally when a man had been licensed to preach, the next step was to accept opportunities to preach within the presbytery that had licensed him. This would allow him to become better known to parish churches and to their patrons, who would be responsible for appointing him to serve a particular parish. But Thomas chose a different path.

Despite the fact that he received a number of offers to preach within the presbytery, he turned all of them down. Instead, he left for England for a reunion with four of his

brothers. He preached his first sermon at Chapel Lane
Chapel in Wigan on 25 August 1799 and then preached the
same sermon the following week in Liverpool. His brother
James wrote to his father and told him that while he was no
expert he believed that Thomas 'would shine in the pulpit'
in years to come.

November 1799 saw Thomas Chalmers in Edinburgh.
He had gone there in pursuit of a tutoring job but was
unsuccessful. His father, who had continued to provide him
with financial support, asked him to return home, where
there was an opportunity for him to be appointed as the
assistant minister in the parish of Logie, which was near St
Andrews. Thomas, however, ignored his father's request,
stating that he wanted to stay in Edinburgh, where he spent
much of his time attending philosophy and mathematics
lectures at the University of Edinburgh.

To his credit, John Chalmers continued to work tirelessly
on his son's behalf. He did everything that he could to use
his connections to procure an ecclesiastical appointment
for his son. John believed that the best opportunity was
to call upon his connections with Sir John Anstruther,
a wealthy landowner who had the power to appoint
ministers in six different parishes. But the Anstruther
family proved to be unreliable, much to the frustration of
John Chalmers and the anger of Thomas.

Thomas's employment prospects did not improve
until 1801, when the parish of Kilmany became vacant.
Kilmany was a rural parish situated nine miles north-

west of St Andrews. The parish was made up of eight hundred people, with an annual stipend for the minister of £200, which was a considerable sum for a recent graduate with no experience. Because it would take some time for the arrangements for his ordination and installation to be completed, in December 1801 Thomas agreed to serve as an assistant in the parish of Cavers. Although he agreed to take on this job, he did not undertake his duties with much zeal or enthusiasm. He wrote to his father that the work was quite easy and even indicated that the lack of work gave him opportunity to work on a series of mathematical lectures that he was going to deliver at St Andrews University. This had been possible because he had managed to get himself appointed to an assistantship at the university. He carried out his church duties at Cavers in a rather half-hearted manner until September 1802. At that point he resigned his church appointment and focused all his energies on his mathematics lectures at St Andrews.

While Chalmers was considered an eloquent lecturer and his students liked him because he was also entertaining, the university authorities were unhappy with his performance. William Vilant (1765–1805), who was the Professor of Mathematics, complained that Chalmers was including as much social commentary as he was mathematics in his lectures, and that the students were not learning the basic material that they should have. Vilant became so concerned that he began to interfere in Chalmers's classes. Chalmers, in headstrong fashion, continued his fanciful lectures, and then took the disastrous step of publicly questioning Vilant's integrity.

Not surprisingly, his assistantship was terminated after just one session. And so, with his academic prospects curtailed, at least for the time being, Chalmers was ordained and installed as the minister of Kilmany on 18 May 1803.

In surveying Thomas Chalmers's early life, we have seen a young man of considerable academic promise and giftedness, but a man who possessed a highly-developed sense of his own importance and giftedness. Despite the piety of his parent's home, he seems to have understood very little of what it really meant to be a Christian. Rather than having a desire to preach the gospel and care for the needs of the people of his parish, he seems to have taken up his ministerial duties as a career rather than a vocation. While this was the way in which his ministry in Kilmany began, a very real change would transform his life and his ministry in the next few years.

3

KILMANY, 1803–1815

Thomas Chalmers's first summer in the parish of Kilmany was a busy one. He wisely decided that he needed to get to know as many people as possible and so he began an active programme of parish visitation. During his first few months in Kilmany he visited all of the 150 families who were connected to the Church of Scotland, as well as conducting regular services and administering the sacrament of baptism as needed. However, as the summer passed, he came to the conclusion that he did not really need to spend much time on caring for the people of his parish. Instead, he decided that his best career prospects lay in St Andrews University. So he announced that he would begin lecturing again, even if he had to do it unofficially. His teaching gifts were such that he did attract students, but the university was unimpressed and sought to discourage these unofficial lectures.

Chalmers's father was disturbed by his son's cavalier attitude to his ministerial duties and tried to persuade him that since he was now a minister of the gospel he should devote himself wholeheartedly to his ministerial labours. Thomas dismissed his father's concerns, saying that no minister found it necessary to devote all of his energies to his parish. During the winter of 1803, Thomas's commitment to his parish weakened even further. He actually moved out of the parish and took lodgings for the winter term in St Andrews, where he believed he would soon become an academic star at the university.

In fairness, we should note that Chalmers was by no means the only minister of the Church of Scotland who took on extra work. However, even by the somewhat relaxed standards of the day, it has to be conceded that he did not take his parish work very seriously. He would return to the parish church to conduct and preach at the worship service on Sunday, but his preparation for preaching was minimal. Most weeks he would prepare his sermons early on Sunday morning, preach them, and then return to St Andrews on Monday morning.

His presbytery, too, was concerned about his ministerial work habits. Questions were raised at presbytery meetings. They went so far as to minute their opinion that he should stop his lectures at St Andrews University and spend more time in his parish. Chalmers reacted with anger. He wrote to the moderator of his presbytery daring him to send a delegation into his parish to determine whether his people were suffering or discontented with their minister. And then, displaying breathtaking contempt for the authority of the Church, he concluded that he would strenuously resist any attempts to curtail his outside activities or threaten his independence.

Despite his protestations of independence, Chalmers did pay some attention to the concerns about his absenteeism. During the winter of 1804 he actually spent five days a week in his parish. While he was more physically present, his heart was still elsewhere. Believing that the ministry provided insufficient intellectual stimulation or public fame for his talents, Chalmers continued to desire academic appointment.

Over the next two years he unsuccessfully campaigned for vacant teaching posts at St Andrews University and the University of Edinburgh. His lack of success in achieving his goals led him to remark that he was

> ... *one of those ill-fated beings whom the malignant touch of ordination has condemned to a life of ignorance and obscurity; a being who must ... drivel out the rest of his days in insignificance.*[4]

His failure to achieve his aspirations did not stop him from informally teaching chemistry around the area and, what is more interesting, he did link his chemistry demonstrations to Christianity. Even though he could hardly claim to be living out the message of the Christian gospel and was barely serving the needs of his parishioners, he still felt able to say that the Christian faith was true and could bring cheer to life and hope for the future.

In April 1807, Chalmers temporarily left his parish and took up residence in London, where he remained until July. He spent his time investigating the sights of the capital and learning as much as he could about the politics and economics of the city. His brother James, who was an accountant at a commercial firm in the city, told his father in a letter that Thomas had seen more of the city in three weeks than he had in three years.

At this time, fashionable London and all of Britain were focused on the struggles with Napoleonic France and, in particular, the impact that the war was having on the British economy. As Thomas spoke with politicians and others in London, he decided that he should devote himself to writing a book that would show the way forward, if Britain should be cut off from continental commerce as a result of the conflict with France. He worked on this project when he returned to Kilmany, and by December 1807 his *Enquiry into the Extent and Stability of National Resources* was ready for publication. In the book he argued that if British society were properly organized and regulated, the economy could flourish based on internal production.

The fact that he did not have a publisher for his book did not discourage him. He had five hundred copies printed at his own expense and then sent copies to all those he deemed to be shapers of public opinion. Then he waited for the reviews. Sadly, most of them were uncomplimentary. One particularly harsh review commented that the author's '... command of language is probably a fatal snare ... for as he seems to be at no loss for words, he is led to mistake fluency of expression for fertility of thought'. While this and other reviews stung him, what hurt the most was that the decision makers and influencers of public opinion he most hoped to impress largely ignored his work. While it is tempting to dismiss this book as a mere footnote to his life, it is important to note that the book did display real concern for the welfare of society in general and particularly for those who were less fortunate. This as we shall see, would later become a major focus of Chalmers's life and ministry.

Somewhat chastened by his unsuccessful publishing venture, Chalmers returned to his parish work. Over the next couple of years he remained in the parish more and seemed to have finally accepted the fact that he was not going to achieve academic notoriety. One project that kept his attention at this time was the construction of a new manse for him to live in as the old one was in a seriously dilapidated condition.

His next campaign was to try to persuade the Church of Scotland that it should work toward increased ministerial stipends. These stipends were set by Act of Parliament and it was up to the Church of Scotland to make the case that increases were needed. In 1809, he presented a petition on behalf of the presbytery of Cupar to the General Assembly of the Church of Scotland in which he attempted to make his case. Chalmers argued that ministers' stipends should be increased so that they could 'maintain their rank in the community'. He also suggested that politicians needed to recognize that ministers were a 'powerful instrument of security against the disaffection of the people' as they sought to teach 'the solid principles of virtue and patriotism'. His petition was not adopted by the Assembly, but his speech did serve to introduce him to the wider church.

Between 1809 and 1811 a series of events took place which dramatically changed Chalmers's life and ministry. In 1809 he came into contact with a number of young evangelicals in the Church of Scotland. One of these men, David Brewster, invited him to contribute a series of scientific articles to a forthcoming encyclopaedia. As *The Edinburgh Encyclopaedia* developed, Chalmers was also offered the article on Christianity, which he took on with considerable enthusiasm, promising that he would conduct 'a careful scientific inquiry into the historical evidence for the Christian revelation'. Thus he also began a period of 'serious study of the Bible and of the early church fathers'.

Then in June 1809 Chalmers became very ill with consumption. The disease had already killed his sister Barbara and his brother George. He had been quite close to his siblings and their deaths caused him to re-examine the course of his own life. During the summer his own condition worsened, until there was very real concern for his life. In a letter written to a friend that summer he stated that his own sickness was giving him serious

pause for thought about the priorities he had established
for himself. He also wrote that he had been reading
Thoughts on Religion, a work by Blaise Pascal, the
French mathematician, physicist, inventor and Christian
philosopher. He told his friend that the work was written
by

> ... *a man who could stop short in the brilliant career of
> discovery, who could resign all the splendours of literary
> reputation, who could renounce without a sigh all the
> distinctions which are conferred upon genius, and resolve
> to devote every talent and every hour to the defence and
> illustration of the Gospel.*[5]

In April 1810 Chalmers's health improved slightly
and he returned to his family's home in Anstruther to
continue his convalescence. While his health improved a
little, he experienced a number of setbacks and tragedies
in his personal life. First of all, his brief but passionate
engagement to Anne Rankine came to an end and then
his sister Lucy died of consumption on 23 December 1810.
As he attempted to deal with his grief, he began reading
William Wilberforce's *Practical View of the Prevailing
Religious System of Professed Christians*. The book had
a profound impact upon him. In it he discovered an
understanding of the Christian faith that he had heard
from his father, but which he had forgotten in his search for
fame. Ten years later he wrote about this period in a letter
to his brother Alexander:

> ... *as I got on in reading it, [I] felt myself on the eve of a*

great revelation in all my opinions about Christianity ... I am now most thoroughly of opinion, and it is an opinion founded on experience, that on the system of—Do this and live, no peace, and even no true and worthy obedience, can ever be attained. It is, Believe in the Lord Jesus Christ, and thou shalt be saved. When this belief enters the heart, joy and confidence enter along with it.[6]

Thomas Chalmers had come to realize that Christianity was not about following rules or moral principles. It was not about earning salvation. Rather, it is a living faith in Jesus' death for sinners and his resurrection from the dead. In later life he would say to his own students that '... there were only two ways of being religious: one way is to try to put God in our debt; the other is simply to acknowledge the greatness of our debt to God'.[7]

Chalmers's conversion had an instant and profound effect upon his parish work in Kilmany. His priorities changed dramatically. Instead of viewing the pastoral ministry as a means to preferment and a way of receiving recognition, he recognized that he was called to preach the gospel and serve his parishioners. His preaching took on a radically different tone. It became more passionate, and the things that he emphasized changed. Instead of preaching moralism, he began to call his people to repentance and faith in Christ. Attendance at services increased dramatically as his fame spread throughout and even beyond the confines of his parish. Some came out of curiosity, wanting to experience the new phenomenon. Others came out of their own feelings of spiritual concern.

And still others came, wanting to hear the man that some were calling 'mad' because of his passionate preaching. While exact numbers were not kept, parish revenue figures suggest that regular attendance at services in Kilmany rose from less than seventy before his conversion, to nearly two hundred by 1814. Chalmers did note in his diary the numbers of tokens that were distributed at some communion services, and there was a notable increase which indicated a greater participation in the sacrament of the Lord's Supper.[8]

While Chalmers had always had considerable oratorical skills, he began now to pay more attention to the needs of the people he was preaching to. Instead of writing his sermons at the last moment, he devoted much more time to reading and sermon preparation. Entries in his journals indicate just how widely he was reading. His reading list included parts of Calvin's *Institutes of the Christian Religion*, many of the Puritans, and other evangelical authors of his day. In addition, he read widely in contemporary literature, mathematics and science. What is also striking is his correspondence and contacts with people outside his own theological tradition. He would always be a man who was open to interaction with those with whom he did not entirely agree.

While his reading and his letters indicate that he embraced the basic understandings of reformed and evangelical theology, he never entirely systematized his theology. He would always be nervous of theological systems and debates which he feared might distract from the basic message of the Bible; that the sinner must turn to Christ in repentance and faith and then live a life of obedience and service. While it is true that Chalmers never wrote a systematic theology, this is not as surprising as it might seem, since the chief concerns of his ministry would always tend toward the practical outworking of the Christian life. After his death, some of his lectures were published as his *Institutes of Theology*, but these do not provide a conventional systematic theology as such.

As his fame spread, he accepted invitations to preach in other places. He always took care to try to preach in a way that would connect with his audience. By his own admission, he found it difficult to communicate with those who were less well educated. Even though he believed he was not as effective communicating with farm workers and labourers, one of the first people who was converted as a result of his preaching was a ploughman. Chalmers also now spent more time preparing and leading new communicants' classes, and the number of people who attended these classes steadily increased after Chalmers's own conversion.

Chalmers also spent a lot more time and energy on doing pastoral work in his parish. The amount of visiting that he did increased and he was very enthusiastic about the catechizing of children. Not all of his energies, however, were devoted to his own parish. He was beginning to have a much larger vision for the work of the church.

In March 1812 Chalmers founded the Kilmany Bible

Society. He believed that the message of the Bible was important to the health of society, and he worked with people of diverse church backgrounds to bring this organization into being. He also wanted the local society to connect with other Bible Societies which had similar aims. He encouraged everyone within his own parish to support the work of the Bible Society even if they were only able to give a small amount of money. In so doing he taught his people that it was not just the wealthy or the minister who could have an impact on the growth of the church and the spread of the gospel. They, too, could help to spread the good news. His belief that the Bible should have the widest possible distribution led him to campaign for support for the Bible Society in other Church of Scotland parishes, which was not always well received by some of his ministerial colleagues. Chalmers's support for Bible Societies eventually evolved into his support for and advocacy of the Victorian missionary movement, which would have a real impact throughout the British Empire and beyond.

In August 1812 Thomas's life underwent another significant change when he married Grace Pratt, the daughter of an army captain, who came from one of the wealthier families in the parish. The Chalmers's marriage was a happy one. The first of their six daughters was born on 5 May 1813. Thomas's wife provided a place of security for him and she was able, over the course of time, to temper some of her husband's more extravagant and impulsive behaviours.

It is hardly surprising that Thomas's work in the parish of Kilmany began to attract attention in the wider church. In 1813 he declined the opportunity of moving to London, but when in 1814 he was asked to consider moving to Glasgow he found it harder to refuse. St Mary's Tron Church in Glasgow had a history of evangelical ministers and so when the pulpit became vacant Chalmers's name was put forward as a candidate.

The elders of the Tron Church were unanimous in their desire to call him, and after much soul searching he eventually agreed that his name could be considered for election. The decision was in the hands of the Town Council of Glasgow, who were the legal patrons of the Tron Church. Vigorous campaigning took place, with Chalmers being the popular choice among the evangelical party. However, the moderates also had their candidate and they pressed the Council to choose their man instead. In spite of this, on 25 November 1814 Chalmers was elected as the next minister of the Tron Church. On 2 January 1815 he officially accepted the call and a date for his installation was set for July of the same year.

The minister who left Kilmany for the city in the summer of 1815 was a very different person from the one who had arrived there twelve years earlier. Instead of someone who was not particularly devoted to the work of the ministry, except as a means of gaining popularity and academic position, Thomas Chalmers was now firmly committed to his evangelical principles, the mission of the church, and his desire to see the church make a difference in the world.

4

THE TRON PARISH, GLASGOW, 1815–1819

The city of Glasgow was divided into eight parishes. Each of these had a parish church that was responsible for providing for the care of the residents in that area. The Tron Church where Chalmers served had a long history. The parish had been established in 1484, and after the Reformation had become Presbyterian in 1592. The church building itself had been rebuilt in 1794 and seated about 1,300. Oddly enough, the actual church building was located just outside the official parish boundary. This was not unheard of, but it does indicate that the original concept of the parish system had broken down. Funding for the work of the parish, including paying the minister's stipend, came from pew rents, which were money paid for the privilege of having an assigned seat in the church. At the time of Chalmers's installation, the total population of the parish was approximately 11,000 people, but nearly half of those were not members of the Church of Scotland. Some of these people attended other churches, while others did not go to church at all, because they either could not afford the pew rents or were not interested in attending. The parish was a very poor one, and it would not be long before the new minister would begin to realize just how big the task was that lay before him.

The people of the Tron parish were very pleased to have acquired their new minister and received him with genuine excitement. His evangelical preaching attracted more people to hear him preach and he quickly became a favourite preacher in Glasgow. The conferring of the degree of Doctor of Divinity by the University of Glasgow on 21 February 1816 also increased his popularity.

Chalmers's first challenge was that most of the people who came to hear him preach on any given Sunday did not actually live within the boundaries of the parish. His congregation at the Tron was drawn from people who lived in the surrounding area and who had been attracted to the church by the previous minister and his evangelical preaching. Because his congregation were paying seat rents which granted them the privilege of attending the church, some came to view the new minister as their property and expected that he would devote much of his time to visiting them and attending their social functions.

Chalmers soon realized that this was a very different

situation from what he had experienced in Kilmany, where he was preaching to people who actually lived close to the church. In his first parish he had been able to devote almost as much time as he wanted to the work of the church, which he saw as preaching, teaching and pastoral care. Now, he was expected to attend social functions and meetings on subjects that had little or nothing to do with the work of the church. Such was Chalmers's frustration at these demands that his letters contain statements of regret that he had ever moved to the city. While there is a note of self-pity in some of these letters, he managed to recover his equilibrium and began to turn his attention to the people who lived within the parish, but who were unable to attend worship services. While he continued to preach to and teach the pew holders who regularly filled the church, his focus became how he and his church could care for those in need immediately outside their walls.

His first step in ministering to his parish was to begin a systematic parish visitation. Beginning in November 1815 Chalmers, along with elders from the church, began visiting the residents of the parish. He spent whole days visiting as many as seventy families a day, and over the course of two years he was able to meet most of his parishioners. Chalmers knew that he would not get to know the people intimately, but he did take care to keep statistics on each family and made careful notes of specific needs that he discovered. It is important to note that his visits were not confined to those who had a connection with the Church of Scotland. He also visited the families of Dissenters (Protestants who did not belong to the national church). More remarkably, he also visited the homes of Roman Catholics. This was unusual at a time when there were deep divides between Catholics and Protestants. The more Chalmers visited, the more he came to recognize that the regular Sunday ministry at the Tron Church could not meet the needs of most of the people. As a result, he began to think about new ways to care for all of the people of his parish.

The first thing that he did was to establish midweek meetings in various parts of the parish. He invited those he had visited to come to these meetings, where he would preach and teach the basic concepts of the Christian faith. While these meetings would only touch a fraction of the parish, his visitation efforts and these special meetings did serve to make him much better known and respected in the area.

He soon recognized that the needs of the parish were so great that that he could not make a difference on his own. As a result, he began to look for help from within his congregation. The Tron parish was divided into twenty-five districts or proportions, and each of these districts was supposed to have an elder who was responsible for pastoral oversight and care. But when Chalmers was installed as minister, there were only eight elders. Eight men could not properly care for the 1,300 who regularly attended the church or the 11,000 outside the church. So during his first year as minister Chalmers began to look for suitable candidates for the eldership.

Twelve younger men were elected to the office of elder. By December 1816, Chalmers had trained and was ready to install them. All of them were well educated and had both the money and the time necessary to devote themselves to the work of the church. At their ordination Chalmers told the new elders that under God it would be up to them to see that the parish system could be made to work in the context of a large city. While he conceded that the parish system had broken down in the cities of Scotland, it did not have to remain that way.

He then went on to give them a threefold charge. First, it was their duty to teach the good news about Jesus through regular visitation. Second, they were to be proactive in looking for those who needed material assistance from the church. Families should be encouraged to help themselves and, wherever possible, care for their own, but the elders were to make sure that people who genuinely needed it would be provided with support. Thirdly, the elders were to encourage others who regularly attended the Tron to become actively involved in parish life. His hope was to mobilize the resources of a middle-class congregation to give of their time, talent and treasure to care for the less fortunate. Chalmers was no revolutionary and was not interested in breaking down class distinctions, but he did believe that social harmony was possible and that it was part of the mission of the church to encourage this harmony within communities. Some have argued that Chalmers's vision of society was outmoded and oppressive to the poor, but he cannot be accused of not caring for the spiritual and physical needs of those outside of the walls of his church. Not all needs were met, but the mobilized and reinvigorated eldership did make a difference. People still fell between the cracks, but the Tron parish and the city of Glasgow were both much better places as a result of Chalmers's initiatives.

Sabbath or Sunday schools were another initiative that Chalmers used to reach out to his parish. It is important to note here that Chalmers did not invent the Sunday school movement, but he did adapt it to meet local needs. One of the things that he noticed during his visitations was that many people had little or no education and that illiteracy rates were very high. He wanted to raise literacy levels so that people would be better equipped to lead a more successful life and so that they could more fully understand the gospel.

What was novel about Chalmers's approach to Sunday Schools was that he took the parish model of oversight and pastoral care and applied this to the Sunday schools. Once he had done this, he then looked within his own congregation for able men who were willing to teach. Because his congregation was largely comprised of middle-class, well-educated people, he had a good pool of talent to draw from. He drew on men like David Stow (1793–1864) and William Collins (1789–1853), who were already involved in education. David Stow was the founder of the Glasgow Education Society, which had had some success in raising literacy levels in Glasgow. Collins had been one of the men involved in attracting Chalmers to Glasgow, and he would eventually become the publisher of most of Chalmers's books when his own publishing firm was established.

A Sunday school society was established in December 1816 with only four teachers. By the time Chalmers left the parish three years later, there were over forty teachers and forty-seven schools, which made up almost half the total number of schools in all of Glasgow. In addition to providing for both basic literacy and the religious education of many young people, Chalmers's Sunday school scheme had another major benefit. Some of the teachers, who previously had been unaware of the difficult living situations of many Glasgow citizens, learned of the state of the inner city and were moved to devote significant efforts to improving the conditions. Also, a number of young men would ultimately decide to go into the ministries of the Church of Scotland, and later the Free Church, as a result of their work experience in the Tron parish's Sunday school work. Another sign of the success of this endeavour was that the organization of the schools would be replicated in other parishes in Scotland.

While this part of Chalmers's parish ministry was a success, it was not always well received. Some in his parish objected to the fact that their minister was spending too much time on this, rather than on visiting them or attending their social gatherings. They took the view that since they were paying his stipend through their pew rents they should have more say in how their minister spent his time. Chalmers did not take well to this criticism. He castigated his congregation for being so inward looking and in January 1817 he announced that he was considering a call to another parish in Stirling. When this news broke, his friends and allies within the congregation mounted a campaign which persuaded him to stay for at least a while longer. While many of those who opposed him ultimately left to worship in other parishes, they were soon replaced by other people who were attracted to the Tron because of Chalmers's preaching.

During his time as the minister of the Tron parish, Chalmers preached a number of sermons which cemented his reputation as one of the great evangelical preachers of his day. Even though Chalmers read his sermons from a manuscript, he was able to lift the words off the page in a way that captivated his audiences.

The first sermons that captured the public's imagination were those that came to be known as the *Astronomical Discourses*. He preached these sermons at midweek meetings between November 1815 and October 1816. In the *Discourses* Chalmers made use of his considerable scientific knowledge to demonstrate that the Christian faith had nothing to fear from modern science. These sermons were a response to society's growing awareness of the vastness of the universe and the claim that Christianity—and especially that the death of Christ on earth could somehow redeem humanity from sin—was implausible. Rather than being daunted by the possibility of other populated worlds, Chalmers persuasively made the case that the death and resurrection of Christ were in fact

God's way of bringing the whole universe back into relation with God.

What is most striking about the *Astronomical Discourses* is not Chalmers's answer to what is a hypothetical question. Rather it is his warning that knowledge from science needs to be kept in proper perspective. Chalmers reminded his hearers that science should be appropriately modest. It was the purpose of science, he argued, to observe the natural and created orders and not to explain them. If one really wanted to understand and explain the world, the only infallible place where that explanation could be found was in God's self-revelation in Scripture. It was in the Bible that God had revealed himself as the creating and redeeming God who had laid down standards by which all should live. Chalmers further warned that if belief in God was replaced with a belief in science, this would lead to each individual doing what was right in their own eyes and becoming a law unto themselves. It was an important warning then and remains so now, nearly two hundred years later.

The *Astronomical Discourses* had an impact on his congregation in Glasgow. They also had a much wider impact through their subsequent publication. When Chalmers approached the Glasgow publisher John Smith (1784–1849) and asked him to consider publishing the *Discourses*, Smith hesitated, fearing that there was little money to be made in the publication of sermons, as historically had been the case. Smith suggested that Chalmers canvass his friends to ask for their financial backing, but Chalmers refused on the grounds that it was demeaning to have to beg people for support. Smith, who was both a friend of Chalmers and a member of his congregation, eventually agreed to the venture and the risks involved, and he must have been glad that he did! Within ten weeks of publication 6,000 copies of *The Discourses on the Christian Revelation, Viewed in Connection with Modern Astronomy* were sold and within a year 20,000 copies in nine editions had been purchased, making a tidy profit for both the author and the publisher.

One of Chalmers's gifts was that he was a good self-promoter. He decided that if his new book was going to sell well he would need to go on what would now be called an author tour. In the spring of 1817 he set out for London, where he preached several sermons and became something of a sensation. While the book was already selling well, his personal appearance certainly helped to spread the word.

Encouraged by his London success, Chalmers returned to his Glasgow parish, more determined than ever to make an impact on the city. Increasingly he began to preach that the social impact of the gospel was being neglected. He told his congregation that the church tended to focus too much on the individual's relationship with Jesus Christ and had not spent enough time and energy showing people how they should live out their faith. He sincerely believed that a revival of the evangelical faith within the Church of Scotland could make this possible, and he also argued that all Protestants should be working together to create what he called 'the godly commonwealth'.

The concept of the godly commonwealth is critical to a proper understanding of Chalmers's thought and life. By it, he meant that through the preaching of the gospel and the inculcation of Christian principles a more moral, equitable and just society would be created. For most of his life, Chalmers would remain suspicious of government schemes to improve the conditions faced by the poor. He believed rather that the church could and should make a difference. Not that the church should simply become an institution for the distribution of welfare, but rather that the church through Christian witness and in reliance on the power of God, would make the rich care more for the poor and the poor to live lives that were shaped by the Christian virtues of industry and responsibility.

Chalmers's desire to include other Protestants in his vision for a renewed Scotland was not particularly controversial, but his attitude toward the Roman Catholic Church was a different matter. In a sermon preached before the Hibernian Society in December 1817 he called for greater tolerance and understanding between Protestants and Catholics. He claimed that much of the Protestant criticism of Catholicism was based on prejudice and a misunderstanding that the abuses of medieval Catholicism still had a grip on the Catholic population. He went on to say that Protestants also had their own failings and had no grounds to feel proud of who they were. He also argued that some of the prejudice directed toward Roman Catholics was based as much on Protestant insecurities and feelings of failure as it was on a clear understanding of Catholicism.

It is hard to square Chalmers's views with the significant differences that did and still do exist between Roman Catholic dogma and Protestant theology. But what he was trying to do was to look for common ground for Catholics and Protestants to work together on educational and social endeavours to improve society. His views were overly romanticised, but he was right to call for deeper understanding between the various branches of Christendom and he was also right to call for increased toleration.

His Hibernian Society sermon created something of a sensation. While some welcomed it, many evangelicals within the Church of Scotland believed that Chalmers had unwisely downplayed the real theological differences that existed between Protestants and Catholics. Some even went so far as to question how any orthodox Church of Scotland minister could preach such a sermon. While this sermon may have given Chalmers a hearing in the wider world, he did find himself isolated for a time from those in the Church of Scotland who should have been his natural allies. This isolation affected him deeply, but it is unclear whether he ever understood that it had largely been of his own making.

His feelings of isolation were further intensified when his father died in July 1818. He felt guilty that he had not treated his father better when he was a young man and deeply regretted that his father's deafness and senility had prevented him from understanding that his son had become a sincere Christian and an evangelical minister.

Chalmers's successful venture into print with the *Astronomical Discourses* persuaded him that there was sufficient interest in his work, and a little money to be made, in the publication of his sermons. So in 1819 he released through John Smith's publishing house a collection entitled *Sermons Preached in the Tron Church Glasgow*. This collection was not a commercial success. Chalmers blamed the publisher for inadequate promotion of the book, but it is just possible that the topic of the sermons—human depravity—did not sound quite as interesting to potential readers. Chalmers's blaming John Smith for the poor sales of this work would ultimately result in him switching publishers. As we shall see later, it would mark the beginning of the very successful William Collins publishing house.

As Chalmers continued his work in the Tron parish, he focused much of his energy on reaching out to the poorer people in the parish. As he did so, he experienced growing frustration that his ideal of what urban parish ministry should look like was not developing as he had hoped. What he really wanted was to recreate, in the urban context, what he had experienced in Kilmany. While this was naïve, Chalmers was passionate about the church meeting the needs of all those who needed help, both physical and spiritual.

He was especially frustrated by the way in which poor relief money was administered. While pew rents covered church expenses including ministerial stipends, separate collections were taken for the relief of the poor. These were controlled by the General Session, which was made up of ministers from each of the parishes. Then money was sent back to individual parishes based on the size of the poor population in the parish. If the needs outweighed the distributed funds then those cases were referred to the Town Hospital, which was funded out of a local assessment.

Chalmers came to view this system as being overly complicated. He began to campaign to keep all collections for the poor within the parish for the exclusive use of the parish. During 1818 and 1819 he increasingly advocated the abolition of the system. In so doing he clashed with other evangelicals in the Church of Scotland who believed that while the current system was not perfect, it was better than what Chalmers was advocating.

One of Chalmers's failings was that he held his views with considerable tenacity and he was not always gracious when debating with others. Therefore, as a result of his views on Roman Catholics and his new proposals for poor relief, he found himself isolated from those who should have been his natural allies in the Church of Scotland.

The Glasgow Town Council had been planning to create a new parish in the east end of Glasgow for some time. They did not create a new parish for Chalmers, but he seized upon the plans as a means of moving forward his vision for parish ministry in Scotland's cities. As he thought about implementing a fuller vision in a new parish, he was careful to ensure that wealthy pew holders at the

Tron would be given the opportunity to move to the new parish if they chose to. He also secured agreement that he could take some of the elders from the Tron to the new parish. This meant that he would be starting with a core congregation which could provide him with the manpower and the financial resources necessary to make the experiment work.

Chalmers ended his ministry at the Tron in July 1819 and planned to be installed as the minister of the new parish of St John's in September. But the St John's experiment almost did not get off the ground. Chalmers had demanded assurances that he would be allowed to implement his own views on poor relief. But the assurances were not forthcoming and, in fact, public opposition to his ideas was growing. As he waited to see what would happen, he left for Edinburgh to investigate the possibility of leaving the ministry entirely and, instead, taking on the Chair of Natural Philosophy at the university.

When it was announced that his name would be put forward for the Chair at the University of Edinburgh, there was intense negative reaction. He was accused by the press of abandoning all principles for the sake of personal advancement. Back in Glasgow, his supporters, who were looking forward to his ministry in the new parish, felt betrayed and the elders who were going to be serving on the Session of the new parish threatened to resign.

Returning to Anstruther for a vacation, Chalmers finally recognized that his impulsive pursuit of the Edinburgh

Chair could result in him obtaining neither the pulpit at St John's nor the academic appointment. Concluding that he needed to do some fence-mending, he reached out to one of his ministerial colleagues, Andrew Thomson (1778–1831). Thomson was one of the leading evangelicals in the Church of Scotland and, although he had disagreed with Chalmers's views on Roman Catholicism and questioned whether his views on poor relief would work, he nevertheless wished Chalmers well in his new parish. As a result, he preached at the first service in St John's and formally introduced the new minister.

Chalmers had behaved impulsively as he explored the possibilities of moving to St John's. He had upset many people in the Church of Scotland and on the Glasgow Town Council, but now he had his parish. He could distribute poor relief in the way that he wanted, through the church, and it was up to him to show whether he could make the model of ministry that he believed in work.

5

St John's Parish, 1819–1823

It is a little startling that St John's was the first new parish church built in Glasgow for thirty years. Despite massive population growth, the Town Council had been reluctant to create new parishes because they were expensive to operate. Also, some argued that because there was little or no unrest in the city no new churches were needed to help control the behaviour of the people. This is a sad commentary on the motives behind church planting in the nineteenth century, but it was the reality.

Because of the reluctance to fund the building of new parishes at the end of the eighteenth century, the Church of Scotland had responded with the creation of chapels of ease. These chapels were not supported financially by town councils or patrons. They relied on the generosity of donors to support the minister. Unlike parish churches, they were not set up along conventional Presbyterian lines. They did not have elders and they enjoyed the right of popularly electing their ministers. While the chapels of ease reached many with the gospel, they were not able to provide for educational and temporal needs and thus were not satisfactory substitutes for fully-fledged parish churches.

While Chalmers's path to the pulpit of St John's parish had not been straightforward, he nonetheless took on the challenges of the new work with his typical enthusiasm and vigour. As he did so, he had a clear idea of what he hoped to achieve. He simply wanted to bring the message of the gospel and the lessons of Christianity into contact with the people of his parish. His first objective was to preach the gospel and through his preaching and teaching invite his hearers to repent of their sins and turn to Christ for salvation.

But there was more. What he had been able to do in Kilmany, partly because of its rural location and small population, he now hoped he would be able to do on a much grander scale. The four years that Chalmers spent as minister of this parish would do much to enhance his reputation. His preaching and writing increased his popularity, and many argue that during this period he revolutionized urban parish ministry in the Church of Scotland.

On 27 September 1819, just one day after his installation

as the minister, Chalmers called the first meeting of the St John's Committee of Education. He donated £100 of his own money and encouraged other people of means to show their commitment to parish education by making similar donations. This was typical of the man. Once he had decided on a course of action, he would begin to work immediately to bring it about. Sufficient funds were raised so that by July of 1820, two schools in the same location were opened. The first school taught reading and English grammar while the second one taught writing, mathematics and book-keeping. School fees were charged, but they were kept very low so as to make education affordable for as many people as possible. Chalmers took a very real interest in the running of the schools by visiting them regularly to encourage the teachers and to get to know the children better. Within a month of opening, the schools were overcrowded and the school masters were required to teach additional classes. By the time that Chalmers left Glasgow for St Andrews in 1823 there were four parish schools that were providing education for 419 boys between the ages of six and fifteen.

One of Chalmers's achievements as minister of the Tron parish had been to reinvigorate the office of elder in the congregation. As we saw in the last chapter, he had recruited young men who had a vision for caring for the spiritual needs of the poor of the parish. Like the Tron parish, St John's was divided into districts or proportions. In each of these Chalmers wanted to have an elder, a deacon and at least one Sunday School teacher. While he already had a good pool of elders to draw from, the situation with the deacons was different. The Church of Scotland had long recognized this office, but it had fallen into disuse, particularly in the cities. However, this was about to change.

Chalmers began actively to recruit men who could fill the ranks of the diaconate. After a period of training he began to ordain these men for the work. Each deacon was required to get to know the people who were in his district through regular visitation. They were not simply the instruments through whom charity was to be distributed; in fact, part of their job was to encourage self-reliance and family and community support for those in need. Chalmers was anxious to show to his critics that with proper support from the church the problem of pauperism could be reduced.

Chalmers expected his deacons to be proactive. They were not to wait until problems presented themselves; rather, they were to be actively looking for opportunities to share their wisdom and provide support from church resources where that was necessary. The distribution of money from church offerings was an important part of their work, but it was not automatically given to all who asked for it. Rather, the deacons would first work with the needy to determine whether there were others in their families who could help them, or to seek out ways for the needy to become more self-sufficient.

As part of their work, the deacons were required to meet together on a monthly basis to discuss common problems that they were facing and to strategize about how their work might be more effective. They were expected to become actively involved in dealing with the many social problems that existed in Glasgow. Their task included encouraging education and looking for ways to improve living conditions through the removal of health hazards and stressing the need for sobriety.

Chalmers's dream for St John's was that lives would be changed through the preaching of the gospel, that his elders would provide pastoral care and oversight, and that the deacons would oversee the physical conditions in which the people were living. One of the side benefits of his plan for the parish was its positive impact on those who were doing the work of pastoral oversight, diaconal care and teaching. Chalmers was able to create a group of people who believed that they were making a difference in the world and their enthusiasm was infectious. To further encourage a positive spirit, Thomas and Grace Chalmers regularly hosted breakfasts and teas in their home for those who were involved in parish work. These meals provided encouragement for the workers and also enabled Thomas to keep his finger on the pulse of the parish.

One of Chalmers's greatest gifts was that he was a very capable organizer. The pastoral work that was carried out in the Tron parish showed to his critics that a well-planned programme of evangelism, education and pastoral care could work. Thomas also led by example. While he was willing to delegate the bulk of the work to parish workers, he regularly made visits with his elders and deacons.

As Chalmers came to grips with the work of his parish, he came to the conclusion that he needed an assistant to help him with the workload of preaching, teaching and visitation. When he heard of a young man by the name Edward Irving (1792–1834) and of his exceptional oratorical abilities, Chalmers went to hear him preach. Irving had graduated from the University of Edinburgh at the age of 14 and had worked as a teacher for a time, while he set his sights on becoming a minister. He was eventually licensed to preach in June of 1815 but was unable to find a church which wanted to call him. Just as he was considering going to the mission field, he was invited to take the Assistantship of St John's. For a period of two years he shared preaching duties with Chalmers and threw himself into parish visitation. Chalmers developed personal fondness for the young man which he was to retain for the rest of his life.

Irving's subsequent career is one of the tragic stories of nineteenth-century church history. After leaving Glasgow, Irving served a church in London, where he developed pronounced premillennial views on the second coming of Christ and taught these beliefs with eloquence and passion. Irving also began to teach ideas that would be precursors of the modern Pentecostal movement's stress on the supernatural gifts of the Spirit. Much more alarmingly, he started teaching a faulty view of Christ's incarnation. He believed that Jesus' human nature was exactly like that of all other people, including the fact that it had 'innate sinful propensities'. He would go on to stress that Jesus was completely indwelt by the Holy Spirit from the moment of his conception, which enabled him to live a holy life. Not surprisingly, his critics pointed out that if Jesus had a sinful human nature, he too needed a saviour and thus was in no position to be offered as the perfect atonement for sin. Irving was deposed from the Church of Scotland ministry in 1833 and went on to found the Catholic Apostolic Church.

Much has been made of Chalmers's response to Irving's later life and particularly his descent into heresy. Some have even argued that Chalmers was unconcerned by Irving's unorthodox views; but there are passages in his diary where he expresses deep concern about Irving's unorthodox preaching and teaching. It is true that Chalmers took no part in any of the ecclesiastical trials which ended Irving's ministry in the Church of Scotland and, in fact, Chalmers and his family retained a cordial relationship with Irving. What seems clear is that Chalmers allowed his feelings of personal affection for Irving to cloud his judgement.

As we saw earlier, Chalmers had become a published author before he came to St John's; but in 1820 he began a new venture. The *Commercial Discourses* or *The application of Christianity to the Commercial and Ordinary Affairs of Life* appeared in 1820 under the imprint of Chalmers and Collins publishers. These eight sermons had formed part of the same series that had given the world the *Astronomical Discourses*. Chalmers took the profits he had made from the hugely successful *Astronomical Discourses* and used them to set up his friend William

Collins in the publishing business. Collins had owned his own school, had been a key supporter of Chalmers at the Tron, and had worked hard as one of his Sunday school teachers. Now he became the primary Scottish publisher of Chalmers's works. The Collins publishing name would eventually become synonymous with quality publishing in Great Britain and around the world.

This was not Chalmers's only publishing endeavour at this time. As he developed and implemented his ministry model, Chalmers released a series of quarterly papers which discussed his approach to the ministry. These quarterly papers, which were eventually gathered together and published in 1826 as *Christian and Civic Economy of Large Towns*, had a wide circulation. These papers received mixed reviews, with some questioning whether the essentially rural model of parish ministry could work in cities. Others welcomed and commended Chalmers's ideas.

By the autumn of 1821 Chalmers was beginning to feel tired because of all his labours in the parish. Although the four Sunday services and pastoral visitation were shared with Irving and the elders, he also had to prepare for impromptu evangelistic meetings that took place in various locations throughout the parish during the week. Some have claimed that his more informal addresses at these meetings had a greater impact than his Sunday sermons. Then, in addition to all of this, there were all the meetings that he had to attend in order to keep all of the parish organizations running.

As he contemplated all of the work that needed to be done, Chalmers came to the conclusion that another congregation was needed. He hoped that by planting another church in the parish his workload would eventually be eased. The problem was that that there were insufficient funds to create a fully-fledged parish and the Glasgow Town Council made it very clear to him that they were not going to erect a new parish. So if a church was going to be built it would have to be done through private donations and be erected as a chapel of ease.

In March 1822 the St John's session created a committee to investigate the situation. Chalmers contributed £500 of his own money and persuaded others to contribute toward the project. He planned to use the donated funds to build the chapel and then pay back the contributions through a portion of the pew rents that the new congregation would generate. The fundraising work was difficult and it was only when someone from outside the parish contributed £1,000 that work on the building of the chapel could begin. Even when the initial funding was secured there were still other problems to deal with.

The majority of the Glasgow presbytery was not happy with the situation. There was bitterness because of the way in which Chalmers had gone about campaigning for his appointment to St John's. Many of the ministers in the presbytery were still unconvinced that Chalmers's scheme for poor relief was working and they found willing supporters on the Town Council and in the press. There were increasing demands from the Council and the press that door collections be handed over for the support of the Town Hospital rather than being used for poor relief in the area. At the Church of Scotland's General Assembly in May 1822 Chalmers successfully argued his case that the new chapel should be allowed to keep the door collections, but it was a hard-fought victory. Chalmers was deeply hurt by the fact that most of the presbytery and the local government didn't share his vision. He took their objections very personally and it would be a very long time before he got over the hurt caused by this dispute.

While the chapel was being constructed, Chalmers was asked whether he would consider accepting a call to a church in Edinburgh. He refused this offer; but it is clear from his diary that he was feeling extremely tired and was beginning to wonder how long he could keep up with the workload. On 16 November 1822 he received a letter from Dr Francis Nicoll (1770–1835), who was the Principal of the United Colleges of St Leonard's and St Salvator's at St Andrews University. Nicoll told Chalmers that St Andrews was seeking to fill the Chair of Moral Philosophy at the university and asked whether Chalmers would accept the Chair if it were offered to him. Chalmers was somewhat surprised by this offer, because Nicoll and the university were unsympathetic to Chalmers's evangelical theology, interests and outlook. Nevertheless, he agreed to an interview, which took place in Edinburgh in January 1823. Further letters were exchanged and later that month Chalmers agreed to the appointment.

On 18 January 1823 Chalmers was unanimously elected to

the Chair and two days later he called a meeting of St John's elders, deacons and Sunday school teachers to inform them of his decision. At the meeting he read them his letter of resignation, in which he told them that his decision was not an impulsive one. Further, he indicated that he had had opportunities to leave St John's earlier but had turned all of them down. So why was he leaving now? He told them that he was resigning from the parish because his health would no longer allow him to keep up the pace of work that was required. It was certainly the case that he had worked very hard, and no one would ever accuse him of simply sitting in his study writing sermons. In fact, as we have seen, there was hardly an area of parish life that he had not involved himself in. He went on to say that with the opening of the chapel of ease and all the other programmes that were running so smoothly in the parish, he believed that the work of the ministry would carry on even if he were not there to oversee it. Another element in Chalmers's decision to move was his family. By now he and his wife had three daughters and Grace Chalmers was pregnant with their fourth daughter. The prospect of moving from Glasgow to a rural location appealed to the whole family. Needless to say, most of his parishioners were very upset at losing their popular minister, but recognized that he would be doing good work for the wider church by teaching at the university, where he would come into contact with those training for the ministry.

Chalmers did not actually move to St Andrews until November 1823, so he was still the minister of St John's when the new chapel of ease was opened in June 1823.

Although Chalmers was pleased that the chapel had finally been opened, it opened with an outstanding debt. Because of this, the pew rents had to be set high so that the running costs of the chapel could be covered and a minister's stipend paid. While Chalmers had begun this project with the very best motives, the struggle to see the chapel completed had been an exhausting one. Then, to his distress, the new chapel did not attract the number of people he had hoped for. It would continue to struggle for stability for many years to come. Worse still from Chalmers's perspective was that the high pew rents meant that many people whom he had hoped to reach with the gospel could not afford to attend the chapel.

Because the chapel was not a fully-fledged parish, it was not allowed a local session of elders, so pastoral care and oversight had to be managed from St John's. Additionally, as we have seen, one of the keys to Chalmers's successful parish ministry model at St John's had been the momentum created by the training of new elders, deacons and teachers. This could not happen at the chapel and so the work was significantly hampered. When the chapel opened, the decision was made to stop evening services at St John's and move them to the chapel. This did not encourage the development of a local congregation for the chapel. In retrospect, the chapel experiment was not a great success and took away from Chalmers's undoubted achievements as the minister of St John's.

There is much to admire in Chalmers's work during his tenure as the minister of St John's. However, it must be conceded that his experiment in using funds raised from within the parish for poor relief was not a total success. Chalmers had incorrectly assumed that the rural parish ministry model could be fully implemented in a large city with a growing and mobile population. Chalmers also staked a good deal of his own reputation on his work, which meant that he found it very difficult to accept even constructive criticism. His writing and lecturing on his ministry model certainly raised his profile, but his greatest achievement at St John's would ultimately prove to be his faithful preaching of the gospel. God blessed his ministry in such a way that many lives were changed and the evangelical party in the Church of Scotland was given a much higher profile and a wider hearing.

6

St Andrews University, 1823–1828

Thomas Chalmers had been a student at St Andrews in the last decade of the eighteenth century; he had taught there briefly and, before his conversion, had desperately wanted to obtain a permanent teaching post. The university was the oldest in Scotland, and the third oldest in Great Britain. The university's roots went back to 1410 when a group of masters, mostly from France, initiated a school of higher studies in St Andrews. By February 1411 the school had established itself sufficiently to receive a charter of incorporation and privileges from the Bishop of St Andrews, Henry Wardlaw. Bishop Wardlaw soon began the process of applying for official university status. Only the Pope or the Emperor could confer this status, and Wardlaw applied to Pope Benedict XIII, who was incarcerated in the Spanish fortress in Pensicola. On 28 August 1413 the Pope agreed to the petition; but it would not be until February 1414 that the official documents arrived in St Andrews to much celebration. The early history of the university was certainly eventful. In 1426, King James unsuccessfully tried to move the whole university to Perth. Then, in 1470, several masters and students were expelled for attacking the dean with bows and arrows. Later in the sixteenth century the university banned beards, the carrying of weapons, gambling and football.

By the time of Chalmers's return to St Andrews in 1823 the town had become something of a backwater. While the pace of the industrial revolution was having a significant impact on Scotland's biggest cities, the same could not be said of St Andrews. In fact, during the first two decades of the nineteenth century the local economy had fallen on hard times. To be sure, the town was rich in history, having seen John Knox preach there and Cardinal Beaton hung from the castle, but now only a feeling of faded grandeur remained.

The university had also seen better days. It had been decaying when Chalmers was there as a student, but now the situation was becoming very serious. Buildings were falling into disrepair and there were charges that money which had been set aside for improvements to the campus had in fact gone to augment the salaries of some of the faculty. As for the faculty, there were excellent teachers in some departments, but appointments were made based on family connections, friendships and political affiliation rather than academic excellence.

If the faculty was not particularly distinguished, neither was the student body. The resident student population was about 220, which was the smallest of Scotland's five universities. There were no entrance exams or requirements and so most students simply transitioned from parish schools to the university at the average age of fourteen or fifteen. It should also be noted that the level of preparedness for university varied considerably among the student body.

The theological makeup of the St Andrews faculty had not changed a great deal since Thomas Chalmers's student days. The moderate party in the Church of Scotland was still very much in control, and they could not have been too enthusiastic about adding an able and strong evangelical to their number. The appointment was in fact a pragmatic one. In voting for Chalmers, the faculty of the university was hoping that the popularity of the city preacher would attract desperately needed students. As we have already seen, Chalmers accepted the appointment partly for personal reasons, but also he believed he would now have an opportunity to have an impact on the lives of young men preparing for ministry.

Chalmers moved by himself to St Andrews in November 1823, leaving his family behind in Glasgow until he could get himself established in his new location. He delivered his introductory lecture on Friday 14 November. He was pleased with how the lecture was received, but indicated in a letter to his wife that he would not feel really settled until his family was able to join him, which they did in January 1824.

His duties as Professor of Moral Philosophy were not exactly arduous. His teaching responsibilities amounted to teaching one course per session. This was in sharp contrast to the exhausting pastoral duties he had just relinquished in Glasgow. If his teaching load was not heavy, he nonetheless made it clear that he was going to take the discipline in a new direction.

The teaching of moral philosophy at St Andrews had long followed in the tradition of the 'Scottish common sense' school. This school of thought focused on the study of the human mind so that it could be demonstrated that the mind had an internal moral regulator or 'common sense' which reflected the divinely-ordained moral dimension in the universe. The school taught that everyone had experiences that provided assurances of the existence of the self, the existence of real objects that could be seen and felt, and principles upon which sound morality and religious beliefs could be established. Perhaps not surprisingly, Chalmers was about to take a very different approach to the subject.

On one level Chalmers accepted that individuals had a moral regulator, but this he called conscience. Where he most differed was in his understanding of what guided the conscience into making choices and decisions. Rather than seeing this as an innate human quality, he recognized that people needed to have their minds directed by God's revelation in Scripture. What most shaped Chalmers's approach to his subject was his evangelical faith. In all that he taught he started with the assumption that salvation was necessary because of sin, and that salvation was only possible through faith in the crucified and risen Christ. He stressed that it was only as people were supernaturally freed from the power of sin and Satan by the work of the Holy Spirit that they were then able to live their lives in the community according to the positive principles taught in Scripture. Chalmers was also eager to show that it really mattered how people lived their lives. He further stressed that there were answers to society's problems which could be found in Scripture, and that it was the duty of mankind to find these answers and to apply them. Rather than focusing in his teaching on epistemology, or the scope and nature of knowledge, Chalmers taught his students that what really mattered was the application of the teachings of Scripture to the everyday problems that people faced in their lives and in society as a whole.

Chalmers was extremely popular with most of his students and was a charismatic teacher. His enthusiasm characterized his teaching. Unlike some of his colleagues, who seemed to be going through the motions as they taught, Chalmers delivered lively lectures. The same skills which he had used in the pulpit to draw large congregations in his Glasgow churches, he now used in teaching his students. Likewise, he used his gifts as a pastor to take a keen interest in the lives of his students.

He was known for very carefully grading student papers. Students came to recognize that when they submitted work to their professor he would take it seriously. His students were also encouraged to present seminars based on their papers. Exploration of new ideas was encouraged and, perhaps most importantly, students were taught how to think for themselves. Although Chalmers was no twenty-first-century democrat in terms of his views on how society should be structured, he was insistent that all his students should treat each other with respect and dignity, regardless of their background. For Chalmers, all his students were valuable and important.

During his second year at St Andrews, he developed a new course on political economy. This gave him an opportunity to introduce his students to his political and economic views and to show them how he had sought to implement his ideas on poor relief during his time in Glasgow. This course was very popular, attracting thirty-five students the first time it was offered. He was seeking to show his students that his ideas were more than just theories; they had been tested and put into practice. Certainly the students were given a somewhat one-sided and very positive view of Chalmers's great urban experiment, but they learned that ideas taught in the classroom needed to be worked out in the real world.

While Chalmers was extremely effective in the classroom, he also took it upon himself to actively mentor a number of the young men. They were invited into his home on Sunday evenings for instruction and fellowship.

While this group started very small and with no fanfare at all, word of it soon spread until there were more students who wanted to come than the Chalmers's home could reasonably accommodate.

Chalmers also took an interest in other areas of the university and the town. Not long after his arrival, he joined the St Andrews Mission Society. Although this society had been in existence since 1812, it had ceased to be an active organization due to lack of interest. Chalmers believed that if it could be revived it could enliven interest in foreign missions and it might also play a key role in increasing the effectiveness of the evangelical party in the Church of Scotland. He presented to the society a picture of the growth of Christian missions around the world, and pressed upon his hearers that it was the duty of the church to go into all the world to preach the gospel. He also expressed confidence in the power of the Holy Spirit to bless the faithful preaching of the gospel and thus he encouraged his hearers to think that there was hope for the world. His exciting presentations soon attracted such large audiences that the society had to change location. The enthusiastic expansion of the town's missionary society soon spilled over into the university, with one society starting up in the Divinity College and another in Chalmers's own moral philosophy class. These two university groups eventually merged to form the St Andrews University Missionary Society, with almost a third of the university's total student enrolment participating.

The St Andrews Missionary society met on a regular basis for prayer and study. They raised funds for foreign mission and most importantly created massive momentum and would eventually provide manpower for mission work. Alexander Duff, who would eventually be responsible for massive educational reform in India, was a member of the Missionary Society. In later life he would say that he could '... trace the dawn, the rise and progress of any feeble Missionary spirit I might possess, to the readings, conversations and essays called for by the student Missionary Association in St Andrews'.[9]

Away from the university, Chalmers busied himself with other activities. He lost little time in establishing a local Sabbath school in one of the poorest sections of the town. He invited the children to his home, where he told them Bible stories and undertook simple catechizing. In doing this, Chalmers was demonstrating his genuine passion for the spread of the gospel to those who may never have been inside a church building. While he was personally engaged in this work, he also actively encouraged some of the young men in his classes to become involved as teachers in Sabbath schools in other parishes of the Church of Scotland. When some of them met resistance, he suggested that they might find greater acceptance if they offered their services to some of the dissenting congregations in the area, that were not part of the Church of Scotland but did have an evangelical outlook.

As this student work built momentum, Chalmers was presented with a proposal to open a summer school that would give free instruction in economics, history, mathematics and philosophy. While he truly appreciated the desire that lay behind this proposal, he was concerned that the students' enthusiasm might be greater than their abilities to make it work and so he reluctantly refused to support it.

All of this activity in St Andrews shows that while Chalmers may have felt the need to leave active parish ministry, he had not escaped into an ivory tower. His lectures were inspiring and instructing a new generation of students and he was, along with his students, putting into practice one of his basic principles that the gospel must be lived out. Faith that remained in the head but did not warm the heart and change lives was not real faith.

While Chalmers's classroom lectures and relationships with students were a success, the same cannot be said for his interactions with the university's faculty and administration or with some in the Church of Scotland. One area of conflict was over the eligibility of Church of Scotland ministers to hold appointments both at the university and also in a parish. In 1824 Francis Nicoll, who was both the Principal of the United Colleges and minister of the college chapel, requested that an assistant minister for the chapel be appointed. Nicoll had come to realize that he could not do both of his jobs well without help and so he proposed that James Hunter (1772–1845), the university's Professor of Logic and Rhetoric, be given the position. Hunter was well liked and the proposal seemed uncontroversial, but Chalmers reacted angrily. He argued strenuously that Hunter should not be appointed the assistant at the chapel unless he was going to resign his academic appointment. He went further and turned on Nicoll, who had been instrumental in his own appointment, and suggested that if he needed help doing two jobs then he should resign as minister of the chapel and devote himself to his academic work.

Nicoll, who had viewed Chalmers as a friend, made a personal appeal to him; but his request went unheeded. Chalmers instead took his complaints to the local presbytery and at the same time began to organize public opposition to the appointment. As tensions built, both moderates and evangelicals appealed to Chalmers to behave appropriately as he was bringing both the church and the university into disrepute. But he pressed on. Eventually Nicoll succumbed to pressure and resigned as the minister of the chapel and Hunter was appointed in his place, while still keeping his academic chair. But this did not end the unpleasantness. Some evangelical students broke university regulations by refusing to attend services in the chapel that were led by Hunter and demanding to be allowed to go to other churches. While Chalmers claimed that he had not put the students up to this, he nevertheless was quietly supportive of them. Eventually tensions eased, but the damage had been done.

Chalmers's behaviour in this incident was motivated by his genuine belief that a minister should not hold plural appointments, and also his suspicion that too many academics were not hard-working enough. But even if he was acting out of principle, he did not conduct himself well. He had drawn students into a dispute that was not their concern and he had paid little attention to his personal relationships with his colleagues on the faculty. He does not seem to have thought very much about how he could remain as an effective member of the university community when he had lost a lot of good will.

Chalmers's relationship with the university faculty and administration deteriorated further when he decided to take up the question of how funds were being spent by the university. It had been the practice since 1784 to pay the faculty an annual dividend to supplement what were admittedly small stipends. Shortly after his arrival at the university, Chalmers came to the principled conclusion that he and the other faculty were not entitled to this money. So he announced that he would not take the money for himself and that he was considering referring the whole matter to the civil courts for investigation. His concern was that funds which should have gone for university improvements were, instead, going into the pockets of the professors.

Eventually the government in London, faced with unrest at St Andrews and other Scottish universities, decided to set up a Royal Commission to investigate the whole matter. Chalmers was called as a witness in the summer of 1827. He gave lengthy evidence in which he spoke out against plural appointments and the special dividend paid to faculty. He further called for reform of the curriculum to bring it more up to date. Before the Commission brought in their final report, they indicated to Chalmers that the payment of the dividend to the faculty was probably legal. On the basis of this he accepted his share of it in 1829. When the final report was delivered in 1831, it was decreed that the dividend should not have been paid and plural appointments were condemned. While the Commission's report provided some vindication for Chalmers's original concerns, he looked totally inconsistent for having accepted the 1829 dividend.

Chalmers's outspoken criticisms of the administration of the university alienated him further from his colleagues, and so he began to wonder whether he should be looking for another position. Through most of 1827 Chalmers seriously considered an offer to move to the University of London to take the Chair of Moral Philosophy there, but then in 1828 he heard that the Edinburgh Town Council had elected him to the prestigious Chair of Theology at the University of Edinburgh. During his years at St Andrews, Chalmers had remained in contact with the people of Edinburgh and Glasgow through regular preaching, and there is little doubt that his oratorical skills contributed as much to his new appointment as they had to the one at St Andrews. With the sense that God was calling him to a new and more important field of labour, he accepted the appointment.

Chalmers's time in St Andrews was something of a mixed blessing for him. There was personal happiness for him as two of his daughters were born there, but he also lost his much-loved mother and sister. He had a major impact on the lives of a number of young people who would subsequently go on to do much good for the church throughout the world, but he had increasingly found himself in the middle of controversy. It was also a period where his inability to get along with people with whom he did not agree became more pronounced.

7

THE UNIVERSITY OF EDINBURGH AND THE SCOTTISH CHURCH CRISIS, 1828–1842

The period from 1828–1842 was among the busiest of Chalmers's life. During this period he occupied the Chair of Theology at the University of Edinburgh, involved in teaching and tutoring students. Just as importantly, he became increasingly involved in the ecclesiastical politics of the Church of Scotland that led to the Disruption of May 1843 and the creation of the Free Church of Scotland.

Chalmers was inaugurated as the Professor of Divinity at the University of Edinburgh on 6 November 1828 and his inaugural lecture took place on the following Monday. William Hanna, Chalmers's nineteenth century biographer, described the scene in these terms:

> The morning of that day was singularly unpropitious, showers of snow and hail sweeping through the College courts; yet from so early an hour as nine, those who had secured that privilege were passing by a private entrance into the class-room, while so great a crowd besieged the outer door, that a string of police found it difficult to restrain the tumult.[10]

During the winter of 1828–29, Chalmers was extremely busy. His lectures at the university were very well received. He was so occupied with work that he asked his household servants to protect him from intruders who merely wanted to have a social visit with him.

In February 1829, one of the most controversial political debates of the early nineteenth century began when it was announced that the government was going to pursue a policy of Roman Catholic emancipation. This was a major change for Britain. In 1661 Parliament had passed a series of laws which were largely designed to protect the realm from the influence of Roman Catholicism. These pieces of legislation prevented all those who were not members of the Established Church, and specifically Roman Catholics, from sitting in Parliament or holding public office. Under the terms of the proposed emancipation legislation, members of the Roman Church and Protestant nonconformists would have the same political rights and freedoms as citizens who belonged to the Established

Church. This decision received a mixed response. Many evangelicals opposed the proposals, but Chalmers was quick to agree with the new policy. His argument was that there was no need, or any theological justification, for preventing Catholics from taking part in the political and public life of the country. In a speech delivered in Edinburgh on 14 March 1829, he argued that the suppression of Catholicism by legal means was wrong. He contended that reason, Scripture and prayer were the weapons that God had given to the church for the propagation of the gospel. Instead of maintaining laws that suppressed others, the Protestant church should rely on the power of the Holy Spirit to advance the cause of Christ.

One of the results of Catholic emancipation and the subsequent Reform Act of 1832, which expanded the electoral franchise, was the weakening of the old assumption that the government had a duty to support the Established Church. While Chalmers did not believe that Catholics and nonconformists should be persecuted for their views, he still held firmly to the belief that it was the duty of the State to support the work of the Established Church, the Church of Scotland.

Increasingly, Chalmers's pastoral and teaching experience, along with his writings, meant that his profile as an important leader and thinker grew. In 1830, he gave evidence before a Select Committee of the House of Commons on the issue of poor relief in Ireland. In his evidence, he argued that the government should be providing support to the Established Churches and then allowing them to administer poor relief through the parish system. Chalmers also told the Committee that the parish system as he had seen it working in Kilmany and as he had tried to implement it in Glasgow was the best way forward. Chalmers firmly believed that those who were in need must first have their character reformed through the teaching of the church and the embracing of Christian values, and only then would they benefit from poor relief. He was also concerned with a broader issue, that of the secularization of society. As he saw the impact of the industrial revolution and rapid population growth, he was becoming increasingly alarmed that the old values were being lost. It was therefore essential to put the church at the heart of the poor relief system so that people could be helped spiritually as well as physically. The Committee chose to ignore most of his advice and, in fact, did not reach any firm conclusions at all, other than to tell Parliament that the issue needed further study!

Undeterred by his failure to persuade Parliament, Chalmers chose to expand his ideas and publish them. These appeared in 1832 in a book entitled *On Political Economy, in Connexion with the Moral State and Moral Prospects of Society.* The book received mixed reviews, with some welcoming Chalmers's argument that the church should be the source of poor relief, while others dismissed it, arguing that it was only the national government which could adequately execute this task. Chalmers's belief that governmental poor relief programmes would only serve to further secularize society may have been correct, but the mood of the day was not in his favour.

This book was just the latest example of Chalmers's prodigious literary output. By the time of his death in 1847, Chalmers's publications would reach an astounding twenty-five volumes, with nine more volumes published after his death. A good deal of the credit for this massive productivity must be given to Grace Chalmers, Thomas's wife. She handled all of the publishing arrangements with his publisher William Collins and answered most of his correspondence. This, in addition to all of the duties of a pastor's and professor's wife and mother of six daughters, indicates what a remarkable woman she was.

On 9 February 1831, the Reverend Andrew Thompson, who had preached the first sermon at St John's Church in Glasgow, died suddenly of a heart attack. At the time of his death, he was the minister of St George's Church in Edinburgh and was considered by many as the leader of the evangelical wing in the Church of Scotland. Although Chalmers and Thompson had much in common, they did not always see eye to eye. Thompson never agreed with Chalmers's idea that poor relief should be distributed through the parish system, and in fact had been a supporter of government plans for the strengthening of the poor laws. Despite these differences, Chalmers assumed Thompson's mantle as the leader of the evangelicals, which impacted the rest of his life and ministry. The first public recognition of his increased prominence was his election as the Moderator of the General Assembly of the Church of Scotland in 1832. He carried out his duties with distinction. He refereed debates with fairness and won the approval of both the moderate and evangelical parties in the Assembly.

During 1833, Chalmers's profile in Edinburgh and throughout the Scottish church continued to grow. He found himself in the middle of a highly contentious debate about how the clergy in Edinburgh should be paid. The Town Council wanted to abolish the Annuity Tax, the revenues that paid clergy stipends. What particularly angered Chalmers was the Council's proposal that the number of clergy in Edinburgh should be reduced and that the rest of the clergy should have their stipends cut. Debate raged both at the Town Council and in the presbytery about the best way forward. Another element of the debate was that the Church of Scotland was increasingly having to contend with the rising tide of voluntarism, the belief that the church should be supported by those who attended and not from government revenues. If the Council's proposals were approved, it would be a direct threat to the privileged position of the Church of Scotland. Chalmers passionately believed that it was the Established Church that could best bring about the vision of the Godly Commonwealth. His dream could only be realized if the church had enough money to be less dependent on pew rents for operating capital. If the church were financially independent, the poor would be able to come to church on the same basis as the wealthy and stability in society would be maintained through Christian teaching and principles.

In April 1833, the presbytery of Edinburgh appointed Chalmers to its committee for the preservation of presbytery's endowments and income. His appointment was due in part to his rising prominence, but it also was because his stipend came to him as a result of his university appointment. As a result, he was perceived as not being directly impacted by the strenuous debate that was taking place.

In January 1834, the Town Council did in fact eliminate the annuity tax and reduced the number of clergy serving Church of Scotland congregations in Edinburgh. Chalmers reacted with anger at this decision. At a meeting of the Edinburgh presbytery on 23 January 1834, he raised the alarm that the mission of the church was under attack from the voluntary movement and the Town Council. He passionately argued that unless the Church of Scotland continued to have proper funding from the government, it would never be able to care for the needs of those who needed the gospel the most. The presbytery was energized by his speech and enthusiastically adopted his committee's report, even though the battle over the annuity tax was lost.

Not only did Chalmers and the Church not achieve their goals, the strain of recent events took an immediate toll on his health. On his way home from the presbytery meeting, he suffered what was, in all probability, a stroke. He was paralyzed on his right side, although he was still able to communicate clearly. There was concern as to whether he would completely recover. Chalmers confided in letters and in his diary his fears that he might lose his mental faculties and might not regain his physical strength. However, he did recover sufficiently that he was able to return to his teaching duties at the University of Edinburgh. Towards the summer he suffered a relapse with what he described as 'considerable and constant noise' in his head. When this occurred, his doctor insisted that he cease all study and spend the summer having a complete rest. Chalmers's restless personality made it difficult for him to relax, but he had little choice. His cousin Charles Cowan (1801–1889), successful businessman, politician and churchman, provided Thomas, his wife and two of his daughters with comfortable accommodation for the summer which allowed for a period of recuperation.

As we saw earlier, when discussing Chalmers's ministry in Glasgow, the Church of Scotland had been almost entirely unsuccessful in the first years of the nineteenth century in gaining government grants for the establishment of new parishes. Everyone recognized that there was a need, but no one wanted to pay for it. As a result, the Church of Scotland began to look for other solutions, and at the 1834 General Assembly plans were put in place in an attempt to move the work of the church forward.

Chalmers was unable to be actively involved in the Assembly because of his health, but this did not stop him from being a very interested observer or expressing his opinions. Despite his poor health and the lack of certainty about his recovery, the Assembly asked Chalmers to chair a new committee on church extension, which was known as the Church Accommodations Committee. The aims of this committee were twofold: first, to lobby the government for more funds, and secondly, to seek private donations if money from the government was not forthcoming. As Chalmers began to recover during the summer months, he set the work of the committee in motion and, as he was able, took an enthusiastic part in its work. Chalmers was very clear on the Committee's goal: to open as many Church of Scotland parishes as were needed to serve the needs of the population so that everyone who wanted to go to church could. It was not too long before what had begun as the work of a church became a movement.

This period coincided with a revival in evangelical religion in Scotland. As Chalmers began his work for this committee, the seed he was sowing fell on hungry and fertile ground. He took every speaking engagement that he could to explain his vision; in addition, he had a captive and motivated audience in his classroom at the University of Edinburgh. For many of his divinity students, the only way that they could ever hope to find a vacant pulpit would be if there was significant expansion within the Church of Scotland. So Chalmers encouraged his students to take his message outside the university classroom to the people of Scotland. The message was a simple one. The Great Commission given by Jesus to his disciples needed to be carried out, and society's good demanded that people should be able to hear the gospel and receive Christian education and discipleship from a local congregation.

Also at the 1834 General Assembly, the *Veto Act* was passed. The purpose of this act was to restrict the power of patronage by giving to male heads of families the right to veto the parish patron's appointment of their local minister. Chalmers enthusiastically supported this piece of legislation and argued for it on the basis that the Church could trust the common sense of its members to make proper appointments. To modern ears, this hardly seems a noteworthy event, but it was very controversial at the time. The first test of the *Veto Act* occurred in 1834 in the parish of Auchterarder, Perthshire, where out of a total of 336 heads of families, only two of them were prepared to sign a call to the laird's preferred candidate, Robert Young. When the call was not then acted upon by the presbytery, Young sued, thus beginning a long legal wrangle.

The same General Assembly also passed the *Chapels Act*. This Act gave official recognition to chapels of ease, granting them similar status to parish churches.[11] This had the immediate effect of swelling the ranks of the evangelical party in the Church of Scotland. With the *Veto Act* and the *Chapels Act* in place, the Church of Scotland began an aggressive and impressive church-extension programme which would see the building of many churches and schools throughout Scotland. Rather than asking for full government financial support for this expansion programme, the Church decided to fund this effort largely through private contributions. They only looked to the government to provide a partial endowment in those areas where poverty was so great that parish residents could not afford to pay the stipends of the local schoolmaster and minister. Chalmers's visionary leadership of the Church Accommodations committee turned it into a movement that produced significant funds for the establishment of new churches.

Chalmers's increasing reputation was recognized by an

important honour he received in 1834. He was surprised to be elected as a corresponding member of the Royal Institute of France. He felt deeply honoured to receive this recognition for his academic work. However, it was not until 1838 that he was able to visit France to accept this award. He travelled with Charles Cowan, who acted as his translator. In Paris he was greeted with real warmth as he preached at the Chapelle Taitbout and also gave a scholarly paper to the Institute. A second honour was given to him in 1835 when the University of Oxford awarded him a Doctor of Laws degree. In doing so, the university singled out his academic work, along with his pioneering work in parish ministry and his leadership in the Church of Scotland.

While Chalmers cannot be faulted for his energy and vision in leading the cause of church extension, he was not as successful in persuading those who disagreed with him to join his cause. Chalmers was a very complex character. He could be very stubborn and possessed a formidable temper which he displayed all too often. His pen, which he had used so successfully to promote the gospel and social change, could sometimes be turned on his foes. In 1834, for example, as the Edinburgh Town Council continued their campaign to reduce the number of ministers, he published a fiery pamphlet entitled, *On the Evils which the Established Church in Edinburgh Has Already Suffered, and Suffers Still, in Virtue of the Seat-Letting Being in the Hands of the Magistrates.* Pamphlets like this one only hardened positions rather than bringing about resolution.

And it was typical of Chalmers's approach when he was challenged or thwarted.

Chalmers's relationship to the British government's Royal Commission on Religious Instruction in Scotland presents another example of the complexity of his character. The Commission was given a broad remit and its composition raised concerns as to its impartiality. But Chalmers counselled patience, believing that the Commission would have enough information to make the correct decision and recommend greater support for the church-extension movement in Scotland. However, when an Edinburgh minister, Robert Lee, gave evidence that Chalmers's parish model did not really work in the cities, Chalmers reacted with fury. His outburst was prompted by the fact that Lee had been nominated as the Moderator of the 1836 General Assembly. Chalmers had initially nominated Lee, but he quickly changed his mind when Lee's evidence contradicted his views. Chalmers was successful in blocking the appointment in 1836, but when the nomination was reissued the following year his opposition became even more pointed. In January 1837 he published another pamphlet called *A Conference with Certain Ministers of the Church of Scotland, on the Subject of the Moderatorship of the Next General Assembly*. Chalmers named Lee in the pamphlet and engaged in a bitter personal attack against his ministerial colleague. Even many of his friends believed he had gone too far, and for a time his image in the public mind was tarnished by his impulsive behaviour. It is unfortunate that his quick temper sometimes got the better of him. While his explosions were often of a public nature they do not present a fully rounded picture of the man. He was much loved by his family and friends and wrote witty and warm letters to his wife and daughters when he was away from them.

Between 1834 and 1843, the church scene in Scotland became increasingly complex as tensions increased both within the Church of Scotland and between the Church, the courts and the British government. While Chalmers was not directly involved in all of these situations, it is important that we understand what was going on in the wider scene.

Within the Church of Scotland, evangelicals were continuing to call for the people to have the freedom to call their own ministers. There were several cases that brought this issue to the forefront of the public's mind. The most notable instance took place in the Parish of Marnoch when John Edwards was presented as the next minister. While he had the support of the patron, the congregation did not want him. The local innkeeper was the only member of the parish to sign the call. This created a major problem for the presbytery, whose job it was to install the new minister. The presbytery asked the Commission of Assembly what they should do. They were instructed to reject the nomination, which they did. The patron accepted this decision, but Mr Edwards did not, and he subsequently took the presbytery to court. The presbytery responded by saying that they would await the result of the court action before making a final decision. In the end, the Court of Session instructed the presbytery of Strathbogie to proceed with Edwards's installation, but the Church's Commission of Assembly told them not to. Faced with the difficult decision of having to choose between obeying the state or the Church of Scotland, the presbytery met and agreed by a vote of seven to four to obey the civil court and sustain Edwards's ordination. The 'Strathbogie Seven' as they were called, were subsequently deposed for disobeying the Church and the minority were called upon to announce the sentence of deposition. Eventually Edwards was admitted as minister of the parish, while the seven suspended ministers constituted themselves as the presbytery and sought court protection to keep those who opposed them out of the area. This case had much wider implications than in the particular parish involved, because it brought into sharp relief divisions within the Church over how ministerial calls should be handled.

On the political front, the British government announced that they would not support the work of the Church of Scotland in the poorer areas where the partial endowments had been sought. This was a blow to the Church, which had hoped to get at least some funding for the creation of much-needed parishes. Then the Court of Session in Scotland decided that the Church's *Veto Act* was illegal, since it infringed on the rights of parish patrons to decide on who the minister should be. These decisions effectively killed the momentum that had been created by the church-extension movement. Undoubtedly, there had been real progress. From the time that the campaign started until Chalmers resigned from the committee in 1841, over

£300,000 was raised and 222 new churches were built. To even the most critical or cynical observer, the scheme was a massive success.

By 1842 the situation was reaching a breaking point. Frustration was growing because of the fact that the state, through the courts, was inserting itself into issues that were none of its business. Over the next eighteen months events were set in motion which would change the face of the church in Scotland. And Thomas Chalmers stood at the centre of these events.

8

THE DISRUPTION,
1842–1843

As if the divisions between the moderates, who were more or less happy with the status quo, and the evangelicals, who wanted change, were not enough, it became increasingly apparent during 1842 that the evangelicals were not in total agreement on the way forward for the Church of Scotland. As we have seen, Chalmers was firmly opposed to those who believed that patrons should be left alone to choose parish ministers. However, he also wanted to maintain government financing for an Established Church. While the evangelicals were all agreed that congregations should have a direct say in the appointment of their ministers and wanted the Church to be spiritually independent, not everyone was convinced that an Established Church was a good idea.

Robert Candlish (1806–1873), the minister of St George's Church in Edinburgh, was just one influential figure who came to believe that a connection with the state might be detrimental to the Church of Scotland. At a meeting of the Edinburgh presbytery in January 1842, he stated that the only way to end the uncertainties and disputes currently raging would be for the Church to recognize that patronage and connection to the state needed to end. He went on to argue that the really important thing was that the Church should never compromise on the principle of spiritual independence. He told the presbytery that

> I prefer the downfall of the Establishment infinitely rather than any compromise of principle. Of the two things—the Church existing as a Voluntary Church, or existing as a Church Establishment with even an apparent sacrifice of honour of principle—I am convinced that her existence as a Voluntary Church is far more likely to promote the glory of God and to win souls to Christ.[12]

Hugh Miller (1802–1856) was another important figure at this time. He was a stone mason by profession, an accomplished amateur geologist, and a journalist. As the dispute over the spiritual independence of the church continued, he wrote strenuously in support of the evangelical cause. His opinions were expressed so strongly that he would eventually be encouraged to launch his own newspaper, *The Witness*. Starting with only six hundred subscribers, the paper would eventually rival *The Scotsman* as a shaper of public opinion. It is important to note here that the debates taking place in presbytery meetings were becoming much more public. Through Miller's colourful journalism, popular support for the spiritual independence of the church was increasing.

In March 1842, yet another group in the Church emerged. The 'middle party' claimed that they did not want the state intruding in the affairs of the Church, but advocated further negotiations with the government in hopes that compromises could be reached. They called for calm since they believed that Chalmers and other leading evangelicals were being far too strident. This group attracted a number of leading moderate evangelicals to their cause and their ranks eventually comprised about forty ministers, some from quite prominent churches. Chalmers was not impressed by their argument for moderation, and neither were most of his followers. In the pages of *The Witness*, Hugh Miller accused these men of wanting to compromise only so that they could retain their stipends and their manses. He accused them of selling out the cause and dubbed them 'the forty thieves'. Despite Miller's attacks, there were suggestions that the government might hear the pleas from the middle party and agree to recognize the stipulations of the *Veto Act* as long as the Church would not continue to be so outspoken on the issue of spiritual independence. However, events were reaching the point of no return.

The future direction of the Church of Scotland came into sharper focus during the General Assembly which took place in Edinburgh in May 1842. The tone of the assembly was set at the very beginning when there was a wrangle over which representatives from the presbytery of Strathbogie should be seated. Rival groups from the presbytery appeared, each claiming the right to take part. On the one side were representatives of those who had obeyed the civil courts and installed John Edwards as the minister of the parish of Marnoch, even though this was against the majority opinion of the parish. On the other side was a delegation representing those who had deposed the so-called 'Strathbogie Seven' for disobeying the Church.

Some argued that the representatives of those who had obeyed the Commission of Assembly, and had deposed the 'Strathbogie Seven', should be allowed to take their seats and take part in the Assembly. The moderate minority of the Church argued that neither should be seated because the Church was so divided on the issue. Further, there were still appeals to be heard on the merits of the original case. Chalmers argued that the Assembly had no choice but to seat those who had been obedient to the Church. He also stated that if the moderates did not like this, they should either secede from the Church or themselves face disciplinary action. The Assembly backed Chalmers, but that was not the end of the story. The Court of Session ruled that the Assembly was acting illegally and forbade the members of the Strathbogie presbytery from participating. In response, the Assembly ignored the ruling of the court, claiming that their decision was just another example of unjust civil interference in the affairs of the Church. If anyone had thought that this Assembly might bring about a peaceful resolution to the crisis, it was now clear that this was not going to be the case.

The Assembly of 1842 has come to be associated with two pieces of legislation. First, a resolution was passed which called on the government to abolish patronage totally. This motion was proposed by William Cunningham (1805–1861), who would go on to be one of the most influential Scottish theologians of the nineteenth century. Chalmers was not enthusiastic about this measure because he still held out hope that the government might recognize the spiritual independence of the church while still maintaining some form of financial support for the Church of Scotland. However, he was concerned that the evangelical wing of the Church was beginning to fragment so, against his better judgement, he supported this motion.

On Tuesday May 24, Thomas Chalmers moved the adoption of the other important piece of legislation: *The Claim Declaration and Protest anent the Encroachments of the Court of Session.* It was the clearest possible statement that the Church of Scotland should be free from all interference on spiritual matters, such as the selection of ministers and issues of church discipline. After reciting the history of church and state relations, the document concluded by recognizing

> ... *the absolute jurisdiction of the Civil Courts in relation to all matters whatsoever of a civil nature, and especially in relation to all the temporalities conferred by the State upon the Church, and the civil consequences attached by law to*

the decisions, in matters spiritual, of the Church Courts,—DO, in name and on behalf of this Church, and of the nation and people of Scotland, and under the sanction of the several statutes, and the Treaty of Union herein before recited, CLAIM, as of RIGHT, that she shall freely possess and enjoy her liberties, government, discipline, rights, and privileges, according to law, especially for the defence of the spiritual liberties of her people, and that she shall be protected therein from the foresaid unconstitutional and illegal encroachments of the said Court of Session, and her people secured in their Christian and constitutional rights and liberties. [13]

In his speech supporting this legislation, Chalmers made the point that the Church of Scotland would never surrender its historic rights, but if the British (and here he actually used the word English) government continued on the present course, there would be no option but for evangelicals within the Church to give up state support. The *Claim of Right*, as the Act came to be known, easily passed the General Assembly and was dispatched to London. The Conservative government in London responded almost immediately by admitting that they could not find an immediate solution to the problem and leaving it to the civil courts to determine the rights and wrongs of the various cases in dispute.

Thomas Chalmers and his family headed for Ireland after the Assembly for a period of rest, but as he left Scotland, he kept a careful eye on the fast-developing events. In August, the House of Lords in London made a decision which effectively quashed any hopes for the spiritual independence of the church. In effect, they said that any minister or elder who believed in the arguments presented in the *Claim of Right* no longer belonged in the Church of Scotland.

Returning from Ireland, Chalmers and his colleagues began to make plans for what would not be another minor secession from the Church of Scotland, but which had the potential to reshape the entire church landscape. As they began planning the next steps, it was not entirely clear how many ministers, elders and congregations would be prepared to sacrifice their livelihoods, church buildings and manses for the sake of principle. There were probably those in the government in London, serving on courts in Scotland and within the Church, who hoped that this was all a bluff and that Chalmers and the other leaders would never be able to keep their supporters with them. It is at this point that many people underestimated just how effective a leader Chalmers was.

Chalmers returned to Scotland at the beginning of September 1842. Over the course of the autumn, he began reaching out to as many prominent ministers as he could. By November he was ready to have an organizational meeting to put together a clear plan of action. The Convocation opened in St George's Church in Edinburgh on Thursday November 17. As Chalmers preached at the opening meeting he found himself speaking to 465 ministers, a significant portion of the entire Church. While there were no official minutes taken of the Convocation, it is possible to piece together what took place from the diaries and letters of Chalmers and the other participants.

There was lively debate at the Convocation on what was the best way forward. The earlier divisions among the evangelicals remained, although the increasing intransigence of the courts and the government were bringing more people together. After the opening worship service, the delegates moved from St George's Church to the less prominent Roxburgh Church where, it was hoped, there would be more privacy. Chalmers was asked to chair the Convocation. From this position, he laid out a very clear vision for the future. Everyone present was aware of the fact that they were about to take a decision that would require personal sacrifice, so Chalmers sought to calm their fears.

He told his audience that the new denomination could be economically viable. Chalmers argued that no minister would receive an annual stipend of less than £200, that there would be an active campaign to raise funds to build new churches and schools where they were needed, and that this would be a missionary-minded denomination both at home and abroad. And, to prevent anyone from thinking he was simply dreaming, he told them that this programme could all be financed through the giving of the laity and the sharing of resources. He went further and made a personal pledge that he would undertake personally to raise the staggering amount of £100,000 each year to support the new denomination. At the end of the week of meetings, 423 ministers signed a statement listing all the grievances that had been inflicted on the Church of Scotland at the hands of the courts and the government. Then another document was signed which stated that unless there was redress, the signatories would resign their offices in the Church. This second document received 354 signatures. It subsequently emerged that some participants felt intimidated by Chalmers's personality and oratory, but it is still remarkable that after a week of meetings so many were prepared to sacrifice their secure livelihoods.

In January 1843, the government announced that they were rejecting the 'Claim of Right'. Further, the Court of Session declared that the 1834 *Chapels Act*, which had set the church-extension plan in motion, was illegal. The effect was to legally abolish all the new parishes that had been created by the Church. This decision only strengthened the resolve of Chalmers and his followers. A second Convocation was held in February and, as a result, local committees were created to raise funds for what would soon be a new denomination. Chalmers led the Finance Committee and was able to announce by the middle of February that in Edinburgh alone £18,550 had already been raised and that donations were flowing in at the rate of £1,000 a day! During the next two and a half months local committees were established throughout Scotland to prepare for the inevitable split. With such substantial financial backing encouraging the evangelical clergymen, by May, when the General Assembly met, there was no turning back.

The people of Scotland, and particularly of Edinburgh,

were in a high state of anticipation as the General Assembly began its meetings on 18 May 1843. In fact, as early as five o'clock in the morning, the public galleries of St Andrew's Church were full of people who were waiting for the opening of the Assembly, which was due to start just before three in the afternoon. At noon the Marquess of Bute, the Lord High Commissioner, representing the Queen, set out from Holyrood for St Giles' (the High Church) for the opening sermon of the Assembly. Arriving at St Giles' at 12:45, the High Commissioner and his retinue, along with delegates to the Assembly, listened to a sermon delivered by Dr David Welsh, the Moderator of the previous General Assembly and a prominent member of the evangelical party. Welsh's sermon was based on words from Romans 14:5: 'Each one should be fully convinced in his own mind.' In the course of his sermon, Welsh made frequent references to the crisis in the Church; it was clear that something momentous was about to happen.

Following the conclusion of the sermon, Dr Welsh led the Assembly from St Giles' to St Andrew's Church for the work of the Assembly to begin. Just before three o'clock, the Lord High Commissioner and his party took their places and Dr Welsh rose to open the General Assembly's first session with prayer. Custom then dictated that the names of new commissioners should be read out, but this was not to be. Instead, Welsh read a lengthy protest against the state's intrusion into the affairs of the Church. He announced that because of this state of affairs, he and the many others who were making this protest were being forced to separate from the Established Church. Welsh bowed to the Marquess of Bute, placed the document containing the protest on the clerk's table, and walked slowly toward the door of the church. Thomas Chalmers and over two hundred other ministers and elders quickly followed them. A cheer broke out briefly in the gallery and then stopped as the spectators realized that this gesture was inappropriate. However, the cheers started again outside the church as the departing ministers and elders left St Andrew's. A contemporary account of the event described the scene that followed.

[As] Dr Welsh, Dr Chalmers, and Dr Gordon made their appearance outside, they were received with a tremendous burst of applause from the masses assembled in George Street, which was continued and reiterated with the most extraordinary enthusiasm as they went along. All the windows and staircases were filled with ladies ... the very housetops, were covered with groups of spectators, and the universal waving of hats and handkerchiefs from all quarters, mingled with the shouts below, had a very imposing effect. The whole body formed into a line of procession, four abreast, and proceeded ... to the Hall at Tanfield, Canonmills—preceded, accompanied, and followed by immense multitudes of people—... When they reached Tanfield, they were greeted with a loud and continued burst of cheering from the multitudes which had assembled to receive them; and on entering the Hall, the part of it assigned to the public was found filled to overflowing... Those parts of the Hall devoted to ministers and elders were soon also filled, and when the business commenced, the sight of the immense mass of people congregated, upwards of 3000 persons, had a most magnificent effect.[14]

Thomas Chalmers was quickly elected as the first Moderator of the Free Church. He began by calling upon all those assembled to sing part of Psalm 43 from the Scottish Psalter. Contemporary accounts record that a sudden burst of light filled the building as the assembly sang the words:

> O send thy light forth and thy truth;
>   Let them be guides to me,
> And bring me to thine holy hill,
>   Ev'n where thy dwellings be.

Whether or not we accept the historical accuracy of the burst of sunlight, there is no doubt that there was a very positive mood among those who had left the Church of Scotland.

In his moderatorial address, Chalmers was quick to point out that the departure of most of the evangelicals from the Church of Scotland was not because of deep theological differences. It was, instead, a breaking of the relationship between the Church of Scotland and the state. This was because the state had broken its promises to maintain the spiritual independence of the church. The Free Church was being formed because the state was imposing illegal and unbiblical demands on the church, which were intolerable and which had to be resisted. In effect, it was the actions of the British government that forced the evangelicals to act in the way that they had.

Chalmers acknowledged that all those who were forming

the Free Church were making very real sacrifices, but he
went on to say this:

> *It is well that ... in the issue of the contest between a
> sacrifice of principle and a sacrifice of your worldly possessions,
> you have resolved upon the latter; and while to the eye of sense
> you are without a provision and a home, embarked upon a wide
> ocean of uncertainty, save that great and generous certainty
> which is apprehended by the eye of faith—that God reigneth,
> and that He will not forsake the families of the faithful.*[15]

Despite the optimism, there were huge challenges facing
Chalmers and the other leaders in the denomination.
Financial matters were a main priority as stipends had
to be provided and plans for building churches, manses
and schools had to be set in motion. But this was not
just a business meeting. Throughout the proceedings, the
Assembly focused its energies on how best it could carry
forward the mission of the church, to bring the gospel to
Scotland and, through its foreign mission agencies, take the
gospel to the rest of the world.

9

THE FREE CHURCH, 1843–1847

Thomas Chalmers was that interesting combination of the romantic and the realist. His romanticism sometimes caused him to be far too optimistic about what was achievable in his own life and ministry, but as the Free Church was launched, he looked upon the work that needed to be done in a very realistic fashion. Providing funds for stipends and for church-building projects was the immediate need and so, as the Assembly rose from its work, prominent ministers from the Free Church undertook fund-raising tours in England, Ireland and as far afield as Canada and the United States.

Chalmers, believing that his talents could best be used by spreading word of the Free Church's needs at home, set off on a frenetic tour of Scotland to raise support. During

August and September 1843, he visited a number of places where he knew there were supporters of the cause, who could themselves provide needed funds or who had the necessary connections to raise money. While he was not starting without any resources, because local committees had been hard at work raising money before the disruption took place, there was still a lot of money needed.

Chalmers correctly recognized that the first duty of the Free Church was to provide for church buildings, ministers and pastoral care for all those who associated themselves with the new denomination. By May 1843, there was a total amount of £76,253 in the building fund which was used as seed money, providing at least 20% of the funds needed for the construction of new church buildings. Chalmers was content to leave most of the work surrounding this building boom to other people. Where he did become involved was in cases where local landowners were unsympathetic to the Free Church, and therefore were unwilling either to sell or to give land for new church buildings. When faced with this problem, Chalmers used all of his connections and powers of persuasion to try to obtain suitable sites for churches.

Every minister and congregation which left the Church of Scotland suffered pain and loss. The most difficult problems were experienced by those in the Highlands of Scotland and in other rural areas. Where sites for churches were not forthcoming, it was not uncommon to find groups of Christians meeting for worship in some makeshift situations, and many congregations were forced, for a time, to worship in the open air.

Despite these difficulties, there was amazing progress. Buildings were erected at a remarkably fast pace, in part because of the generosity of some local businessmen who were supporters of the Free Church, and also through the donation of free labour from a number of tradesmen. Just one year after the Disruption, 470 buildings were completed. Within four years, the number had risen to 730. As well as erecting new churches, the Free Church also went to court and had some success regaining control of buildings which had been opened during the church-extension campaign. One of the side benefits of the building programme was its positive impact on the Scottish economy. In the years immediately prior to the Disruption, there had been little building taking place, so all of the activity surrounding the new construction actually helped to lower unemployment.

Chalmers assumed that the initial enthusiasm created by the Disruption would, in all likelihood, provide the necessary funds for buildings and perhaps even for pastoral stipends for a time. But after the initial enthusiasm had worn off, then what? By separating from the Established Church, the Free Church had, in effect, turned itself into a denomination that was based on voluntary contributions. This was anathema to Chalmers's belief in the establishment principle and vision of the Godly Commonwealth, where the state should be providing support for the work of the church. Given this circumstance, Chalmers, Charles Cowan and others had planned for what they called 'the sustentation fund'. This fund, which had been discussed at the Convocation in November 1842, was set up to help pay clergy stipends. It was designed so that each congregation would have a role to play in the financial stability of the whole denomination.

The fund worked in this way. Each year local congregations collected as much money as they could for the work of the entire Free Church. These collections were then sent four times a year to Edinburgh, where they were invested. Then, on an annual basis, every minister was paid an equal amount from the fund, which guaranteed that a basic stipend was provided for all clergy. In 1844, one year after the formation of the Free Church, the sustentation fund had collected £68,000, which provided a basic stipend of £100 to nearly six hundred ministers. Local congregations were free to give additional amounts to their minister if they wished, as happened in many parishes, although these amounts varied considerably. With the combined generosity of local churches and the help of the sustentation fund, it was possible for some ministers to at least equal the stipends they had received prior to 1843. There was one final component of the sustentation fund. Not all the money collected each year was spent. A proportion was kept back and then invested in church extension so that the Free Church could continue to grow and meet the needs of the people of Scotland.

Providing education for the people of Scotland was also a key component of Chalmers's strategy for the Free Church.

He recognized that unless parish schools were established, many children would be left attending schools that were still connected with the Church of Scotland. Chalmers was concerned that if this situation was allowed to continue, children from Free Church homes would not understand where their church came from, and why the principles it had stood for were important. At the same time, there were teachers in Church of Scotland parish schools who, having expressed support for the Free Church, were losing their jobs. As a result, a national education strategy was needed. At a meeting of the Assembly in October 1843, a proposal was put forward to raise £50,000 which would be used to provide stipends for teachers and construct schools in as many parishes as possible. While this was not Chalmers's idea, he was happy to support it. To some at the Assembly, this seemed an overly optimistic target. But again, the people of Scotland demonstrated the depth of their support for the Free Church. Six months later, the collection had reached a total of £52,000 and a permanent Education Fund was established. Within four years of the start of this project, there were in the region of 44,000 children attending Free Church Schools with 513 teachers receiving stipends.

There was also a real need for the Free Church to provide for the education of its ministers. Even before the first General Assembly, a committee was put in place to plan for a seminary. Thomas Chalmers, who had resigned his position at the University of Edinburgh when the Disruption took place, was named Principal and Senior Professor of Theology. By November 1843, the

Education Committee had secured rooms at 80 George Street in Edinburgh and 168 students were enrolled in the new seminary. These rooms were seen as a temporary measure, and soon much larger plans were in place to build a permanent college that would provide instruction in the arts as well as theology. When Chalmers laid the foundation stone for 'New College' on 4 June 1846, he told the assembled audience that the College would produce students who had excellent qualifications for the gospel ministry as well as to hold a place at the very top of society. But he went on to say that what was really wanted and needed were humble ministers who would be willing to spend time with the poorest members of their parishes, especially sitting beside them as they died. Chalmers's point was that the education offered at the college was not an end in itself; rather, it was intended to prepare men for as wide a sphere of gospel service as possible.

While much of Chalmers's time was spent on helping to raise funds for the Free Church while also teaching divinity students, he still had energy to become involved in other projects as well. He remained committed to his vision of parish ministry and church extension. In the summer of 1844, he gave a series of lectures in which he again argued that the territorial or parish system was the most effective means of helping those in society who were most in need. Despite the fact that the Glasgow experiments at both the Tron and St John's parishes had not been entirely successful, Chalmers pressed on with his ideal. This time he chose the West Port area of Edinburgh, which was among the poorest in the whole city.

While the West Port area was poor by anyone's standards, with large populations of paupers, the homeless and prostitutes, this was not the reason most people had heard of the area. Its notoriety was due to the appalling crimes perpetrated by the Irish criminals Burke and Hare. In 1828, they had killed seventeen people and then sold their cadavers to the University of Edinburgh's medical faculty. When they were caught and put on trial, their appalling crimes shed a light on just how difficult life on the streets of Scotland's capital could be. While some had questioned whether the needs of the Tron and St John's parishes in Glasgow were as great as Chalmers had portrayed them, there could be no doubt about the desperate need that existed in this part of Edinburgh.

One of the major differences in Chalmers's plan for the West Port area was that he intentionally chose to work with Christians from different backgrounds. He still wanted there to be a Free Church parish with a church and a school, but he recognized that the need was so great that outside help would be required. He first contacted the Edinburgh City Mission, which already had significant experience in the area. With their blessing, the West Port Local Society came into being. Its first meeting was held on 27 July 1844. The area was divided into twenty districts with approximately twenty families in each district. It was agreed that a survey should be taken to assess the depth of the problems. The results were not encouraging.

The survey covered 411 families and demonstrated the size of the challenge. The population was extremely mobile, with those who were employed moving frequently to find work. Few school age children actually attended school, and church attendance was very low among both Catholics and Protestants. To say that there was no sense of community would be an understatement, and those surveyed saw little if any value in religious instruction.

Chalmers was able to recruit a number of 'visitors', whose job it would be to visit families within a designated area. They were to become acquainted with the people, to begin to teach them moral and religious principles, and to encourage a community spirit. It was not their purpose to distribute charity, but rather to help in other specific ways. For example, they were told to help the unemployed find work and arrange for apprenticeships for young people. They were also to lobby the Town Council to close the many taverns and to bring other social problems to the attention of local authorities.

Work in the West Port area was slow and difficult. It was hard to find enough visitors to work directly with the people who needed help the most. This was because crime rates were high and it was not particularly safe for individuals to undertake the visitations alone. Chalmers's plan therefore depended on building teams of two people who would work together. The teams then met on a weekly basis to discuss progress and plan strategy. Chalmers's role in the earliest stages of the project was different from the approach he had taken in Glasgow. He was much more hands off. It is probable that he was anxious to avoid the criticisms that had been levelled at him during his time in

Glasgow; that he was so important to the efforts there that once he was gone, they would collapse.

Worship services began in December of 1844. The following April, Chalmers persuaded one of his best students, William Tasker (1809–1879),[16] to become the pastor of the West Port Free Church. Tasker had been a school teacher before entering seminary and had also worked as a home missionary in Glasgow. With his appointment, work in the West Port area picked up momentum. Tasker soon was conducting three worship services every Sunday and threw himself into the visitation that Chalmers believed was central to the success of the project. In addition to the worship services and visitation programme, a school, a library, a laundry and a savings bank were opened, and there were some signs that progress was being made. Securing funding for this work remained a priority, and this was helped by Chalmers's occasional preaching in the new congregation, which drew large crowds. Funding was also supplied by the Sustentation Fund and from wealthy philanthropists from as far away as New York City.

Chalmers had a real sense of satisfaction when in February 1847 the West Port Territorial Church was received into the Free Church of Scotland, and William Tasker was ordained to the Free Church ministry. With some justification, Chalmers could look on this congregation, which he had helped to plan but which others had largely carried out, as evidence that his territorial model of ministry could work. While there is no question that the West Port experiment did make a significant difference to the lives of many people, it would be too much to say that it had permanently solved the systemic problems which made the West Port such an impoverished area of Edinburgh. Some have claimed that the inability to fix the systemic problem demonstrates that Chalmers's model was wrong. Instead, it is better to see that the social problems were so enormous that no one congregation or denomination, however successful, could possibly fix them.

During the period 1845–1847, Chalmers spent considerable energies trying to raise interest in and support for his vision for territorial ministry in Scotland. He travelled, spoke and wrote as much as he could in an attempt to show that the West Port experiment was making progress and could be made to work. Sadly, his vision for interdenominational cooperation never got off the ground, and the funds necessary to multiply the kind of work that had begun in the West Port were not forthcoming.

The widespread famines of 1845 and 1846 placed major strains upon both church and state as they sought to meet a very real need. First, in 1845, the potato crop failed in Ireland and then in 1846, the failure was even more widespread, impacting the Highlands of Scotland. In the autumn of 1846, Chalmers was instrumental in raising more than £15,000 from within the Free Church for famine relief, which placed the Free Church at the forefront of relief efforts. By early 1847, the situation was made even worse by the outbreak of typhoid. It was clear that private philanthropy, either from individuals or churches, could not meet the need. There were calls among some just to let the epidemic run its course. This appalling lack of concern was based on the bizarre idea that the moral failure of the inhabitants of the affected areas of Ireland and the Highlands of Scotland had brought on the famine and the plague. Chalmers angrily denounced this unfeeling attitude in a letter published in the *Witness* on 6 March 1847. Chalmers bluntly called these attitudes unchristian. Rather than spending time blaming the poor for this terrible situation, he argued, Christians should be doing all that they could to alleviate the distress.

Then, in what must be seen as a major change in his views, Chalmers argued in an article for the May issue of *The North British Review* that a crisis of the proportions that was currently being faced could only be dealt with by direct government intervention. He went on to argue that if this meant increased taxation on the more wealthy, then the government should take this action. It has been argued that this is evidence that Chalmers was completely abandoning his ideal of the Godly Commonwealth. However, this is an overstatement. It is better to see Chalmers's views as being adapted to a moment of crisis in Ireland and Scotland.

In May 1847, Chalmers visited London. He had gone there to appear before a parliamentary committee that was investigating the difficulties some Free Church congregations were experiencing in obtaining proper sites for churches. Four years after the Disruption, there were still many landowners who had neither forgiven nor forgotten the events of May 1843 and they were going out of their way to make life as difficult as possible for the Free Church. Sir James Graham (1792–1862) took the opportunity to question Chalmers aggressively on the very existence of the Free Church, hoping to force Chalmers into making concessions admitting that the Disruption had been wrong. But Chalmers held his ground. He used the rest of his time in London to visit a number of friends and relatives and he continued to visit various people in England on his return journey to Scotland. Unfortunately, the visit had taken a toll on his health. He returned to Scotland clearly exhausted and many of his family and friends expressed real concern for his wellbeing.

On Sunday May 30, he attended church as usual but went to bed early that night after leading family worship. When his housekeeper went to wake him up the next morning because he was late for an appointment, he was found dead in his bed, having died of a heart attack sometime in the night. Thomas Chalmers was sixty-seven years old.

10

THE LEGACY OF
THOMAS CHALMERS

The grief expressed at the death of Thomas Chalmers was deep and genuine. There was a very real sense that someone important had died. Because the Free Church's General Assembly was in session at the time of Chalmers's death, Edinburgh was filled with ministers and elders who all wanted to be present for his funeral.

The funeral took place on Friday 4 June. The *Scotsman* newspaper, which was not always sympathetic to Chalmers, commented that there had never been a larger funeral procession in the entire history of Edinburgh. Private devotions were held at the Chalmers home beginning at noon. At the same time, separate services were held at Free St Andrew's, Free St George's and New College. After the services in these various locations were

completed at around 1 p.m., the congregations formed
processions which came together outside Chalmers's
home. When the coffin was removed from the house, a
procession of at least two thousand formed for the journey
to the Grange Cemetery where he was to be buried. This
procession included members of the Town Council in
full regalia, commissioners to the Free Church's General
Assembly, and many other Free Church ministers and laity.
There were also representatives of many other Scottish
denominations, which showed the respect that many had
for Chalmers. Most of the city's businesses and shops
were closed for the day and the streets were lined by an
estimated 100,000 people. Hugh Miller's newspaper, the
Witness, summarized the day's events when he wrote that

> *[The day's proceedings] ... spoke more eloquently than by
> words, of the dignity of the intrinsic excellence, and of the
> height to which a true man may attain. It was the dust of a
> Presbyterian minister which the coffin contained; and yet they
> were burying him amid the tears of a nation and with more
> than kingly honours.* [17]

In the weeks which followed, many memorial services
were held throughout the country amid feelings that
Scotland would never be quite the same again. Tributes to
Chalmers flowed in from all over Scotland, as well as from
England and North America. The *Spectator,* published in
London, commented on his death:

> *It is not often that a man can be said to have "lived all
> his days," so truly as in the case of Thomas Chalmers. The*

oldest reminiscences of him that have been preserved, present the image of a young and ardent spirit luxuriating in the exercise of its powers, scarcely able to confine itself within the conventional sphere of activity prescribed to those of the profession which was nevertheless of all within his reach the best suited to his tastes and faculties: and he has been taken away while still earnestly toiling in his vocation, before any symptoms of mental weakness or of lassitude and aversion to work had become visible.[18]

While the *Spectator* then went on to question some of Chalmers's ideas and accomplishments, it generously concluded its obituary with these words:

His earnest benevolence ... was contagious. He was the Socrates of the school of Christian pastors he has founded: the value and importance of what he taught will be more apparent in the intellects he has formed than in any work he has left us.[19]

Five years later, the Scottish philosopher and essayist Thomas Carlyle (1795–1881) would sum up his life in a letter to Chalmers's son-in-law William Hanna. Carlyle wrote that

It is not often that the world sees men like Thomas Chalmers; nor can the world afford to forget them, or in its most careless mood be willing to do it, when they do appear, in whatever guise that be. Probably the time is coming when it will be more apparent than it now is to everyone that here intrinsically was the chief Scottish man of his time.[20]

It was certainly true that the Free Church lost its principal driving force when Chalmers died. While there would be many able ministers and laity who would carry on the work of the denomination, there would never be anyone to fully replace him. As the Free Church continued to expand both at home and on the mission field in the years to come, any who were being honest would acknowledge that without Chalmers's life and ministry, their own work would not have been possible.

Thomas Chalmers has now been dead for over 160 years. It is appropriate that we should ask ourselves why his life mattered, and whether twenty-first century Christians can learn anything of value from him? I would suggest that there are both positive and negative lessons that can be learned from him.

Thomas Chalmers was, first and foremost, committed to the local church. After his conversion, God used his efforts to revitalize the parish of Kilmany. Because of his preaching and pastoral care, commitment to the local church increased and Chalmers began to test his territorial model of ministry. Much has been written about his ministry in Glasgow. It would be fair to concede that his work at the Tron and St John's parishes was never quite as successful as Chalmers or his friends claimed it was. However, it is an unfair over-simplification to suggest that Chalmers's life was '... in one sense a tragic disappointment'[21] because his territorial model of ministry was never entirely successful and his vision for a flourishing Scottish evangelical church did not reach the heights he had hoped for.

The churches that he served in Glasgow did make a positive difference in their communities. Through his preaching, the light of the gospel shone forth; through the schools and the work carried out by an active eldership and diaconate, lives were changed. Chalmers also clearly recognized that for the local church to succeed, the work of the ministry had to be shared. His Glasgow parishes only succeeded because there were small armies of people who had caught Chalmers's vision for the church, and who were prepared to devote themselves wholeheartedly to the work of the church.

We are now living in a time when the prevailing philosophy of ministry appears to be that the bigger something is the better it will necessarily be. Also, we tend to look to megastars on the conference circuit to lead the church. The problem with this view is that it devalues the ministry and mission of the local church, which has been tasked to take the gospel to the community where God has placed it. Chalmers always understood that if Christianity was going to transform lives, it had to happen through the presence of a faithful, worshipping and caring church in every community. He also understood that it was the faithful preaching of the gospel that was central to the mission of the local church. We would do well to recover his focus on the value of the preached word if we want the church to have a greater impact on the world.

As we have seen, Chalmers spent a significant portion of his life working in academia. In doing so, he understood that the academy was never an end itself, but rather, it was the place where training for ministry and missionary endeavours took place. His years at St Andrews University are chiefly remembered because he inspired and helped prepare a generation of ministers and missionaries for the Church of Scotland and the Free Church. He may have been lecturing on moral philosophy at St Andrews, or on theology at the University of Edinburgh or New College, but what he was really doing was teaching practical theology to his students. For Chalmers, all of his teaching was intended to be intensely practical.

His years in academia also produced a vast literature on everything from astronomy to economics, to politics and to what we would now call sociology. We do not need to embrace all of his conclusions in these areas to see that his investigations make an important point. What Chalmers showed very clearly was that Christians do not need to be afraid of the world of ideas; in fact, the more we speak into these spheres the better off the world will be.

Another important aspect of Chalmers's life was his role in addressing the wider issues of his day. He frequently spoke about issues as diverse as who should have the right to vote, poverty, homelessness and education, to name but a few. In doing so, he was living out his belief that the gospel was not just about matters of spiritual concern. While he was careful not to take explicitly political sides in these discussions, his theology did have a public face. And he believed strongly that, with God's help, the church's views would be heard. Chalmers would not have recognized the prevailing pessimism of many twenty-first century Christians. Instead of lamenting the secularization of society and the marginalization of the church, he would be telling us to get busy and bring the gospel to bear on every area of life.

There is much that can be learned from Chalmers's style of leadership. The Disruption of 1843 and the creation of the Free Church were used by God to reinvigorate the church in Scotland. The Free Church came into existence largely because Chalmers would not give in to state interference in the affairs of the church. Positively, he had the vision and ability to propose an alternative way forward and bring many people along with him. He was not only gifted in being able to set forth a vision, he knew how to motivate people to support it. Chalmers understood that leadership meant not only pointing in a particular direction, but also taking people step-by-step through the process so that they, too, could understand the vision and carry it out.

However, one of his greatest weaknesses can also be seen in his leadership style. When he faced opposition, he could be ruthless. He tended to push forward regardless of opposition and seems to have been unable to consider the possibility that those who disagreed with him might have something to teach him. All leaders need to be prepared to listen to the perspectives of others. It is just possible that some of the conflict Chalmers faced in his life could have been avoided had he taken more time, exercised more patience, and been willing to concede that the perspectives of others could be valuable.

But whatever his faults, there can be little doubt that Chalmers's faith in the power of the gospel remained strong all of his life, and it was this faith which animated his ministry. In a sermon based on Ecclesiastes 4:13, Chalmers made this powerful statement about the power of the gospel to change the lives of individuals and the world. The gospel, he said, is

> ... the great instrument for ... elevating the poor... Let the testimony of God be simply taken in, that on his own Son he has laid the iniquities of us all ... Jesus Christ died, the just for the unjust, to bring us unto God. This is a truth, which, when all the world shall receive it, all the world will be renovated. Many do not see how a principle, so mighty in operation, should be enveloped in a proposition so simple of utterance. But let a man, by his faith in this utterance, come to know that God is his friend, and that heaven is the home of his fondest expectation; and in contact with such new elements as these, he will evince the reach, and the habit, and the desire of a new creature. It is this doctrine which is the alone instrument of God for the moral transformation of our species.[22]

BIBLIOGRAPHY

Ewing, William, ed. *Annals of the Free Church of Scotland, 1843–1900*. Edinburgh: T. & T. Clark, 1914.

Baillie, John, ed. *Proceedings of the General Assembly of the Free Church of Scotland With a Sketch of the Proceedings of the Residuary Assembly*. Edinburgh: W.P. Kennedy, 1843.

Brown, Stewart J. *Thomas Chalmers and the Godly Commonwealth*. Oxford: Oxford University Press, 1982.

Carlyle, Thomas. 'Letter to William Hanna 7 June 1852'. *The Carlyle Letters Online*. http://carlyleletters.dukejournals. org/cgi/content/full/27/1/lt-18520607-TC-WH-01 (accessed 20 June 2013).

Chalmers, Thomas. *Observations on a Passage in Mr. Playfair's Letter to the Lord Provost of Edinburgh relative to the mathematical pretensions of the Scottish Clergy*. Cupar, Fife: R. Tullis, 1867.

Chalmers, Thomas. 'On the Advantages of Christian

Knowledge to the Lower Orders of Society' in *Sermons and Discourses by Thomas Chalmers, DD. LL.D now completed by the introduction of his posthumous sermons.* 2 vols. New York: Robert Carter and Brothers, 1853.

Cheyne, A. C., ed. *The Practical and the Pious: Essays on Thomas Chalmers (1780–1847).* Edinburgh : Saint Andrew Press, 1985.

'Claim, Declaration and Protest, Anent the Encroachments of the Court of Session'.

Free Presbyterian Church of Scotland, http://www.fpchurch.org.uk/Beliefs/HistoricalDocuments (accessed 9 May 2013).

Hanna, William. *Memoirs of the Life and Writings of Thomas Chalmers.* 2 vols. Edinburgh: Edmonston and Douglas, 1867.

Piggin, Stewart and John Roxborogh. *The St Andrews Seven: the Finest Flowering of Missionary Zeal in Scottish History.* Edinburgh: Banner of Truth, 1985.

'Thomas Chalmers'. *The Spectator* no. 988 (7 June 1847), http://archive.spectator.co.uk/article/5th-june-1847/11/it-is-not-often-that-a-man-can-be-said (accessed 20 June 2013).

Watt, Hugh. *Thomas Chalmers and the Disruption.* Edinburgh: Thomas Nelson and Sons, 1943.

Wilson, William. *Memorials of Robert Smith Candlish.*
Edinburgh: Adam and Charles Black, 1880.

ENDNOTES

1   For more information on this period of Scottish church history see Sandy Finlayson, *Unity and Diversity the Founders of the Free Church of Scotland* (Fearn, Ross-shire: Christian Focus, 2010). I am grateful to Christian Focus for their permission to use some of the material from this work.

2   Quoted in Hugh Watt, *Thomas Chalmers and the Disruption* (Edinburgh: Thomas Nelson and Sons, 1943), p.6. While this pithy saying has often been attributed to Chalmers, I have been unable to trace it in one of his published works.

3   William Hanna, *Memoirs of the Life and Writings of Thomas Chalmers* (Edinburgh: Edmonston and Douglas, 1867), vol. 1, p.13. William Hanna (1808–1882) was married to Thomas Chalmers's eldest daughter Anne (1813–1891) and he was a minister in the Church of Scotland and later the Free Church. While Hanna was very proud of his father-in-law and his achievements, which is clearly reflected in this biography, it is still a valuable resource. This is partly because it reproduces lengthy sections from Chalmers's diary and correspondence. Hanna's life of Thomas Chalmers was originally published in four volumes. References in this book are to the two-volume edition.

4   Thomas Chalmers, *Observations on a Passage in Mr. Playfair's Letter to the Lord Provost of Edinburgh relative to the Mathematical Pretensions of the Scottish Clergy* (Cupar, Fife: R. Tullis, 1867), p.48.

5   Hanna, *Memoirs of the Life and Writings of Thomas Chalmers*, vol. 1, p.112.

6   Ibid., p.138.

7   Quoted in Hugh Watt, *Thomas Chalmers and the Disruption*, p.33.

8   At every celebration of the Lord's Supper, people who intended to receive the sacrament had to receive a token from the Minister and Kirk Session which indicated that they had been examined and found fit to participate in the sacrament.

9   Stewart Piggin and John Roxborogh, *The St Andrews Seven: the Finest Flowering of Missionary Zeal in Scottish History* (Edinburgh: Banner of Truth, 1985), p.48.

10   Hanna, *Memoirs of the Life and Writings of Thomas Chalmers*, vol. 2, p.177.

11   These new parishes were officially known as *quad sacra* parishes, which meant that they had been established by an act of the Church rather than by the civil authorities.

12   William Wilson, *Memorials of Robert Smith Candlish* (Edinburgh: Adam and Charles Black, 1880), p.171.

13   'Claim, Declaration and Protest, Anent the Encroachments of the Court

of Session', Free Presbyterian Church of Scotland, http://www.fpchurch.
org.uk/Beliefs/HistoricalDocuments (accessed 9 May 2013).

14 *Proceedings of the General Assembly of the Free Church of Scotland With
    a Sketch of the Proceedings of the Residuary Assembly*, ed. John Baillie
    (Edinburgh: W. P. Kennedy, 1843), p.8.

15 Hanna, *Memoirs of the Life and Writings of Thomas Chalmers*, vol. 2,
    pp.645–46.

16 There is some doubt about Tasker's date of birth. The date chosen here
    is based on its appearance in the *Old Parish Register of Births and
    Baptisms*. W. Ewing's *Annals of the Free Church of Scotland* suggests a
    later date of 1811.

17 Hanna, *Memoirs of the Life and Writings of Thomas Chalmers*, vol. 2,
    p.780.

18 "Thomas Chalmers", *The Spectator* no. 988 (7 June 1847), http://archive.
    spectator.co.uk/article/5th-june-1847/11/it-is-not-often-that-a-man-can-
    be-said (accessed 20 June 2013).

19 Ibid.

20 Thomas Carlyle, "Letter to William Hanna 7 June 1852", *The Carlyle
    Letters Online*, http://carlyleletters.dukejournals.org/cgi/content/
    full/27/1/lt-18520607-TC-WH-01 (accessed June 20, 2013).

21 Stewart J. Brown, *Thomas Chalmers and the Godly Commonwealth*
    (Oxford: Oxford University Press, 1982), p.378.

22 Thomas Chalmers, 'On the Advantages of Christian Knowledge to
    the Lower Orders of Society' in *Sermons and Discourses by Thomas
    Chalmers, D.D. LL.D now completed by the introduction of his
    posthumous sermons* (New York: Robert Carter and Brothers, 1853), vol.
    2, pp.343–44.

he was the sun

Lauren Vinn

Cover Design by Luke Buxton | www.lukebuxton.com
From an original concept by Jamie Vinn
Photography by Russell Vinn
Encouragement by Lacey Vinn
All made possible by Tina Vinn

To Nanny Jean and Nanny Jill

For holding my hand until I found my own way,
but for holding my heart forever

Asher

I told myself it would be okay. But there's a difference between telling and knowing. And I knew I was lying. It wouldn't be okay, not without her.

She didn't want this life and I don't blame her. I wanted extraordinary and she wanted normal. Normal isn't a bad thing; it represents peace and tranquillity and answers. Opportunity. Maybe I ask for too much. In this moment that I shared with the ocean and the feeling of an empty, purposeless life, it didn't matter what I wanted anymore. It won't make her want this life and I, still, will not blame her.

I felt this way for the many hours that I sat, dangling my legs off the pier, contemplating the last two months I'd spent at this stupid camp. My thoughts were spiralling through deep episodes of sadness, to a burning rage that even the thought of her no longer extinguished. Not this time, anyway. The words escaped my mouth and the ocean swept them away into nothingness.

"It's funny really, isn't it? A boy gifted with magic, but still not powerful enough to make her stay. What did I do wrong? Maybe I should've told her everything I knew from the start. That way, the truth wouldn't have overwhelmed her as much as it did. She'd have trusted me quicker. Or, maybe, I should've pretended I didn't believe in magic, and

1

that she was silly for bringing it up. Maybe then we could've lived happily ever after, both having secrets, but together."

The ocean became the outlet for my rage, listening to the pain in my voice.

"Together is better than strangers, which is what we'll be now. Happily ever never, that's how this story ends."

I felt my voice growing louder. The rage was dominating me. Anger growing like a wave. I threw my head back, confronting the blazing sun and the tropical sky, yelling at them with a hurting heart and uncontrollable fury.

"She should've kept the pendant!" I shut my eyes and lowered my voice again.

"I wish she'd kept the pendant."

Two months before...

Brannon

The flames from the bonfire were jumping frantically. The burnt orange glow stretched for the night sky, falling back down towards the fire pit as its reach proved too ambitious. We all stood together, yet subtly segregated into small groups of our own choosing. The sound of chattering, singing and crackling firewood. The smell of heat and freedom. And youth.

"You need a break from real life, Brannon. Summer camp is the perfect opportunity for that. A change in scenery from England to a Greek Island will be fantastic. I'm sorry, but it's not up for discussion. Pack your bags, you're going!"

The wise words of my mother, a couple of weeks before this very moment. What she said was ironic and almost comical. I had breaks from 'real life' all the time, just not the type of breaks she wanted for me. I told her I thought summer camps were cringe-worthy and an attempt to recreate childhood movie scenes. The type that I had no interest in. But, to my surprise and deepest displeasure, my mother had been right; I was enjoying myself.

Smoke from a fire has always been one of my favourite smells. It lingers on your clothing for days after, causing you to hold onto the feeling of togetherness for a little while longer. I've always found that scents have stronger connections to memories than pictures ever have. Pictures are still and only capture moments that are intended to be remembered. That type of control cannot be said for scents. They catch you off guard, like when you're walking down the street and smell the aftershave of an ex-boyfriend. Nobody wants to be reminded of their ex-boyfriend. They're usually an 'ex' for a reason. But whether you like it or not, that smell will awaken memories that you spent months trying to forget. It will leave you in a pool of emotions, making you question every decision you've made since the last time you smelt the same thing. Wouldn't it have been so much easier if the scent was never there? Exactly. A smell is more powerful than a picture. After all, it's easy to grab a pair of scissors and cut him out.

Fortunately for me, the bonfire was offering memories in the form of a smell and in pictures. It's a good job I have no emotional attachments. These memories will never go stale.

"We need some more wood, who's volunteering?" asked one of the summer camp leaders, making direct eye contact with me, "Perfect, Brannon! And who else? Mr Curator, you're up."

I passed my drink to Blain, my best friend of 17 years, and left for the shed in the forest where the wood was kept. It would have been unfortunate if I'd experienced one of my breaks from 'real life' on my trek. It's not really an ideal place for someone like me to be. Especially not by myself.

It was only when I heard, "Why are you in such a rush?" that I remembered another student was sent to help me.

"Hey, my name's Asher."

"Hi, I'm…"

"Brannon?"

"Yes, Brannon."

Asher was confident, and clearly a good listener if he had heard my name over the sound of excited teenagers and the group of lads singing or shouting (depending on how you interpreted the noise) '*Sweet Caroline*' at the very top of their lungs. The rips in his jeans were knotted with bits of twig and branch, and his hooded jacket coal black. When he came close, he smelt of freshly laundered linen with a musky overtone of aftershave. He couldn't have been at the bonfire for very long. I decided to make conversation. As my mother told me before I left, "Reach out, Brannon. The world is far bigger than Heston."

"So, what school are you from? I've never seen you before," I asked him, despite feeling somewhat intimidated by his presence. I couldn't say exactly why he made me feel this way, but he did. There was just something about him.

"I don't go to school. I live here, at the camp. My Father owns it. The site has been passed down through generations, and I'm home schooled."

"Home schooled? That must get lonely."

"It does, but it's the safest option for people like me."

People like him. I wondered what he meant by that, but we'd only known each other for a couple of minutes. I didn't want to bombard him with questions or make him feel uncomfortable. Or, maybe, I didn't want to make him feel like I was interested. I've never liked being close to people or knowing more than I need to know. The only

5

person I know and who kind of knows me is Blain. My intention to keep it that way is the reason mum encourages me to 'reach out'.

Asher sparked the next conversation.

"What made you come to summer camp then?" he asked with a mocking grin. His chestnut hair, a nest of flattened curls with a few hairs straying, blended seamlessly into his olive tanned face.

"My mum, mainly. She wanted me to take a break from life and I—" he was looking at me intensely. His deep turquoise eyes stared at me whilst I walked.

Asher

She carried on.

"I graciously agreed. That and the peer pressure from my friends."

She laughed a little nervously. I could tell I was making her nervous. I suppose she didn't know that this was accidental of me. She was fiddling with her fingers. I stared into her eyes. I'd never seen anything like them; a pastel purple mixed with a glistening silver. An exact colour match to her hair that fell like waves over her shoulders and halfway down her back.

"Are you enjoying it?" I asked her.

"So far. Bonfires and the ocean and the greenery. It's pleasant."

Nature gave her a sense of freedom that I understood, because it gave me freedom too. The natural world is beautiful, if you pay attention to it. For a moment she wasn't mine to entertain. Her thoughts stole her from me. I watched as she inhaled the warmth of the summer breeze, naturally.

My hands were buried in my pockets, eyes locked on her, conscious that I might stumble over a tree stump and fall.

She resumed our conversation. "I'd ask you the same, but I guess you've done this a million times before if you live here?" She stepped over a fallen trunk.

"Actually, this is the first time my father has let me join in with the camp. He, too, wanted me to take a break. A real one. I have an important milestone that I'm reaching in a couple of months. I guess he wants me to enjoy my youth whilst I can."

She smiled but didn't reply. I thought she'd question the important milestone, but she didn't. It seemed like everyone wanted to know about it, but not her. She wasn't invasive. I liked that.

We wandered in a comfortable silence until we reached the shed. Her floral dress, which rested halfway down her shoulders, pulled into her waist, accentuating her figure. The flowing skirt of it came down to just above her knees. She bent to make a pile out of some blocks of wood. I picked it up.

"Hey! Get your own next time," she laughed as she spoke. One might even think she was flirting. I didn't want to assume. She made another pile, and we headed back. She led the way.

She smelt of fire smoke and perfume, sweet but not fruity. It was faintly exotic. Floral, clean and I guessed, a little expensive. I looked again at the dress she was wearing; blue with yellow flowers. I'd never paid attention to someone's clothing before. But with her, I couldn't help but notice every detail. I needed to know more.

"Brannon. That's a unique name."

"I know. My dad told me it stands for the descendant of the sad one. Depressing, right?"

"Interesting, actually. Where does it come from? My family also love symbolic names."

She said, less confident in her own answer, "I've been told my family was once a powerful source of dark magic." She examined the response of my facial expressions. She was surprised that I was not. "There's a lot of supernatural mythology in my family. It's crazy." She laughed nervously again.

"Asher is a name that stands for fortunate, blessed and happy," I told her.

"You were luckier than me then."

"I think Brannon is a beautiful name. Normal is boring."

She pressed her lips together and shook her head lightly, looking at the ground.

"Not always."

The conversation ended abruptly. Only someone with a chaotic life would find comfort in 'normal'. Maybe I offended her. I could tell she was someone who didn't like talking to people. She was falsely confident. I could tell it was false because she was so obviously shy. But I find it best to not tell people what they are, as it is not mine or anyone else's place but their own. Her own. Yet, I still wanted to know more.

Brannon

We gave the firewood to the camp leader and I headed back to Blain. He passed me my drink and asked me, "Who is he then?"

"Asher Curator. His Father owns the camp and it's his first time joining in with the summer activities."

"What's he like?" he questioned, a little too excited that I'd interacted with this boy.

"He's nice."

"Nice looking!" Blain smiled, staring him up and down from the corner of his eyes.

"He's nice to talk too. I'm just glad I didn't have to go on my own."

"I bet," he replied, winking at me.

"Blain!"

He'd been my best friend since we were born. As much as I hate it sometimes, he knows me better than I know myself. Which means he knew that by 'nice', I meant he was warming and safe and the human version of a 'break from real life'. What Asher doesn't know, is that I'm someone who doesn't like talking to people, especially people I don't know. But for some reason I didn't regret that I told him about my family's beliefs. What I didn't tell him is that they were my beliefs too.

After I, Blain and our other friends indulged in hot marshmallows that we caramelised over the fire, the group came together for a clichéd summer camp picture. We bundled together, symbolising the togetherness that the smell of bonfire on my clothes would remind me of the next day. I felt an arm wrap around my neck and shoulders. A firm squeeze. A mix of musky, metallic aftershave and washing machine powder that I already recognised as Asher. I didn't think to pull away. I didn't want to. I felt strangely comfortable. This surprised me probably as much as it surprised Blain, who was nudging my shoulder from the other side. Is it too soon to say that this felt like home? Between my best friend...and him.

"Smile, Brannon," Asher said sarcastically, and, more quietly, in my ear, "I wanted to stand next to the pretty one."

His words painted the smile on my face that I observed as I looked at the picture later that night in bed. I looked happy. His eyes stood out, even on paper. I hoped, in this moment, that I wouldn't have to cut him out of it one day.

I flicked through the pictures that I'd been sent from the bonfire. We only printed the big group photo but there were more on my phone. Me and Blain with twins that we'd only met the day before. Toasting marshmallows. Lads singing loudly. My group and Asher's group together. Me and Asher holding firewood. I zoomed in. I hadn't noticed that at the shed, he had removed his jacket and tied it round his waist. He must've done it before we left. I zoomed in further. This time I felt a rush of fear and confusion. My heart plummeted like it would do on one of those theme parks rides that lift you to the top and drop you suddenly. I observed the chain hanging from his chest. The half-circle pendant stood out on his black t-shirt. My hand, slowly and uncertain, moved towards my own neck. I held it in my hand. My pendant. Half a circle. The other half of his.

I woke up from a restless night's sleep to my phone ringing. Mum, checking that I was okay.

"We had a bonfire last night. It was fun. I'm not sure what we are doing today. Maybe water sports or a hike."

"It sounds like so much fun, sweetie! How are you feeling?"

"I'm fine so far. I've had one episode, but it was short and less painful than most. How's Dad? I miss you both."

"Dad is okay, although he does have a bit of a cold. We miss you lots."

"Won't be long and I'll be home. I love you, Mum."

"I love you too, Brannon. One last thing. If you are doing water sports, make sure your pendant doesn't fall off please."

"Okay. Bye."

I hung up, got out of bed, showered and dressed. I was right. The choice of activities today was water sports or a hike. I chose a hike, the safer option.

Asher

She smiled at me as we all met outside to leave for the hike. Beautiful, I thought. Most people chose water sports. Even that boy she spends most of her time with. Blain, I think. She was standing with two girls, but she didn't seem as comfortable as normal.

"Find a partner, choose a trail, and be back before it's dark," were the instructions we were given.

I looked at her to get her attention, but she was already looking at me. Relying on me. Desperate to escape 'girl chat' for an adventure with me. I strolled over to her.

"Sorry girls, I'm stealing Brannon. I've heard she's good with directions. I don't want to get lost."

Suddenly, a rush of excitement raced through my bones. More time with her. People don't usually excite me in this way. But she did.

Her hair was still falling elegantly, but she'd ditched the dress for shorts and a vest top. It was warm, especially in the forest. I similarly wore shorts and a t-shirt, an instant regret as we were attacked by stinging nettles at the entrance.

"How did you sleep?" I asked her.

"Fine thank you," she seemed unsure of me today.

"How was breakfast? My Dad asked me to ask around, get some feedback for—"

"What do you think happens after death?"

Okay. She didn't fancy small talk today. If she'd had the same realisation as I had last night, then I knew why she was asking me this question.

"I don't know. I hope there's peace. I guess I believe that something happens. I mean, we can't be gifted with this magical life for it to end in, well, nothing."

She analysed what I said. To avoid interrogation of my answer, I asked her the same thing. She was careful with her reply.

"It would be good if it was painless. Maybe even an escape to a utopia." She paused for a moment before continuing, "Do you have any siblings?"

"I'm an only child," I told her, trying to keep up with the changing conversation.

Her answer hadn't been what I expected. I thought she'd lie, or at least try to. She was testing me. Annoying but attractive. She knew what happened after death. She knew that I knew, too.

Our conversation was much calmer after this. We chose the trail that led up the mountain because she was adamant that the view from the top would leave us speechless and it was easier to believe her. We spoke about pointless things that you don't necessarily care about but should know. She had a younger brother called Marley. She was clever, though didn't want to admit it for fear of sounding condescending. She'd been in *sort-of* love. Just shallow relationships with boys that she held at a distance. She asked where my favourite place was, and I told her I hadn't found it yet. Although, for the first time in my life, I

14

predicted that I'd soon find my favourite place was not a place at all, but a person. She loves walking, she told me. And writing. Something that I loved too. She sounded excited when she spoke about these things. She told me as we approached the top of the mountain, "I like listening to people. We learn more from listening than talking."

Again, I agreed. We weren't the same, though. I like playing the guitar and watching sports. She didn't. But we were similar. Very.

We both sat crossed legged at the top of the mountain.

She asked me to describe the view. An orange glow stretched over the peaceful sea. Simple, but amazing. I couldn't find words to say out loud.

"I told you," she said, "you'd be speechless."

"How'd you know? You've never been up here before."

"Because have you ever been disappointed in a view with a sunset?"

She was right.

She turned pale quickly. Her skin now translucent and her eye lids flickering until they closed. She fell back. I caught her head with my hands and laid her down. I'm not freaking out because I know what's happening. She needs me to be calm, so that is what I will be.

After a few minutes her eyes opened faster than they shut. She held her hand to her head and sat up.

"Was it painful?" I asked, confused that she appeared to be hurting.

"A little. But it's worth it. You know that."

I stood up and reached my hand out to hers. She grabbed it and I helped her up. I placed my hands on her waist and turned her to face the view, standing close behind her.

"Come on then, Brannon. Give me one word to describe your experience today."

She smiled and spoke shyly, like she did last night, indicating to me that she felt comfortable as she had dropped the fake confidence.

"Extraordinary."

I'd never heard it described in this way before. Although, I'd never met someone quite like her before either. I couldn't tell what experience she was describing. Of course, she could be describing the view. It was, after all, extraordinary, to stand at the top of the mountain, looking down on the world and breathing in the freshest air. But she could also be describing the moment she had when her eyes shut, and she escaped to a place only we know. It wasn't remotely like the mountain view. It was quite pleasant to look at. It wasn't enjoyable to experience, in the slightest. But she was right. Extraordinary. The opposite of ordinary; normal.

We set back down the trail. Every so often, sunlight bounced off her pendant, causing it to glitter on her chest. We knew each other's secrets without saying them out loud. Maybe we should address it. Maybe it's better left untouched. Ignored. It couldn't be forgotten, though. Sooner or later, we'd have to. Surely. But, for now, we enjoyed asking each other more pointless questions, pretending that we didn't know what we knew.

Brannon

We spent the following day together, too. This time there were no questions or seriousness in the air. I liked Asher, and that was enough.

Today, we were building a friendship from a shared humour and mutual understanding of each other. We were also going on a zip wire, from one mountain top to another. He was worried that I'd be scared, but heights are something that I enjoy. The adrenaline brings a sense of thrill and an escape from normality.

Normal. Something that neither Asher or I were. I'd always struggled with this, because normal appealed to me. No secrets. Friendships where the other person can know the real me. A less painful existence. One can't appreciate normal until it's gone. But I also disliked normal. Normal connotes boring and ordinary. I liked being more than that. If it came to it though, I'd always choose normal. Simply because I've never had the chance to choose it before. My mind works in complex ways, but this I have always been sure on.

He'd made me laugh all the way to the top of the mountain. His dopey, fun sense of humour was powerful enough to make the muscles in my stomach ache. The pressure from yesterday had dissolved amongst the trust we were building with each other.

We reached the top, standing speechless at the view, again. After a while he spoke, with less confidence in his voice than before, "That's a long way down."

"It's a mountain, Asher, what did you expect?" I enjoyed winding him up.

Two men began harnessing us and strapping us to the zip wire. There was two metal lines beside each other. As the men were buckling us in, I noticed Asher's eyes on me for brief moments, looking away as soon as I acknowledged the attention he was giving me. We were given no instructions other than to go when we were ready. The men, who were more like moody teenagers, sat back on their stools and returned to their phone screens. This didn't feel like the safest thing I'd ever done. I loved that.

"Are you ready?" I asked him, seeing his heart racing through his chest and his eyes working out the distance to our destination. It wasn't far.

"One minute," he replied, definitely not calm.

Asher

She reached out and gripped my arm. I was glad. My personal crisis of masculinity wouldn't have been a problem if I didn't let my confidence lie about my fear of heights. This wasn't my idea of fun, but she'd mentioned it yesterday and, well, anything to make her happy. I assume she'd have this effect on anyone. Making them feel a desire to see a smile dance on her pretty face.

The reassurance she gave me was unexpected.

"Hey, what's the worst that could happen?" she asked, as if our lives were not at risk.

"We could fall, Brannon!"

She was looking up to me with eyes that I could trust. I got lost in the purple mist of her stare, comforting myself with her.

"Wrong. The worst that could happen is you decide not to do it because you're scared of a possibility. Then you go home and regret it. Plus, if you don't do it, I'll have to go alone, and then you'll have a really long walk to find me again."

I giggled, a little bit and took a deep breath in, "I guess you're right."

We walked towards the end of the wooden plank hovering on the mountain, overlooking the drop. Her face was the definition of exhilarated. She loved being on the edge.

"Are you ready now?"

"I think so," I said.

"Good. At least if we die, it will be with a good view," she smiled, teasing me and terrifying me. And then, without hesitation, she pushed her feet from the edge and glided off through the warm air.

Accidentally my feet copied hers and I, too, was gliding. Flying, possibly to my death, as she found necessary to remind me.

I seemed to follow her in this way. Her thoughts convinced me. Her words persuaded me. Her actions forced me. I was a ball of playdough, and she was modelling me to her own liking, without knowing - I think.

Her legs were still as they dangled high above the lake. Her hair waved through the breeze, like a flag. It was more lilac in the sunlight. I used my vision to trace her shoulder bone down to her back, bronze and glittering. Her beauty captured me like the view of a sunset. She was a free spirit.

I caught up to her, crossing her like an eclipse. She smiled at me, so elegantly, and released her arms from her rope, spread them out like wings and closed her eyes, feeling the freedom in the danger. At first, I was desperate for her to just hold the rope and return to safety. But then, as she tilted her head back and her hair fell like a waterfall into the emptiness around us, I wanted her to carry on. She was walking a tightrope, balancing on a fine line between life and death and, in this moment, I wanted that for her.

That moment soon went though, and now I wanted her to hold on again, for my sake. I chose to distract her.

"Look at that!" I said with a voice of excitement.

Quickly, she leant forward again, looking where I was looking.

"It's beautiful."

She was right. It was beautiful. But I never told her where to look. I admired how she found beauty in everything. But all along, I wasn't looking at anything other than her.

Brannon

I got back to my room at camp in the late afternoon. The cabin was built from logs of wood, as expected of a typical summer camp. But this camp was better. It was near the beach, and a forest, and a mountain range. It was beautiful. I hadn't quite decided yet if the camp was better because Asher was here. I hadn't decided anything about him.

The cabin was lit with the warm yellow glow of the corner lamps. Two beds, two chests of drawers, a bathroom. I shared mine with Jessy, another friend of mine. I wanted to share with Blain, but the outdated opinions of boys and girls sharing rooms still exist, despite the fact that Blain wasn't into girls, at all. Still, I wasn't unhappy to be paired with Jessy. She was a sweet girl, with ginger plaits and freckles that created a dot-to-dot puzzle on her cheeks. We'd known each other since the first day of secondary school. She knew me well enough, as I her. But with limits. She knew that I fainted sometimes, and that the best thing to do was to leave me there until I came round.

"How was it, Bran?" she asked me after I'd washed the grass on my legs, and the desire I had to know more about him, off in the shower.

"The view was amazing," I answered and thought to myself, did I mean the clear aqua waters beneath us, the blue canvas of a sky above, or him?

"It's the party tonight," she reminded me. "What are you going to wear?"

I'd forgotten about the party. I've been used to homework, or Netflix, as my night-time activities. The camp had something on most nights.

I pulled on a black dress with thin straps over my shoulders, and black sandals because the party was on the beach. I chose the outfit purposely. My pendant was exposed, and I wanted to see if he'd ask me about it. I knew after today that it wasn't confidential. He knew me now. But still. There was a secret.

I'd noticed him staring at my eyes all day. Not into them – at them. It wasn't a moment that we were connected, it was a moment of confusion for him, as it is for most people. My eyes are silver and a light purple. My hair is too. At first, I felt strange for having this. Now I like it. It was one thing about me that you couldn't find in anyone else.

Asher

There were so many things about her. Things I knew I'd never find in anyone else.

"Dad, I need to talk to you." I felt nervous, but I wasn't sure why. "I think I've found her. She has the pendant."

"I know, son."

"How?"

"The air feels different. There's an energy about it that only occurs when the pendants are in the same area. The people of our kind have waited centuries for this."

"Why? It isn't going to change their lives."

I knew this because my father had explained it to me since I was born. Since I was given the pendant. It was because of this I knew there was an element of danger in knowing her. Brannon.

"You're 18 in two months, Ash. That means she is, too. This is the way of the universe. Have you spoken to her about it?" he questioned me.

"Not directly, but she isn't stupid. And she had an episode the other day, in front of me. She called it 'extraordinary'. I liked that."

My thoughts had taken me back to the moment she opened her eyes again. I knew she'd come back, but for the first time in forever, I found myself hoping for someone.

Worried, almost. I was drowning in images of her. Her tanned skin and eyes like exotic pearls. Her teeth white, shining as she smiled. Her smile. That was extraordinary. My father's face looked concerned and I knew why. We'd both have to make a decision soon that would determine the fate of our lives. Of us. Together, or not. If she or I chose wrong, or got too close, it could lead to heartbreak.

"Talk to her about it," he advised. "There's no harm in that. Find out more about her. Not because you have to, but because she's the only person who will understand."

"Okay."

"But Asher, please remember that this doesn't have to be a love story."

He said this with piercing eye contact that signalled the importance of his message. He's right. This is not a love story. Not yet. Maybe never.

Brannon

The wind was moving his khaki shirt over his beige t-shirt. He liked layers. I guess that was an accurate representation of him. Like an onion. So many layers, so many versions of him that I wanted to know. Although, I hope he doesn't make my eyes stream in an onion way.

I thought he'd come over to me straight away, or at least look in my direction. I was excited to see him after the last two days. I thought he'd feel the same. We all gathered on the golden sand, faint music playing in the background. Maybe my expectations were too high but tonight, he was distanced. He didn't look at me. He kept his back to me. He didn't wave. He didn't smile. He just didn't. Strangers again. I was standing in my group of friends, surrounded by a crowd of people, feeling a type of loneliness that, for some reason, I knew only he could fix. But no. It wasn't going to be like that. A realisation I came to after the fourth hour crawled by with no acknowledgment of me by him. Had he found out everything he needed to know? I was that girl that had the other half to his pendant. Was I just a great discovery to him? I didn't care.

But then I did. As the sun rested under the horizon and the empty sky became a mixture of dark blues and greys, he came over. The breeze was slightly cold instead of warm, and he asked if I wanted to go for 'a chat'. He was treating me in a way that screamed 'normal'. His aura felt reserved. He didn't want to be close with me.

"I told my dad about you," he began.

I didn't have to ask him why. Instead, I just listened.

"He said I should talk to you about, well, you know what." He's right, I know what. "Our pendants. They go together, as I'm sure you've already noticed."

We were sitting on the pier, dangling our legs over the water.

"Yes. They make a circle." I felt stupid, he knew they made a circle because they were two semi-circles. "I don't know much about it. I just know that I'm like an anchor for the Myst, and you are too."

"What was your first experience like? And don't say extraordinary," he said, half smiling. I felt comfortable in the moment.

"For the first seven years, I didn't really know what was happening. Sometimes I fainted, and I thought nothing of it. I remember dreaming, seeing people, talking to them. On my eighth birthday, I realised I wasn't dreaming. My eyes closed and I entered this whole other place."

He knew the place.

I paused. I've never spoken about this with anyone besides my parents before. I've never felt what I do right now, knowing that this makes sense to him.

"I was blown away by the place. A sun setting behind the sea. Is it the same for you?" He nodded. I carried on, "I couldn't look behind me, only in front. The moment I realised it wasn't a dream was when I saw the same woman I'd seen the day before. She was 82, and she told me that she wasn't ready to go yet. I didn't know what to tell her. I was eight, but I told her that it's easy. And she wouldn't feel any pain, because I would. She was sad that I hadn't found the other pendant yet, because she'd never be able to practise again. I felt bad. She wished me luck and wandered into the sea and then disappeared. I felt a burning sensation in my head and then I woke."

I felt like I'd said too much. I felt the breeze up my spine. It was cold now.

Asher

I noticed as the goosebumps raced over her skin. She was looking down. We didn't make eye contact and I knew she didn't feel as safe with me as she had done before. It was my fault. I was scared. I didn't want to know her anymore. But I did.

This isn't a love story. I repeated this to myself over and over as I listened to her pretty voice open up about a sensitive time of her life. The pendants were made to be together, not us. She sat so stiff and uncomfortable. Her eyes were still glistening, but they were sad. I wondered what she thought of me in this moment.

She rubbed her hands on her arms. Her cold skin did not warm. I took off my over shirt and wrapped it around her shoulders. She jumped at my touch and lifted her head. She was looking at me now. Smiling. This isn't a love story. It doesn't have to be.

"Thank you," her delicate voice whispered.

We both felt guilty for knowing each other. We didn't mean to.

She carried on talking, "My father told me that when my vision blurred and I felt dizzy, I was passing through into the Myst. I was terrified. I didn't want to feel every supernatural death. I didn't even know these things existed.

He told me I'm not the only one and that the other pendant was out there, but they hadn't found each other in centuries. I accepted that this was my life a few years ago."

She pulled my shirt around her shoulders, so that it was hugging her. It felt weird hearing these things out loud. There were moments I wished we were normal teenagers. That our relationship could blossom like an innocent flower. I didn't feel the pain of the deaths. I wasn't like her in that way. But I couldn't bring myself to tell her yet. All I wanted to do was make her smile again. We didn't cover everything. But for tonight, that was enough. Besides, I enjoyed the secrets we shared. Without a second thought, I placed my hand on her leg. She wasn't alone. I was here, with her, for as long as she wanted me to be.

She asked me a question. It surprised me. She was good at that.

"Do you regret meeting me?"

I hated that she even considered this possibility. I should have spoken to her straight away tonight. Before anyone else. We had a special few days and I neglected it so carelessly. I should've thought about her. Not just me and my desperate need to follow my dad's advice. What we are is not normal. It was a miracle for us to meet. It was not right for me to shatter her hopes. Of course, she'd be worried. We found each other. Of course, she'd think this.

"Brannon Amory," she looked up at me with those eyes that made me weak, "I will never regret meeting you. With or without the pendant, you are extraordinary."

I'd only known her for a few days, yet I was confident in what I said. I hadn't known a life with her in it since the other night. Now, I can't imagine one without her. This shouldn't be a love story, but maybe it is.

Brannon

Suddenly, I felt better. I don't know why I needed his reassurance, but I did. Then it struck me. Brannon Amory. I hadn't told him my last name.

Part of me wanted to ask him, but most of me didn't want to ruin this moment. People like us, me and him, are used to pain and darkness. This moment was compassionate. Two supernatural beings, being normal. Super. Natural.

The salty air was refreshing. We were now pointing at the stars. This felt right. The crashing waves danced with anger. Beauty and chaos. Drops of water started reaching for our feet as they collided with the pier. We stood up.

"Was your dad happy that we'd met?" I asked him.

"I don't think he knew what to feel. He said the air felt different. This hasn't happened in many lifetimes. Have you told your parents?"

My answer should be yes. This is important. But it's the opposite of yes. "No. They don't need to know yet."

We stood in silence, shoulder to shoulder, pretending that we couldn't feel droplets of rain landing on us. We liked to pretend. Maybe that's our thing.

I understood why his dad didn't know how to feel. But that's not what I wanted to know.

"Asher, do you know how *you* feel?"

My stomach became a butterfly enclosure as he turned me to face him. His confidence was inspiring.

"It's only been a day, Brannon."

My heart sunk a little - a lot.

He continued, "and I know, already, that there is no one else I'd rather be here with, standing in the rain."

He smiled as he spoke, and then turned his head so that he was looking out to sea. Then back at me, tracing me up and down with his vision. He spoke softly, and quietly, brushing his hands down my arms until they were gripping mine, "You've made me feel. That's something I've never done before."

"But Asher, you're right. It's only been a day and you could feel different tomorrow and then this would be—"

Asher

I kissed her. The rain was now pouring. My shirt dripped around her shoulders and her hair became a dark grey. Her lips were cold and wet, so was her face as I held it in my hands. The rain was insignificant to us. A rush of adrenaline, and satisfaction took over my body.

I couldn't find the words to tell her how I felt. Part of me felt silly knowing it had only been a few days since she'd entered my life. Other parts of me felt like she wouldn't believe me, even if I could find the words. Kissing her felt like the best option.

Brannon

I was going to say, 'a waste of time'. How wrong I'd have been. Meeting Asher is not and will never be a waste of time. Forty-eight hours is not a long time, but it is long enough to know that, whether our pendants completed each other or not, a part of him completed me.

It was fireworks. Incredible and terrifying. The rain was smacking against our skin now. He took my hand, and we ran down the pier, finding shelter. We didn't speak anymore. He took me to my cabin, watched as I closed the door behind me, and ran back to his own.

I'd told him too much tonight. This would change everything between us. But, finally, I was sure on something. This wasn't a waste of time.

***

The next few days were what the camp called 'your choice' days. There were no set activities. The idea was that we chose things to do for ourselves, making the most of the area that we were in. Me and Jessy met up with Blain and Red, the boy he shared his cabin with. Red wasn't really called Red. His name was Diago Redding, but he asked to be called Red. This group was safe. We all got along well and had a laugh whilst doing so.

On the first day, we chose to venture into the forest. We walked for miles, talking about school and what we want to do when we're older. Every question made me wonder what he'd do. Asher. I assumed he'd be given the camp, passed down by his father. I hoped he'd take it and continue this opportunity given to students, to meet new people and see new places. I knew he'd make something of his life, whatever he did. Me, on the other hand? I have no idea what I want to do with my life. Most jobs seem impractical considering I take, 'breaks from real life' far too often. I just hope to be happy. I think that's what we all hope for.

We discovered a small lagoon further into the forest. It was, surprisingly, clean and enticing. We got in and splashed around like children until the skin on our fingertips revealed patterns, symbolising that we'd spent enough time in the water. We walked back in slip on shoes with towels around our shoulders. It was fun. The type of fun that can only be had with good friends and I felt lucky.

It also made me feel independent. I don't need you, Asher. I have people who love me and that is enough. I wanted him, though.

The day after, we had a beach day, the four of us. We enjoyed the temperate water and the clear skies. The white lines left from our swimming suits were evidence of the hot sun. We floated on blow-up lilos, letting the gentle waves lift us up and down freely in the open sea.

I was far away from home. In fact, it took me hours to get here. I live in Heston, a small village in Cornwall where everyone knows everyone. Summer camp was abroad. A chance for students from the United Kingdom to explore.

Being away from home felt strange but the freedom was exhilarating.

We finished the day with a barbeque on the beach. The smell of smoke and burning food. The type of smell I loved. We stayed until the sun set, a neon pink surrounding a falling orange mist, then headed back to our cabins for a much-needed early night.

Asher was also out and about with his friends. We could've spent these days together, but that wasn't the point of coming to camp. I've always had the most fun with my friends and I didn't intend on neglecting them now. Not over a boy. Though he isn't just a boy, he's Asher.

Blain and I spent the following day together, without the other two. Blain wanted to go to the camp's spa, and I decided that it would be nice. I knew he had many questions for me that couldn't be asked in front of the other two. Blain spent a lot of his time caring for me. If I had an episode, he'd make sure I was comfortable and that no one asked questions. He didn't ask questions either. It was just easier that way. But his questions in the spa were not about that.

As we unwound in the hot tub, Blain asked, "You haven't seen Asher much these past days? Missing him?"

"I don't need to see him. I'm fine without him, you know."

"I know. Do you like him?" the interrogation had begun. "Actually, don't answer that. I already know that you do. It's not like you to disappear at a party. I wasn't worried though, because I knew you wanted to be with him."

I hadn't told Blain this. He just knew because that's what best friends do. They know, without the need to be told.

"I enjoy spending time with him, but I won't get my hopes up." It was only half a lie. I had enjoyed spending time with him.

"You spent a whole day hiking with him, he must be special. And special is a must. Nothing less for you, Brannon."

Blain admired me and I admired him. We'd helped each other through the hardest times of our lives. He made the situation with Asher easier, because if it didn't end in happily ever after, I'd be okay. Blain would make sure of it.

"There's nothing wrong with getting your hopes up, Bran. Or admitting that you want something..." He paused, staring at me, trying to get me to admit to my feelings. "Blain, back off. Yes, I want him, a bit, but I don't need him..." 'Yet,' I thought to myself. Instead, I managed to say, "I don't need to rush."

"Rush like kissing someone 48 hours after meeting them?" he found himself hilarious.

"I didn't tell you about that so you could use it against me!" We were laughing now.

Blain and I spent the remainder of the day making the most of the spa. The pools, the jacuzzi, the treatments. Each other. It was needed, a day of just us. I felt better afterwards. My mind was clearer.

We got back to our cabins late that night, mostly because we hadn't got out of bed until late afternoon. When we did get back, everyone was sitting on the grass in the middle of the circle of cabins. They were talking and singing. Apparently, we had been encouraged to spend the evening together, socialising.

Jessy and Red called us over. They were with a group of our friends; some from school, some from the camp. It amazed me how a group of people who had known each other for less than a week created a feeling of community and home. Mum was right. I needed this break.

Asher

I missed Brannon on the days I didn't see her. She had fun without me. I liked that she didn't want to spend every day with me. She had her own life. Her own priorities. I wanted her to want me, I didn't want her to need me. And I loved seeing her happy. It made me happy.

She sat with her friends at the evening gathering on the green. Summer camp was amazing, and I was thankful to finally be a part of it. She perched herself down and then searched for me. It didn't take long because I was already looking at her. Her glowing skin and rosy lips. I disappoint myself in my descriptions of her. I don't do her justice. Words don't. She smiled at me. I smiled back, accompanied with a discreet wink that made her blush. I enjoyed having this effect on her because I could tell that not many did.

My confidence dominated my next move. I got up and walked across to join her group of friends. I sat down beside her, close to her, so that our knees were touching. Although we were surrounded by people, it was just us two.

"You should all come to the beach tomorrow. There'll be a game of beach volleyball," I informed them.

"Brannon, you up for that?" her friend Blain asked her.

She looked at him, and then at me. How I wish I could read her mind.

"Sure," she replied, a sense of competitiveness echoing through.

"She likes to win Asher, I have to warn you," Blain said.

"Is that right Brannon? Well, I have to warn you, I like winning too. And I normally get what I want."

I smirked at her. The type of smirk that would warm her chest because she had my undivided attention. Now. Tomorrow. Forever.

Getting attention from girls is something that I'm used to. My mother tells me it's the curly brown hair and blue eyes. An 'irresistible combination'. I've never cared before, though. Brannon can hear my heartbeat and the words I do not say out loud. Other girls cannot.

She stood up and announced that she was going to bed. She needed a good night's sleep to ensure her victory tomorrow. I watched her as she walked off, knowing that I'd see her again soon. Hoping that I'd know this, always.

Brannon

The game of beach volleyball was fun but cut short. I enjoyed the flirtatious stares that me and Asher were sharing. He didn't do this with anyone else. But then I had an episode. My team was winning. We scored another point, and in the moments of celebration, I could no longer see Asher. I could see several people, blurred like pixels. And that's all I remember.

Asher

I ran to her as soon as she fell. I scooped her in my arms and took her to my house. My house is behind the cabins, a short walk from the beach. Blain offered to help but I suggested he stayed in case anyone asked questions.

I couldn't help but feel guilty. Seeing her like this wasn't pleasant. Not because she'd collapsed. I do that, too. But because I knew she was in pain and this was something I did not know. My family is not like hers. I feel sorry for that.

I left her on the sofa whilst I went to get her a glass of water and something to eat. She must've returned soon after I left the room, because when I came back, she was gone. It was only when my father explained to me their conversation that I understood why.

Brannon

I felt uncomfortable when I woke. I didn't know where I was, or who the man was sitting in the armchair beside me. Although I guessed from his eyes. Turquoise like Asher's. I sat up with vigour and combed my fingers through my hair to quickly brush out any tangles. This wasn't the way I wanted to meet him. I didn't even want to meet him, really.

"Hi, I'm Roger Curator, Asher's father."

I timidly replied, "Hi. I'm Brannon."

He examined my appearance for a while. Did he recognise me from somewhere?

"How are you feeling?" he asked. "What does it feel like?" I didn't expect him to ask me this. Surely Asher would've told him.

"I'm okay thanks. It was painful, like a migraine, you know?"

"I wouldn't know," he laughed to himself. His body language was much like Asher's. Trying to disguise what he was thinking, not realising that his thoughts were painted in neon green, for everyone to see.

"Does Asher not tell you?"

It felt strange that we could talk of it so openly. As though the human world was not the only world to exist.

As though the Myst was a destination that everyone went to.

"Asher wouldn't know either. He doesn't feel pain from the deaths. An advantage of being from our blood line, I guess."

I didn't know what he was talking about. I didn't know the blood line mattered. Asher hadn't told me this. No. Asher held me in his arms as I drifted into the Myst. He asked if I was okay, if it hurt, like he understood. I was under the impression that he could relate to me in every way and trusting him came naturally. All that Asher had done was find out about me. He didn't tell me anything about himself. How naïve of me to think we were close. I didn't know anything about him. Except from his smell. I knew that would haunt me one day. Was today that day?

"I'm sorry, I don't understand." I was fully awake now. The frustration that Asher might have played me was beginning to crowd my thoughts. I didn't understand what this man meant. I felt my fists tightening as I pushed myself to the edge of the sofa. Perching, tensing, I forced a deep breath. "Why wouldn't Asher feel the deaths? What does his blood line matter?"

He wasn't quick to reply. He was calculating what to say. Or what not to say. "What has your father told you, Brannon?"

I answered quickly. My words tumbling out as my emotions heightened. "He told me about my responsibility to anchor the Myst. And that my pendant was one of two. They hadn't been connected in centuries and that if they were to connect, the Myst would be fixed. That's all. I didn't think there was anything else to know."

He could hear the growing anger in my voice. I knew it wasn't Rogers' fault. Or Asher's. Though he could've been more honest.

"I don't think it's my place to tell you any more than you already know," Roger said.

There obviously was more to know. I'd been deprived of the truth. By my own family? I stood up.

"Tell Asher I said thank you for bringing me here."

"Of course."

I left the house, marched into the forest, sat on a fallen tree and dialled my father's number. I had some questions that needed answering.

"Dad?"

He was my best friend and had been since the day I was born. The person I looked up to and admired. My hero. My first love. I didn't think we did secrets. I was angry. More than that, I was infuriated. I'd been sheltered from my own past. The history which made me, but that was the thing; I'd been sheltered. That was a form of protection. I couldn't help but wonder, what if?

"Brannon, is everything alright? How's camp sweetie?" I'd missed his voice and it was the closest to home I'd felt in days. His voice sounded like bed-time stories and 'Brannon, dinner's ready'.

"Camp is fine. Is there any way I can come home?"

Immediately, I felt sad. Asher wouldn't be at home. But I wanted answers more than I wanted him, right now.

"No, sorry. There isn't," his voice was serious, something I didn't hear much of amongst the laughter from his jokes and the singing in the car. I forgot to ask why. I was caught up in my own thoughts. I normally am.

He answered without me questioning, "I know you have chosen not to inform me and your mother about your pendant. Well, the pendants. The thing is, when they find each other, people like us know."

"Let me guess...the air feels different?"

I didn't feel like I was sat, uncomfortably, on a tree trunk near a burnt-out fire pit. The dappling sun warming my back translated to the warmth of my father's presence. I felt like he was beside me. I always found myself making links between him and the sun. I knew he was always there. Through my episodes, through boy dramas, through everything. Subtle, though. Like the sun behind the night sky. You can't see it, but it's never gone.

"Yes, it does. The Myst is," he paused to think, "it's awake. It gives off energy. Hope."

We both paused to think. The pendants were important. I knew that much.

"Why did you call, Brannon? You just missing me?" he asked in a sarcastic tone. We laughed. And within the laughter, my anger melted away.

"I was just speaking to Asher's father. Asher is the boy with the pendant," slight fear travelled through my body. I'd just mentioned a boy to my dad, my biggest protector. "He told me that Asher didn't feel pain when he fainted. Something to do with his blood line. Dad, I know there are things you're not telling me. I could tell by his father's face. He was concerned that I didn't already know."

I could hear the tremble in my voice as my anger solidified again. Now, I was wondering why I couldn't go home.

"Brannon, there are things you do not know because I didn't choose to tell you. It's my fault. And I'm sorry. I just wanted to protect you from this."

Shelter.

He spoke carefully, "You were only a child when you truly understood what was happening. I couldn't bring myself to tell you more. You accepted it. Internalised it as who you are. To say I was proud would be an understatement."

"But I'm not a child anymore, Dad. Now, I'm just a nearly-adult who doesn't know her own self."

I never expected something like this to affect me as much. I had a dad and a mum and Marley, my beautiful little brother. Blain. I didn't need anything else. But being a product of supernatural happenings has never been easy for me. It's not even as if I had to accept that the myths were real. The stories told to most children, the threats used to scare them into eating their vegetables, had always been my life. My real life. If I am capable enough to free the pain from supernatural beings that die and pass through me, then I am capable enough to handle the truth about why my life is like this. Why I am not a normal teenage girl, living a normal teenage life?

"You're right," Dad said. "If you want me to tell you everything, just say the word."

"Yes. I'd like to know."

At this point, I questioned if I really did want to know. If I hadn't met Asher, nothing would have changed. What if this did change…everything.

Dad told me that the Ancestors of the Old World, the ones who absorbed Earth's magic, ran out of substance.

"But how did the magic get there?" I asked.

"We are, quite literally, floating on a ball in space, Brannon. The thought of magic should not surprise anyone.

"The witches sacrificed their magic and gave it to the strongest two. They believed it was what the universe wanted. The idea of giving up magic was not even an idea at all, so it was given to two witches…" He stopped and coughed, holding his phone away from his face. "Sorry," he said and then continued, "The Amory Ancestor and the Curator Ancestor. The magic was absorbed into two pendants."

"So Asher and I have the collected power of the ancient witches dangling around our necks every day? Half a circle each?"

"Yes. It's a symbol of Earth."

"I've always thought of it as a whole." Meeting Asher suggested to me my interpretation had some truth, but I kept that last thought to myself.

"You're right Bran. It was decided that magic would not be practised in the New World. The one we are in now. Magic would simply be used to manipulate fate."

"Manipulate? That word's got some fairly negative connotations."

"Again, Bran, you're right. But let me finish. The rest of the Ancestors slowly passed on, into the Myst, a chance for supernatural beings to find peace. The power of their deaths, the loss of their lives from Earth, sparked immortality in the two remaining. Their eternal life was gifted for their ability to ensure the most deserving people lived lives full of blessings. They were puppet masters, controlling fate as if it was a wooden man on a string. The problem with splitting fate between the two most powerful witches to walk the Earth, was that they had to agree." He paused, and coughed again. I heard him draw a deep, laboured breath. "And they didn't," he said with the most chilling tone.

"Whilst the male ancestor used his power to cure sickness and influence better choices, the female ancestor plagued her enemies and cursed evil."

"Cursing evil can't have been too bad. If they didn't deserve good things, they deserved bad things, surely?" I asked.

"Hate breeds hate. If that was the case, there'd be no point in trying to restore goodness into our world."

"So what happened?" I asked and waited for my dad to continue the story he probably should have told me long ago.

"Despite their difference in opinion, the remaining two were madly in love. Darkness dominated light. It always does. It always has been more powerful. A white piece of paper that is painted black, can never be white again, no matter how many times it is washed and painted over. The light within one was towered over by the darkness of the other. He did not care to fight her. He loved her. She loved darkness. She was sad without her family, who had died for her immortality. She was so sad that it made her hateful. Angry. As for him, love makes you do stupid things." Another pause. Another cough. This time it turned into an extended fit of coughing. I waited and then listened to my dad's sigh from so far away. I thought about Asher. It's true. Love does make you do stupid things.

Dad continued, "The Ancestors in the Myst decided that this was not what the universe planned. As a result, they sacrificed their ability to practise magic on the other side of death in order to diminish the magic of the remaining two in a powerful spell that drained the Myst of supernatural magic all together. The power of the Myst was used to take their magic and store it in the pendants, which were given to the next born in each blood line. Their fate was manipulated, placing the pendants miles away from each other. This was now something that magic could not control. If the pendants met again, it would be because the universe deemed it time. Not the Ancestors.

"Until a few days ago, when you and Asher," he said his name with a hint of resentment, "met for the first time, the pendants had been separated. Our bloodline, like Asher's, is gifted with magic that cannot be used. The thing is, we descended from the sad one."

Brannon, the descendant of the sad one.

"We have to repent her sins. Well, you have to now. The pendant has been passed through the generations, each having to suffer the deaths of others because she cursed fate. It's not your fault. It is, however, your duty to right her wrongs."

This was overwhelming. I didn't understand. I didn't want to. Normal seemed welcoming right now. More than it ever had done before. I thought through what I'd been told and then asked, "So, what changes? Now that the pendants are together again."

My arm was aching from holding the phone to my ear. It must've been ages since I sat down. I couldn't tell if it was that making me numb, or if I was choosing to feel numb. I don't think he had wanted to tell me any of this. Especially that I felt death on repeat at the fault of a woman who came centuries before myself. If this is the way of the universe, then I don't much like the universe.

"When you turn 18, you have a big decision to make–" he broke off into another coughing fit. The weather in Cornwall was not always tasteful. It caused coughs and colds and anyway, I wanted to know about this big decision I had to make.

Unbidden he volunteered that he had a headache; that was something I could sympathise with.

"Can I call you back tomorrow, sweetie? This is a long conversation. I want to give you the best support possible. I can't do that right now and it's getting late."

"That's fine. Thank you for telling me what you did. I just wish you'd have told me sooner. I would've handled it, you know?"

"I know. But I wanted to give my girl a chance to feel strong without knowing that your life is a result of someone filled with hatred for the world. Because that is not who you are. You are better than that. Also, I didn't want to risk making you sad. Apparently, that doesn't end too great for our blood line," we laughed together, "I'll speak to you tomorrow Bran. We miss you."

"I miss you too. Bye, Dad."

And then there was me. The descendant of the sad one. Alone. By myself. Waiting for the next time I'd be punished for someone else's dark and distasteful attitude.

Asher

I knew I should've made our differences mutually known the first time I saw her. I didn't because I felt guilty. It wasn't her fault that the Ancestor that painted her blood line was a depressed, angry woman. And that's putting it nicely. I blamed myself. Welcome to my pity party.

I felt as though she trusted me too soon. I was a stranger one day and her hiking partner the next. I now feel as though she'll regret trusting me, at all. I knew who she was from her name, not her pendant. My family knows almost every meaning to every name. It's a witch thing, apparently. She didn't pay attention to my name or question me until she saw the pendant which signified to me that she was not raised on the mystical learnings that I was. Though that's not an excuse to hide the very thing that separates us from her. I don't have one.

I told my Dad he should've kept his mouth shut and not asked questions. He asked me why her hair was silver and her eyes purple. I told him I didn't know. It was just another thing that made her magical.

When he told me she'd left, I was scared. I was scared that she wouldn't come back. I didn't think she'd blame me, but I knew she'd feel somewhat betrayed. Was it fair to expect me to tell her though? That wasn't my duty. If she was annoyed at me, I'd be annoyed back. But she wasn't annoyed – she was overwhelmed.

When I finally saw her the sun was setting. I waited on the steps up to her cabin. Her walking pace drastically slowed down when she noticed me. I guessed she wasn't in the mood to talk. I also chose to ignore my intuition, because I wanted to talk to her anyway.

I stood up to greet her. We felt like strangers.

"Not now Asher, I'm done with talking for tonight."

"Did you speak to your dad? Or mum?"

"My dad, yes. And he told me everything, so you don't have to."

We stood in silence. I was preventing her from going up the stairs into her cabin, with my body. I couldn't look at her directly, I was staring at the ground, playing with my hands. I wanted to throw my arms around her and make her laugh. I didn't.

"I'm not mad at you, Asher. It was never your place to tell me we were different. It's not even that big of a deal. It's just a lot to take in at once and, to be honest, I wish you didn't pretend that we related as much as we did when you knew that we didn't."

"I couldn't tell you that my episodes were painless when you were in pain. I've had 17 years of seeing people into peace and enjoying that I could make a difference to the end of their story. You have had 17 years of feeling their pain so that they didn't have to. If I was you, I wouldn't enjoy it. I'd be angry at me, just for that." I was sharing my thoughts with her in a way I hadn't before. I'd always been so reserved, because this shouldn't be a love story.

She smiled, "I'm not angry. But I feel like I don't really know you. At all. That makes me not want to spend time with you because—"

"Because you don't know who I am."

She sighed.

"You are Asher. And that was enough for a while. You excite me and intrigue me and make me feel normal. But now I feel alone again."

She was pouring her thoughts out to me too. My chest ached as she spoke. I ran out of words, but she didn't make me feel like a lost cause, the way I felt about myself. Instead, she moved into me and delicately kissed my cheek.

"Goodnight, Asher."

I moved. She floated up the steps like an angel. I walked back to my house, knowing that she wasn't okay, even though she was pretending like she was. But then, I changed my direction. I headed for Blain's cabin.

Brannon

Although I didn't get up until midday, I hadn't had much sleep at all. Thinking kept me awake. The first thing I did was ring my dad.

"Morning sweetie," it was mum, "Dad is sleeping right now. He's feeling a bit under the weather. He said he'd call you back when he wakes up. How are you?"

I was disappointed and I didn't want to talk about how I was because I wasn't sure.

"I'm okay. Got to go though. I'll talk to you later."

She knew this was a lie because I never rang dad for a *quick* chat.

I left my room soon after but was delayed by a piece of torn paper that I spotted on the floor. It read, 'meet me at the pier, Ash'. I didn't have the chance to think twice. My feet carried me to the pier at a speed that could only be defined as 'excited'. I didn't expect what I saw when I got there.

A red and white checked rug. Pillows by the side. Crustless white sandwiches, cakes set up like afternoon tea, bubbling lemonade and yellow roses. Him.

He was sitting at the edge of the pier, with his back to me. His hair was still in the summer heat. I coughed gently to inform him of my presence and he quickly stood up and walked over to me. His black jean-shorts stuck to his legs and his crisp white shirt rippled in the light breeze that had crept upon us. It was hot today. He didn't have a t-shirt on underneath. But that wasn't important.

Asher

"Good afternoon Brannon," I greeted her. The nerves got the better of me, making me sound awkward. I felt my shoulders and neck tensing.

She looked like an angel. Her hair was silver waves. Like the ripples of a calm, but not still, sea. She was standing in front of me in a white laced dress. If the view from a mountain was enough to make one speechless, then she was more.

She smiled at me. She didn't feel as heavy today. I could tell. Maybe she'd processed a little more.

"Good afternoon Asher."

Her voice made my shoulders fall to their natural position and my legs shake a little less.

"Care to join me for a picnic on the pier?"

"Your use of alliteration is irresistible; how could I realistically refuse?" The sarcasm in her tone was compelling.

I took her hand as she sat down. She didn't sit with her legs crossed, mindful of her dress I assume. She was artwork. A masterpiece. She was also waiting for me to tell her what we were doing here.

"Blain," his name engaged her interest straight away, "helped me do this. It wasn't for me; it was for you. I told him I'd let you down, and if looks could kill I wouldn't be here right now."

She giggled. Adorable.

"But when he realised how desperate I was to fix it, he became less intimidating and helped me. He told me you liked picnics and yellow roses. He had first said you liked to watch the sunset, but I already knew that. So, we are going to sit here until the sun sets, and I'm going to tell you about myself. If that's okay with you?"

Her smile was reassuring. I could feel her relief. She sipped on her lemonade and looked out to sea.

"That would be nice."

I took a breath and began, "I didn't understand the Myst until I was 13. That is the age when I was seen as mature enough to handle it."

I could read her mind. 'Boys don't mature by 13. They don't mature!'

I carried on, even though she didn't ask, "I was met by a middle-aged man who thanked me for my duty and told me he'd had a wonderful life. I watched him tread through the water until the glow from the sun annexed him."

I sounded like I was showing off. I kept talking, despite her distanced stare, "Then I woke up. There was no pain. No headache. I felt fine. Sitting here with you now, I hate that because I wish I could've felt pain. I wish you didn't have to. As my name states, I am fortunate. And blessed."

She looked me up and down, quickly. I think the absence of my t-shirt was throwing her off. I don't think she liked being distracted by me. I was apologising for the way our lives panned out until I noticed the lack of interest in her expression.

"Are you okay?" I asked her, not certain if I wanted to hear her response.

"Stop apologising. You and me, we had nothing to do with this."

"I know, but you wanted to know more about me so-"

"You are not defined by some supernatural legacy. I want to know more about you. The real you, behind the magical life you live. I want to know what makes your heart race, and the things that make you feel safe. I want to know what you see your future being or having."

Little did she know, my answer to all her questions was a single, unspoken, word, 'You'.

Instead, I told her that the thought of being alone scared me. So did the thought of not having a fulfilled life. Nature made me feel safe because it isn't judgemental. I told her I felt insecure sometimes because my blue eyes and brown curls were a rare combination.

She interrupted me, telling me to never feel insecure again, because I was gorgeous.

I think I'd have preferred handsome, but I wasn't about to let my masculinity have a crisis over something so innocent. I told her that working out was an outlet for the anger I feel at the world sometimes. Not for any special reason, but for the same reasons that anyone feels angry. I told her the thing that scared me the most was something I'd only feared since the moment I met her.

She focussed completely on me at that point.

The thought of her making me feel negative in any type of way upset her in an instant. It wasn't like that though. It was the decision we'd have to make in several weeks. As soon as we met, I knew I'd have to make this decision. But she didn't.

I thought she must know by now because her father had told her everything last night. But then she slipped away. Eyes flickering, head falling in all directions, before I caught her, again, and placed her head on my knee. I turned to face the ocean with my idea of perfection laying elegantly on my leg. I thought to myself, 'you have to stop bailing on me like this Brannon. I'm starting to think you'd rather be there than here.' I laughed to myself. I knew where she really wanted to be.

Brannon

The Myst called for me at an inconvenient time. He was finally opening up to me. I was finally getting to know him. I told myself to make this quick.

When I enter the Myst, I am immediately placed sitting on the sand. It's white sand and it doesn't stick to me, which is nice. I face a sunset. Orange, red, pink and yellow. That's a poor description, but words cannot do it justice. Picture the biggest and best sunset you could imagine. That was what I was looking at. It made the experience better.

I waited until I saw someone walking towards me. I planned to talk to them, comfort them and watch them as they find peace in a place I do not know. The person walking towards me this time is a man. He has dusty grey hair. Silver, really. He doesn't look old, he looks able. I'd guess late 40's, maybe early 50's. He's wearing brown lace up shoes. Not trainers, shoes. Beige shorts and a white shirt. The type of outfit you'd wear to the beach, which is convenient, at night-time, for a stroll under the star light.

The man started waving, which puzzled me. People don't normally wave, but this man seemed happy. 'Good. This will be quick and easy,' I thought. His teeth were shining as he smiled. His smile was contagious, I smiled too. He radiated happiness. It warmed me up. He was glowing, like the sun. As he got closer, his face familiarised with me. And then it hit me. Like a sun beam in the eye.

"Dad?" the word came out as a whisper, although I was happy to see him. That is my dad. Why am I still sitting here? I stood up and ran to him. It had been a couple of weeks since I'd left. To say I missed him was an understatement. I felt the excitement bubble up inside of me. I wondered what joke he would tell me first. I wondered if it would be one I'd heard a thousand times before. Or maybe he'd thought of something new whilst I've been gone.

He picked me up and swung me round, squeezing me. He smelt of home. And cough sweets. That was a new scent. He put me down and held my face in his hands. I felt like a child again, delighted to see my dad. Safe.

He must have felt my skin when it turned ice cold. When the heat vanished. When the warmth was vacuumed away. When this moment of pure happiness became a moment of – why? Why are you here, Dad?

My head was held in his hands still as he said, "There's my girl. My beautiful Brannon."

I'll ask again, why are you here, Dad? I couldn't say the words out loud because I'd already refused to believe the answer. My eyes were a broken sink. Water filling up quickly, some dripping through a plug that had lost its grip. My forehead clenched into itself with confusion. He knew why.

"You shouldn't be here. Please go," I began to beg, anger in my voice.

"Now you know that's not how this works," his voice sounded deep and musky. Like bed-time stories and 'Brannon, dinner's... '.

I sat back down, still denying his presence. He shouldn't be here with me. He wasn't. I decided. But then I felt his hand grip mine and I turned to see him sat beside me. How to feel? I didn't know. He shared my supernatural blood line. He'd been me before. But he isn't dead.

"Why are you here, Dad?"

"It's my time, I guess." He was looking at the sunset. I was angry at him and full of love.

"What happened?" the ball in my throat became unbearably tight and forced my voice to break, as another tear fell.

"I died," he said, smiling.

I didn't know if this was supposed to be funny. He was smiling and I was furious that he'd even deem this an appropriate time to make jokes. He noticed the absence of my laughter and started to explain himself.

"You anchor the Myst because you came from my blood line. The power of the pendants gets passed down with it, to every generation. When the pendants met, and the power awoke, I felt it. As the last owner of the dark pendant, it is my responsibility to endure this power."

Okay. But that didn't explain why he was still sitting next to me. Still holding my hand. Still dead.

"I couldn't handle it, Brannon. I'm so sorry. After centuries of being passed down, I guess the power grew. I couldn't withstand it. It was stronger than me. It started with a cough and then I was in and out of sleep. I'm guessing this time I didn't wake up."

Another joke? Seriously? I couldn't find the words. What do you say to the man who raised you to be strong and independent and forgiving when you're the reason he is dying? Dead? I don't know.

"I hope you're not angry with me, Bran."

I could never be, but I couldn't phrase my feelings.

"I tried as hard as I could. I felt it attacking my body and I wanted to fight it for you and Marley and Mum."

I couldn't do it. The anger was replaced by sadness I'd never felt. His voice broke like mine. He was gasping for strength. He didn't want me to see him like this.

"I'm not angry Dad," I sobbed, "I just don't want you to be here. I don't want you to go. I can't. I can't do it. I don't know what. What I'm doing. Without you," the sob became a shout, breathless and ugly, "Don't. Please don't leave me."

He sheltered me. I was screaming into his arms. I did this until my chest was a razor blade, piercing my heart. He forced me up and looked me in the eyes.

No words came out. I spoke for him,

"You can stay. Like that old lady did the first time I came here. She stayed until she was ready."

He shook his head.

"No, you can. And I'll come back tomorrow, and the next day and the day after that. That way you won't get bored because I'll be here to talk to."

"And waste your precious time in the real world?"

"Yes. Yes, absolutely."

"Is that really the best option, Brannon?"

"It's the only option Dad! This will not be the last time I see you. Please. Don't make me say goodbye today." I was still sobbing.

"I need to tell you something important," he was mentoring me again like he used to. I was prepared to listen for as long as he wanted me to.

"On your 18th birthday, you have a decision to make. Now that the pendants are together again, the Myst is repairing. You and Asher will have the same birthday. The pendants have to be passed on the same day. He was the only one born of that blood line on the same day as you. That's why it is almost impossible to find the other half of the pendant. Now that you have, you get to decide what to do with it."

Asher's milestone that he told me about. This was what he was referencing on the day we met.

Dad continued, "You have to choose whether to keep the pendant or not. If you choose to keep it, you will suffer more episodes. They may even be more painful. And you will still have access to the Myst. You won't be able to be far away from Asher, or the pendants will stop working. If you keep it, the Myst will allow supernatural beings to practise their gifts in their peace. If you choose to get rid of it, you must throw it into the ocean at sunset on your birthday. You will not be able to see Asher. Ever again. The Myst will still exist but it won't be your duty anymore. It will be given to someone new in the generation after you. You won't have to feel any more pain or the burden of any more lives. You'll be free and you'll have a normal life again. But you must make the final decision on your birthday."

Like the last time we spoke, I was overwhelmed. My dad's dead. I have to choose Asher or a normal life, pain free. My dad is still dead.

"You should go now, sweetie. You've been here for too long. I don't want to cause you anymore pain."

As if that was possible.

"I'm not going. Not unless you promise me you will not go into that sea. Not until we both agree."

"I promise," he said reluctantly.

Okay, that's fine. I can still see him. I'll come back tomorrow. I'll have to feel his death every time I do, but it's worth it. He knows that. And even though I knew I'd see him again; I didn't quite know how to say goodbye. For now.

He stood up, guiding me with him. He hugged me. I buried myself in his neck. In his scent.

"See you soon," he said as he let go of my hand.

He better not break this promise.

Asher

She was out for hours. I didn't leave her side, though I was confused. My episodes never lasted this long. She looked fine, then distressed, then so still. And cold. Her hand felt cold.

When she came around, she sat up straight away. She looked at me. Her eyes were raw. So red. And her cheeks, wet and shiny. She stared through me.

"My Dad's dead."

I didn't know how to react. Then she started crying. Her crying was a light rain shower. It then became heavy enough to flood streets. And then it became a storm. She was screaming. Shouting. Using all the breath in her lungs to cry for him.

"My Dad is dead!"

She cried and cried. I held her. I held her until her grip became the lightest of touches and her rage burned out. Until her strength was weakness. Until she couldn't make a sound. Until the sun set, on what had become the worst day of her life.

Brannon

It's been three weeks now. I haven't left my cabin, other than when Blain has dragged me to the canteen. What does one say when the programmed human interaction always consists of, 'Hello, how are you?' And, due to my lack of ability to filter my words in times like this, my response could only be, 'Hi, my Dad's dead, not great.'

My mother has been calling ruthlessly throughout the day. The first one went something like this.

"Good morning sweetie. How are you?" pretending that the most important man in our lives was still here, and foolishly believing that I would pretend back.

"Can I come home?"

"I wish you could."

I couldn't go home because if the pendants were disconnected after meeting, then the Myst would fall apart, and I'd lose Dad for good. Everyone in the Myst would turn to dust and, after losing my own, I couldn't simply let someone else's father lose his shot at the afterlife.

After our first few calls, I stopped picking up. I left a message saying I was okay and that I loved her, but I didn't want to talk. I knew it was selfish because she needed me too, but I couldn't be there for her right now.

I spent most days forcing myself into the Myst, to make sure he hadn't lied and left me. It was the only place I could be. Halfway between the real world and the 'almost' world. The ones who 'almost' survived but didn't, 'almost' dead but not just yet. I'm lucky really. Most people get one goodbye, or no goodbyes at all.

My father had one rule. If I was going to spend all day with him, then I wasn't allowed to cry. Instead, he asked me about my day. I'd lie and say I'd been hiking again, or to a water park. I told him I had delicious meals and eight hours sleep. He'd lie and say he believed me. It was just easier this way.

Something that Asher was quickly learning about me was that I don't deal very well with sadness. Instead of talking, I lock myself away. I deal with things in my own time. Besides, what could he, or anyone, have said? *It will be okay? Time heals everything. It won't hurt forever.* No. I wasn't going to listen to it. It won't be okay because, no matter how many times I see my dad, he's still dead. Time wouldn't heal because ten years from now, he'll still be dead. And it will hurt forever, because that's how long he'll be gone for.

***

Three weeks later and I can get through the day without crying. Just about. I'm pretending that I've accepted the fact that he's gone. Pretending is my thing. I am ready to admit how fortunate I am to still be able to see him. And I'm ready to let Blain see me. The guilt was starting to get to me that I'd abandoned my best friend for three weeks. And this room was starting to smell of depression and loneliness. A scent I've come to know very well.

I was scared to leave my room. I asked Jessy to make sure no one else knew. She was the one person I couldn't escape from. I was scared for the pity. But, when it feels scary to jump, that's exactly when you jump. Otherwise, you end up staying in the same place, and that I can't do.

Asher

It was lonely without her. Her presence was sorely missed. Everyone loved Brannon. She loved everyone. She made us cry with laughter and made everything fun. I regret not telling her this.

I didn't know how to act or what to do. I sat on her cabin's steps every night for the following week, praying she would let me in. She never did, and I understood this. I asked Blain how she was every day but got the same response. A blank face, shaking, telling me she wasn't okay with no words needed.

My heart ached at the pain she was going through. I knew she'd be visiting her dad in the Myst and I knew how much this would hurt her, physically and emotionally.

It was three weeks before I saw her. It was breakfast and she finally came down to the canteen, with Blain. She didn't eat, she just forced a smile at her friend. I could tell she was comforting him more than he was her. Blain had been sad, too. The real reason was that she couldn't risk being sad for too long, in fear that she would never escape.

Her skin was now a violent pale and so tight that her cheek bones cut through. Her eyes were heavy, but still glistened purple and silver, although I feared that was due to the tears that she was desperately holding in.

Her hair still fell in cascades, like a fountain. A beautiful fountain on a hill side.

When she walked in, I was glued to her. The most gorgeous, saddest person I'd seen. Immediately, I stood up to talk to her, but the lack of eye contact or acknowledgement of my existence pushed me back into my seat. I decided she'd come to me when she was ready.

Brannon

I didn't think I was ready. I wanted to look at him, but I found myself avoiding eye contact. When I looked at him, I was reminded of the one thing I was desperate to forget. That night. Where I cried viscously into his arms, and then disappeared without a word for three weeks.

Blain didn't ask me how I was feeling. He didn't ask any questions about it, which suited me very much. I needed to be distracted, not reminded. I ate an apple for breakfast and a glass of water, more than I'd had in a single sitting for 21 days. I knew I wasn't okay because I was shedding weight like a malting dog. But I was ready to try now. Another thing about me, I'm deeply sad for weeks but when I decide that it's time to try, I really do.

We then headed to the beach. Everyone did. I'd missed the camp activities for the summer. We now had two weeks of free time. Except for the Summer Ball, which wasn't sounding like something I wanted to attend right now.

It was hot. The sun was radiating warmth like never before. The scent of sun cream and salty water floated in the air, along with laughter from the camp attendees. The laughter was comforting. I hadn't heard it in a long time and sometimes we forget that we don't have to be the one laughing for it to make us happy. I think I convinced myself that happiness was out of the picture to the point that I forgot what it was. What it felt like. It was coming easier than expected. I knew dad would be happy when he found out that I actually did something today.

I bathed in my blue bikini for hours. Listening to people around me made me feel like I wasn't lonely and that was enough for now. But I felt Asher's glare as much as I felt the heat tanning my skin. I couldn't avoid him forever. Today, I was trying. I had to try with him, too.

I waited until lunch time when everyone headed for the canteen. I told Blain that I'd wait here for him, and I promised I would join him for dinner. I wasn't hungry and this was the perfect opportunity to talk to Asher. I wondered what he'd say. Maybe he'd ask how much I'd travelled to the Myst, because he knew it would have hurt my head. I'd been a lot, and the pain was excruciating at this point. Maybe he'd ask if I've been sleeping. Maybe he'd hug me. Maybe I'd even let him. Maybe I should stop wondering and just get on with it.

I sat on the sun bed, sipping my passionfruit lemonade, toes buried in the tropical sand, waiting. For him.

Asher

I walked over to her. Today we were matching. Royal blue swimming costume and my royal blue trunks. Her skin was still pale, but it amazed me how quick her olive tone was returning. She was beautiful. Inside and out.

My stomach was electric. My hands were sweating. My heart was racing. Then she saw me, and smiled. A rush of calmness and relief blanketed my body.

She stood up, which suggested to me that we weren't going to stay here. My mind was empty. I couldn't find the words to say that I was sorry and that I'd missed her more than I imagined to be possible. That I thought about her every day and I felt the absence of her humour making me laugh. Words couldn't say that. Instead, I just hugged her. So tight, that I felt her heart beat slow and her face find safety in my neck.

We walked silently to the pier. I think this was our place now. She laid a beach towel out so we wouldn't burn on the scorching wood and we sat down, dangling our legs above the crystal water. The tide was coming in so the waves rushed forward, curling and crashing, becoming a bubbly froth as they met the shore.

She stared into the distance. I admired her full, reddish lips as she sipped on her sunset-coloured drink. Her jawline like a blade and her eyelashes stretching to meet the tidy hairs on her eyebrows. I found myself questioning what I did to deserve this. To be sat with her.

She started the conversation, which came as a surprise, "The sky is clear. There's going to be a good sunset tonight."

I'd spent weeks worrying that she'd lose sight of everything she loved. I was wrong. Then she looked at me and smiled. I swallowed the intimidation she made me feel, "I'm sorry, Brannon." These words escaped my mouth.

"Don't be."

Maybe I shouldn't have brought it up. In fact, I definitely shouldn't have brought it up. She didn't come here to be reminded of this. Her strength melted away as she stopped pretending and her eyes became rock pools.

She spoke quietly, "I've blamed myself. If we didn't meet and the pendants stayed separated, then he wouldn't have died trying to withstand all the power. Then I realised that the universe decided, and the time was right, apparently."

I could hear in her voice, the regret she felt. Meeting me had been a mistake.

Brannon

I couldn't understand. I found myself talking to him. I found myself wanting to talk to him. He was safe.

He looked sad when I spoke. Like I'd shot an arrow through his heart. I carried on talking, "It's been so hard. To lay in bed thinking of all the ways this could've gone differently. Ways that could've kept him alive. But now I've realised that in order to be happy, we have to let every situation be what it is instead of what we think it should be, and then make the best of it. If that makes me sound heartless, then so be it. But no power in the world can bring back the dead."

He looked shocked. He expected me to be a tragic mess, which part of me was. Most of me was sick of hearing my dad lecturing me to keep going. Ironic coming from someone who's gone. But I had listened and I wanted to make my dad happy. I could tell in his tone recently that he wasn't. He was worried about me, and I didn't want this. I'm not here for Asher or for myself, I'm here for my dad.

My thoughts were pulled back to the now. "I've missed you, Brannon."

My heart smiled.

"I've missed you too, Asher."

He reached his arm around me, and I let my head fall onto his shoulder. Lightly, his lips pressed against my forehead. Suddenly, everything felt okay.

***

I returned to my cabin after dinner. I was done for the day. I didn't want to go out anymore. I had other plans.

I lay on my duvet, rested my closed eyes and focused. When I opened them again, I was sat on marble sands, looking at half a ball of orange heat, setting behind the tranquil sea.

"Hey, Dad."

He was sitting beside me, smiling at the tropical glow. He was the sun.

"There's my girl. How was today? Please tell me you left your room."

I was excited to tell him, "I did! I spent the day at the beach."

He looked at me with disbelief. "Promise me you're telling the truth."

Recently, I have been responding to this with a nod full of lies. Today, I didn't. "I promise."

He squeezed me with a growing smile. "I am so proud of you, Bran. I really am."

In my head, I hit pause and lived in this moment for a while. The smell of home and his warmth surrounding me. I told myself I'd remember this moment, forever.

"It was better than I thought. I had an okay day."

"Good! And did that have anything to do with a certain Asher?"

"Dad, I'm not talking about this with you!"

"Oh, come on Bran! I'm not there to threaten him for stealing the love of my little girl, I need to know what he's like."

Love. That's an intense word. "He looks after me, okay. That's all you need to be worried about."

"He better do, or I'll come back and haunt him," he laughed every word out of his mouth.

Through visiting dad every day, I soon came to realise that nothing would stop him making jokes. Instead of being angry at him about it, I just laughed too. Laughing at your dad's jokes and seeing their face light up knowing they made you laugh is a priceless gift in life. Why not the afterlife, too?

"Brannon, make sure you never stop now."

"Never stop what?"

"Trying. Moving on."

"I am not moving on. I will never move on." He was stupid to think I'd just forget about him.

"I'm not asking you to forget about me. I'm asking you to get out of bed every morning and enjoy your life. Live, don't just exist. The hardest part is starting, and you've done that now. Never look back. For me?"

There was a reason you couldn't look behind in the Myst. It was symbolism of the exact lesson my dad was currently teaching me. Looking behind only stops you from looking forward. And moving forward is the only way to reach your destination. In this case, it was peace. Peace after a fulfilled life. Peace that I wasn't letting my dad find yet.

"I won't, Dad, for you."

My head rested on his shoulder. We stared at the sunset, which never actually sets. For the first time in what felt like forever, I felt like I could sleep.

I heard him whisper, "Goodnight, sweetie," as I drifted off. When I woke up again, it was the morning, and I was laying on top of my duvet. The sun was dappling through the window and the birds were singing from the treetops. Today, I was going to carry on. I was going to get out of bed and enjoy life. I was going to hug Blain and thank Asher. The one thing I was not going to do was look back. For dad.

Asher

"Two weeks Asher. Fourteen days, and you need to know what you're doing with that pendant," my father advised me, like he hadn't been reminding me every day for the past three weeks. I think he assumed that Brannon's loss would alter my decision. He was mistaken.

"I know what I'm doing, Dad. It's not a hard decision."

He was talking about how, on my 18th birthday, I had to choose whether to keep the pendant or throw it into the sea. The choice was simple. I either loose Brannon, or I don't. And I picked 'don't'. I'd made my mind up at the bonfire, after our first conversation. When I looked at her, every love song suddenly made sense. Of course I was going to keep the pendant.

"It should be a hard decision Asher," he sounded angry, "You can't just decide to keep it because you like her! If you keep it then you will carry on having episodes for the rest of your life. And God knows how long that'll be! All we know is what the old legends have passed through history. The pendants have never been reconnected in this way. Anything could happen, do you know how much of a risk that is?"

Now I was angry. I was becoming an adult, and he still didn't think I could make my own choices. I've never stood up to my dad before but apparently that was about to change.

"It is a risk, yes, but it is very much worth taking! And she's not just a girl that I like, you don't even know her."

"Invite her round for dinner then. Let me get to know her before you tie your life to hers!"

"Fine, I will!"

Now I had to invite her round for dinner. With my parents. Maybe I should have thought that one through.

He was calmer in his next statement, "Asher, it doesn't make you a bad person for putting yourself first. If that's what you wanted to do, then you are still a good person."

That's what he'd always taught me. Be a good person, but don't waste time proving it.

"It's not what I want to do, okay."

"And what if she chooses to get rid of it?"

I didn't quite know how to respond to this. I hadn't thought about it. Purposely, I avoided playing that guessing game.

"Then she gets rid of it. It doesn't change the fact that I..." What do I?

"That you what?"

"I don't know. Please just get off my back about it. I've made my decision. End of."

***

I headed to Brannon's cabin. I wanted to take her out for the day, if she'd let me. I didn't feel as nervous to ask this time. She was quickly becoming my best friend as well as the girl who made my heart sing. This time I was just excited. I checked with Blain that he hadn't made any plans with her first. His protective nature of her terrified me a little bit. But he said she would be free after midday; he was taking her out for breakfast to 'talk' first. I think he wanted to make sure she was really okay, which he could do better than me. I left at 1pm , skipping to her door.

I knocked, composing a rhythm that I hoped would make her smile. She opened the door, pushing her hand through her hair, making it fall in every direction. She was energetic, signifying that her chat must have gone well. Her eyes twinkled at me and she smirked. I loved that smirk.

"Hey, pretty," I greeted her with confidence that might annoy her.

I could tell she wasn't nervous either today. She didn't shy away; she held eye contact and rolled her eyes at me. I melted into a puddle of desire at her feet as she spoke.

"Hey, you."

I leant against the doorway.

"Fancy joining me for the afternoon?" I asked her, realising, now, that I was more nervous than I anticipated. I wish she didn't have this control over me. Then again, I'm glad she does.

This time, her smile was sweet. Her teeth did not show but her cheeks lifted, and her eyes danced. She opened the door to let me in. I guess that means yes.

Her room smelt of mango and coconut. Her hair normally smelt like that too. Her bed was a mess, but I sat on it anyway.

"Sorry about the mess. I'm usually a tidy person, just haven't managed that stage yet," she looked at me to make sure I knew she meant emotionally. She had managed to get out of bed, but not make it. It reflected her mental state perfectly. She wasn't drowning in sadness anymore, but it was still there.

"So, where are we going?" she asked me, mirroring my internal excitement in her tone.

"I thought, maybe, we could take one of those little boats out on the lagoon in the forest. If you wanted to. If not, then anything really. I don't mind at—"

"That sounds perfect. You do know that stretch of water is only small though? There's nowhere to go but the middle."

"Brannon?"

She looked away. She always did this when I said her name in this way. Maybe I had control over her too, "Do you really think I want to tire myself out trying to move a boat down a lake? I'm here to see you. The middle is fine. In fact, it's more than fine. It's great!"

She giggled. I screenshot it with my mind.

"Okay, let me go and get changed and we can leave."

She searched aggressively through her drawers, making more of a mess, and then took herself to the bathroom. I moved so that my back was against the wall, legs hanging off the side of her single bed, waiting.

I found myself wondering how she does it. How she continues to smile in a time like this. Her phone, which she left on the bed next to me, lit up and I noticed her home screen. A picture of a man with silver hair, who I guessed to be her dad, and her, their cheeks against each other's, laughing. Blain had gone to see her as soon as he found out the day after it happened. She spoke to him sometimes, that's how I found out that her dad was waiting in the Myst. I hadn't had an episode in weeks. Her constant availability meant that I didn't have to. I felt bad for this. I also wondered if she was planning on keeping him there forever. I could ask her about it, or perhaps it wasn't my place to judge. Or my place to pretend that, if I was her, I wouldn't have done the exact same thing. Anyway, the message was from her mum, but I didn't read it. I didn't even mean to see it; I just couldn't help but notice her smile in the photo on her phone and hoped that I could bring her that today.

She walked out of the bathroom like I wasn't there. She was in loose white shorts that exaggerated her sun kissed skin, and a black bikini top. It was wrong for me to stare at her in this way, but I couldn't disconnect my eyes from her. It was hot again today.

Brannon

We headed to the lagoon, walking close by each other. Close enough that our hands were brushing against each other. If only one of us would grab the other's, but we wouldn't. We enjoyed the intimacy of a near touch.

I hadn't been nervous until I had to get in the boat. There were two boats that were tied to the pole of a wooden board that stretched a little over the water, like a mini pier. The water wasn't as clear as the sea but it wasn't mucky. It was enticing, especially in this heat. Asher sorted out the boat by leaning over and untying it. I watched him, until he stood up again, notifying me that it was ready.

"After you," he said, dropping a tonne of pressure on me without knowing.

Why do we do this? Us girls. Convince ourselves that something as easy as climbing into a boat was a make-or-break moment. Ask ourselves stupid questions, like what if the boat tips and I fall in?

I did it quickly. One leg after the other. Sit on the wooden bench inside. Relax.

The boat was deeper than it looked. The planks of wood stopped just above my hips. I waited for him to climb in opposite me, wondering if he'd kiss me again today.

There was only a single pair of oars, so we took one each. We glided them through the cool water, laughing as we lost control of the direction. By the time we reached the middle, we were both holding our stomachs, feeling the ache of pure happiness. A feeling I hadn't felt in a while. He was funnier than he realised, in a rare Ash-like way. But when we stopped laughing, he started speaking to me, in his alluring voice. I could tell this was going to be a full-on conversation rather than small talk.

"How was your breakfast with Blain?" he asked. He and Blain had built a friendship over their shared desire of making sure I was okay. I guessed he knew about my breakfast through conversing with him.

"It was needed."

"What did you talk about?"

I knew this was his way of saying, 'tell me everything you told him', because he was too scared to ask me the same questions himself.

"We spoke about my dad, and how I'm coping."

"How are you coping?"

"I'm doing okay. When the initial shock went, it got a bit easier. By no means did it get easy though. The last three weeks have been a blur, to be honest. I just remember the pain in my throat from crying and the agony in my chest when I was trying to catch my breath. I've never felt pain like it. But after Dad reassured me that he was okay a hundred and one times, I started to feel okay too. And then he begged me to leave my room and do something for the last two weeks, so that's what I'm doing. If I didn't think it would make him happy, then trust me, I wouldn't be here."

He listened to every word I said, intensely. His face moved between concern, relief and gratitude. I assumed the gratitude was towards my dad, for forcing me to leave my room.

I'd learnt that the recovery is quicker if you give in to the hurt. Sometimes you just need to cry and be sad. You need to break down and be torn apart. You need to learn how to pick yourself up and put yourself back together. Sometimes, the only way to be happy is to give into sadness first.

"I'm sorry about what you're having to go through. And I'm sorry that I was there when it happened. I'm sure you'd much rather have been alone."

He was wrong. Although we didn't feel as close as we do right now when it had happened, there was nowhere else I'd have rather been than in his arms. Safe.

He continued, "I'm so glad he convinced you to come out though and enjoy your last two weeks here with me."

I knew what his aim was in saying a sentence such as that. He was digging. He wanted answers. He wanted to know if this was going to be our last two weeks together. What I was going to do with the pendant on the 4th of July, our 18th birthday. Was this the beginning of the end, or the end of the beginning?

I didn't answer. I just smiled and waited for him to fill the silence.

"So, I hope you don't mind me asking this, but is your dad going to stay in the Myst forever?"

If you were anyone else Asher, I would mind.

"For now. I guess he'll tell me when he gets bored. I'm not ready yet. I don't really want to talk about it. Sorry," I ended this conversation because I felt a dark rain cloud hover above my head.

"Of course, I'm sorry," he said, whilst squeezing my hand.

I was leaning my elbows against my knees, closer to him than I realised. His black vest top hugged his defined body, whilst his, also black, shorts sat loose on his thighs. He lifted his other hand and messed it through his hair, making his tight nut-brown curls wave through his fingers. As he did this, his head tilted upwards towards the towering branches of the treetops that hovered above the tranquil lagoon, and his jawline cut through the air like a blade. The ball in his throat stuck out behind his bronze skin. His eyelids hid his aquamarine eyes, resting below his bushy yet well-shaped eyebrows. The sun light streaking through the gaps in the jungle ceiling made his face glow. He was gorgeous. Inside and out.

When time finally caught up with me, I watched as his arm dived into the water and splashed over me. Droplets of water hit my skin. He was smiling, hard, with his perfectly lined teeth. I splashed him back. And then he got me again. So, I got him. And then we found ourselves in a momentary water fight. The giggling returned and the dark rain cloud dissolved into nothing. The boat started to rock as we attacked each other with the water. His arm was moving us like we were in the middle of a storm on the sea. I grabbed his shoulders as I felt us toppling over. He stopped immediately and steadied the boat. My grip on his arms brought us even closer. Everything slowed down at an instant. I heard him swallow and felt his breath against my lips. We were staring each other directly in the eye, appreciating us. I thought he was going to kiss me, until he said,

"Brannon, how would you feel about coming to dinner with my parents tonight?"

My hands stopped gripping and I sat back up. Moment over. Could he not have asked me a few seconds later? Typical.

It's not that I didn't want to meet his parents. I did, I just wasn't sure how I'd handle it. And I wasn't sure of something else.

"Asher, what are we?"

I could tell by the dramatic widening of his eyes that he was surprised and uncertain about this question.

"Well, I guess that depends on how you feel about me, Brannon."

I didn't know how I felt. Actually, that's a lie. I didn't know if I wanted to tell him how I felt. How did he manage to turn this on me?

"I feel like..." I stopped and thought about this, "I feel like if I lost you, I'd have lost the safest place on Earth."

We both looked at each other, more serious than ever before.

"How do you feel about me, Asher?"

"I feel like...when I look at you," he grinned, talking slowly to keep me waiting, "I see everything I have ever wanted, and more."

We were both smiling now. I broke eye contact. He was irresistible, but I was choosing to resist. We sat comfortably in our silence.

He was the one to speak again, "So, what are we then, Bran?"

Our eyes met again.

"I'd say we're pretty extraordinary. Would you agree?"

Asher

The front door of my house is glass. I stared at her standing behind it. I noticed that she had straightened her hair. It looked silky and stretched to the middle of her stomach. She flicked it behind her head, and it fell perfectly like neat curtains, past her black t-shirt, almost reaching the high wasted seam of her denim skirt. Her pearl eyes were mind maps. If I could draw an inference from them to state how she felt right now, I'd write nervous and edgy and timid. To be honest, I was feeling the same. I'd never introduced a girl to my parents before and I knew my dad would ask her questions that she probably wouldn't want to answer. And my mum would most likely fuss over her and make her feel uncomfortable. But I knew I couldn't commit to her without passing this stage.

My parents had only seen me as a 'lad'. Messing about with the few friends that live around here, not taking life too seriously. Never being concerned with a girl. I hadn't even seen myself like this. I liked to take each day as it came. Now I plan my days. Usually around when I get to see her. Where can I 'accidentally' cross paths with her?

My mum always said to me, "when you meet the one, you'll know". And if meeting 'the one' didn't feel the way I felt after meeting Brannon, then there was no one for me.

I opened the door and smiled at her. I was on a mission to make her feel comfortable amongst the chaos she was about to walk into. I hugged her but she didn't squeeze me as tight as usual. I felt her trembling like a little leaf clinging on to a branch in a winter breeze. Her nerves calmed me down. This was a time when she needed me to be her guide. Whatever she needs me to be, I am.

Brannon

His house was colossal. I'd ventured through hanging trees, much like a rain forest, to reach the door of his secluded home. The front of the house was mostly glass with yellow warmth shining out. Dark wood joined the windows together. When I walked in, I struggled to notice anything but the chandelier in the middle of the hall, hanging above the spiralling staircase and lighting up the entrance like a ball room. The house was clean and smelt like fresh linen and white candles.

Asher stood in front of me, in jeans, a white t-shirt and confidence that compensated for the nervous state I was in.

"Are you okay?" Asher asked, in a calming voice.

Before I had the chance to answer, his mum dashed out from behind a door. I guess she'd heard him speaking. She was bouncing. It was overwhelming but it was nice to receive this reception.

She had blonde bobbed hair, with streaks of lighter and darker shades. Her eyes were brown, not like Asher's. She approached me, mouth open with excitement. Her black shirt smelt floral, and she wore fluffy white slippers. She hugged me. Well, pounced on me and I tried to hug her back.

"Brannon, hi! I'm Asher's Mum, Tammy, it's so great to finally meet you!"

She looked like a Tammy. Her kindness made me less shy.

"You too, your house is lovely," I didn't know if this was the right thing to say. I felt awkward. I always did when I met someone new. I slipped off my shoes, revealing my crisp white socks. I felt oddly conscious about this.

Asher looked slightly traumatised by his mother's greeting. It made me giggle under my breath.

"Dinner won't be long. We're having pasta, I hope you like it. But if you don't that's fine too, I have other things in the freezer. I don't mind cooking something else?"

"Pasta is great, thank you!"

Asher placed his hands on my shoulder. He was taller than me but not a lot. He started to push me towards the door in front.

"Let's just go sit down, shall we?" he suggested, eyeballing his mum, silently telling her to not embarrass him. She was a lot, but she was welcoming, and I liked that. Her presence was comforting, much like Asher's.

The kitchen was white and marble grey, like the ones you'd see on a 'luxury kitchen's page' on Pinterest. The yellow glow from subtle lamps infused the room, along with the faint smell of bleach, though the overwhelming smell was of boiling tomato sauce. This relaxed me, knowing that I liked what we were about to eat for dinner.

I walked in, scared to see Asher's dad again. He didn't turn around from the oven until Asher had already pulled my seat out and I'd sat down. I was sitting stiff, leg bouncing, but my top half like an ice sculpture.

His dad turned around with a smile, "Hi Brannon, how are you?"

Tammy gave him a stern look and shook her head. Then I realised, this question must've been on the 'do not ask, her dad just died' list of questions.

"I'm well thank you, how are you?"

"Not bad at all!" he had enthusiasm in his voice that I hadn't heard last time we had spoken. Asher looked stunned as his father spoke. Maybe he expected different.

Asher

We swapped small talk until Brannon had dropped her shoulders and the bubble of fear that she was sitting in had popped. It didn't take her long to start making conversation with my parents. Some moments I felt like I wasn't in the room. I could tell my mum loved her as they laughed together. My dad was joining in more than I'd expected of him, but I could tell he was waiting for the right time to ask Brannon the serious stuff.

We ate the pasta from china bowls, continuing the banal small talk. Brannon kept looking at me throughout dinner, using her eyes to tell me she felt nervous again. I knew she hadn't been eating full meals since what happened, so I warned my dad earlier to give her a small portion.

"Do you have any siblings, Brannon?" my father asked.

Her voice was elegant when talking to my parents. A little fake, but I'd be the same.

"I have a brother, Marley."

"How old is he?"

"He's ten."

"And does he know?"

A cold silence fell upon us. Everyone looked up from their meals, Brannon looked to me. I didn't know what to say because even if I told my dad to not ask the questions, he was going to ask them anyway. Instead, I squeezed her leg under the table to tell her I was here and to calm her.

I knew she didn't want to talk about this stuff because she'd only just found out the depths of it. However, she was the owner of the other pendent. It would be strange if the questions weren't asked. My family deserve to know the girl I'm going to spend forever with.

"Kind of. He knows that I faint sometimes and that I'm in pain quite a lot, but my dad thinks he is too young to know anything else right now. They will tell him when he can understand the seriousness of it and be trusted to not tell anyone else."

The mention of her father caused unease. My mother's face became a poster for pity and my father, for once, looked as though he was struggling to find the words to say.

I spoke for them, "I think that's a sensible decision. It's a lot for a young boy to have to deal with. Are you close with your brother?"

She smiled, "Very. He's such a caring boy. If I have an episode in front of him, I always wake up to him playing with toys next to me so that I'm not alone. He's funny, too. You'll like him."

She spoke about the future with certainty that I'd be in it. I was certain too. We carried on eating, the tension soothing and the small talk, about her school this time, began again.

After dinner, I escorted her to the lounge room where my mother suggested we all sit.

"How are you doing?" I asked before the interrogators joined us again.

She exhaled deeply, "I don't know, how am I doing?"

"I think you're coping great. My mum seems to really like you."

She smiled, noticing the lack of mention of my dad.

"What would you like to drink?"

"Just water, please."

I left for the kitchen to grab her a drink. Now that the dinner was over, I felt relaxed. In fact, in the pit of my stomach was buzzing happiness. With or without my parent's approval, I was going to keep the pendant with Brannon, but having their approval would make it easier.

Mum was in the kitchen cleaning up.

"Your Dad's just gone to grab some firewood from the back yard."

I nodded and opened the top cupboard to get a glass.

"Asher, she is a lovely girl. So beautiful too!"

I couldn't stop the smile on my face. It escaped me.

"I know. Do you think Dad likes her?"

Pretending that I didn't care about my dad's opinion was easy to everyone but my mum. She knew that the only reason I ever came to terms with anchoring the Myst was because he helped me. He taught me that being different was special, and strong. That this duty was a blessing, one that only two people on Earth could claim to have. He made me who I am and, despite his inability to filter his mouth in conversation, he was the man who inspired me to be better. Now I wanted to be better for her.

"Yes Asher, I do. I think your Dad is a slow burner. When we first met, he didn't want to know me! He always told me that life wasn't a mission to fulfil silly love stories," she spoke whilst loading plates into the dishwasher, "After some time, he came through. I think he's fascinated in the pendant. I mean, his eyes lit up when he saw it. His interests are disrupting his manners. He'll get over it soon. If you're truly happy, which he can see you are, then it's simple. He's happy, too."

I filled up the glass, watching water droplets splash out, grinning. I hugged her. She hugged me back. I left to find Brannon. My Brannon.

Brannon

I was sitting in his lounge. A small-ish room, with two cream sofas facing each other, a fireplace against the wall and a cream rug in the centre. There was a small lamp by the corner, but the room was lit by the cosy glow of the fire.

The bookshelf beside the sofa was full of old and delicate looking supernatural books. I traced my finger over the red spine of one. *'THE OLD WORLD: The Modern Translation of an Ancient Story'.* Pulling it from the shelf, I opened to a random page and, compelled by own fascination, began reading.

The leading Ancestor, Juno, cast an extraordinary spell and as the sun set, the Myst rose. This construct, on the other side of the sun, set seamlessly behind the ocean, would gift an afterlife to those who possessed supernatural qualities, but one that they could never leave. This last was not seen as a dire consequence. After all, there are worse places to spend eternity.

Passing into the Myst was a natural process. In the beginning. However, when the Earth's magic was exhausted from the core, this once natural transition became impossible. The leading Ancestor had not so much power that allowed the Myst to survive once her magic was also gone. The power to wield Supernatural abilities was about to be lost forever, leaving one question that seemed unanswerable; what would happen to those souls, who although powerless, were still supernatural?

Ancestor Juno created a ritual that would require immense sacrifice. The supernatural community understood this but agreed that the sacrifice was necessary as Juno was not powerful enough to perform the spell without it. They also understood that nothing lasts forever, but the Myst had to.

Every person with any remaining supernatural ability was required to sacrifice their power and superior qualities immediately. No longer a slow decline. Their abilities would be gone in an instant. All power would transfer to two Ancestors, the Curator and the Amory Ancestor.

They alone would be the gatekeepers of the supernatural afterlife, sharing the responsibility for guiding any supernatural being through to the other side of the sunset. One of the chosen two would meet each new soul in a middle ground between life and death, allowing them time to accept their passing and instructing them on the path. They were to walk into the sea when they were ready. Then and only then would they venture through into the Myst, a place where their afterlife would, for eternity, be shared with those who passed before them.

The two chosen Ancestors were assigned the privilege of each wearing a pendant, that had been cast as the repository of power for the Myst. These two then were the only custodians of magical abilities, trusted to use the incredible power in wonderful ways for the highest of purposes. However, this trust was soon broken and the rules for the survival of the Myst were rewritten.

And the breach in trust? The Amory ancestor used her power in unforgiving ways.

I flipped the page. I knew this part of the story already. My Dad had told me. I knew that it was a woman representing my blood line who used her magic for personal reasons; to cause suffering to those she opposed and to bring pain to the people of her choosing. I knew this already, and I dealt with the punishment every day. I didn't need to read it again.

The supernatural population was angry at Ancestor Amory and decided that her bloodline was infected with evil instincts and couldn't be trusted, but the pendant could not be removed from her. The spell was binding and locked the pendants power with the blood of the Amory and the Curator. After much thought the solution was realized. Their blood linked the pendants and so, for their separate bloodline descendants that would also be true.

So it was determined that the pendants would be separated, far away from each other, and as they were passed to the next born in each bloodline, the power of the two Ancestors would be drained.

For the Curator, all would remain as it had. They would assist the passing of those with supernatural genes in a peaceful ceremony. But for the Amory, their duties to the Myst remained but they would suffer indescribable pain as each and every person passed through, as a punishment for what the Amory Ancestor did.

Yet to remake the rules required an immense amount of power and there was none to be had within the Earth's core. So it was that Ancestor Juno called upon the power of the Myst itself. In doing so all knew that the ability to enjoy an afterlife within it would be cast aside. The supernatural souls who had passed into the Myst would fade and die. In the future, the Myst would only hold their souls until perhaps, one day, if the pendants were to meet again in the modern world, their power would spark a reawakening.

In the process, Juno, exhausted by her efforts, died. She used her last remaining magic as leading Ancestor to perform the ritual for the good of the world. It is rumoured that she left the majority of her remaining magic in a talisman, in case the supernatural world thrived once more. Juno continues to reserve the title of the most respected supernatural person to walk the Earth.

Chapter 7: Why were the Curator and Amory ancestors important?

I heard the kitchen door shut and shoved the book back onto the shelf in its exact place. Sitting back on the sofa, I felt rude for looking through Asher's dads' stuff, although I understood my place in the world better than ever before.

His parents joined us and there was more comfort in this room than there had been in the kitchen. Being around them made me miss my parents, who were very similar people. My mum is also overbearing sometimes, and easily excitable. My dad is protective of me like Asher's is of him, but also loving and puts family before everything. I was excited to see him again, later.

"You have the most gorgeous hair, Brannon. Is it coloured?" Tammy asked me. She had complimented me all night which was sweet.

"I was born with it. My Dad has the same colour hair. He reckons it was part of the curse put on our blood line," I giggled, "he didn't enjoy the purpleness of it!"

His dad laughed with me. His laugh was almost the same as Asher's, just deeper and wiser. I felt proud to have done this. Asher looked happy about it, too.

"Your Dad sounds like he was a funny man, Brannon," his father said. What does he mean 'was' a funny man? He is a funny man. Present day.

"Yeah, he is," I corrected him, politely. Asher moved closer to me, so our legs were pushed against each other. He always did something to tell me he was there.

This was a big step for us. It had been six weeks since we'd met, although it was starting to feel like forever. I'm glad we got this out of the way. I intended on spending the rest of camp having fun, making sure I always had good news for Dad. This wasn't bad news, though.

"It can't be easy for you, having to feel the supernatural's deaths." His father was obviously done with small talk.

"It's painful, yeah. But I don't mind. I'm used to it. And knowing that their deaths can be painless and that they might find peace at the end of it makes it worthwhile."

"Not all supernatural people are good, though. They don't always deserve a pain free death," he sounded knowledgeable on this. He must've done a lot of research when he was the owner of Asher's pendant. Or he was hinting at the darkness of my blood line. After all, it was me who descended from 'the sad one'. It was us who manipulated fate in the wrong way. It was me being punished with the curse of the pendent. I wasn't that interested; I just did the job.

"No, probably not. But it would be much worse if supernatural natures and abilities were activated again."

"That would never happen. The magic from the core of the Earth has been drained. The only place where that would be possible is on the other side of the sunset, in peace," he paused and looked into my mind, knowing I was desperate to avoid his next comment, "Of course, that can only happen if you keep the pendant."

Asher's body tightened. Nobody knew how to react. That was my business. I planned on keeping it this way. I wasn't going to announce my decision like this.

"I always wonder what the world would be like if there was still magic in the core. I'd be a witch and there'd be vampires and supernatural things roaming around," I diverted the conversation.

"It sounds ridiculous, doesn't it? Even I can't imagine it, it sounds like fantasy land!"

I laughed at his Father's comment. This stroked his ego and made him sit up straight with pride. He was so much like my dad. Flattered when someone found him funny.

"Your parents did a good job with you, Brannon."

Asher finally loosened up as his dad said this.

"I can't tell you how happy I am that you met our Asher."

His Mum started speaking, "It's true! I've never seen him this happy, or worried, or anything really. I think he really cares about you."

I blushed, noticing Asher blushing more. He pushed his hand through his curls. He did this when he was embarrassed or nervous. I guessed it was a bit of both, this time.

"Cheers Mum, that'll do."

We spent the last hour talking about Asher. They told me funny stories from his childhood. Like how he didn't approve of wearing clothes until he was four years old. And how he stole his mum's hair straighteners to try to get rid of his curls once, when they were untameable. And when he used to get told off as a young teenager and he'd run off to the pier and sulk.

It reached 10pm and I decided it was time to leave.

"I'm going to walk Bran home, won't be long," Asher announced.

"Thank you so much for dinner and having me round, it's been great to meet you both."

"You're more than welcome, Brannon! You can come anytime!" Tammy said, hugging me goodbye at the door.

His dad continued, "Yeah, you're always welcome. And, Brannon, we owe you a thank you, for making our Asher happy."

Asher

That was the first time I'd heard our names in the same sentence. Brannon and Asher. Hm. Sounds like a love story to me.

We were both surrounded by satisfaction. She was pleased that my parents liked her, as was I. We didn't need to reflect on it any more than that. Now, on our walk back, we could be less serious and more us.

"I can't believe I was forced to come to a camp and six weeks later I'm meeting a boy's parents!"

She was right, this was quick.

"Is that all I am to you, Brannon Amory? Just a boy..."

Her face turned serious. "Asher, how do you know my second name is Amory. I've never told you that before."

She was perceptive. She didn't miss a thing.

"I'm sorry, I didn't even think about how weird that must seem to you. My dad taught me our history since I was a child. The sir name of the Ancestor who played with fate in bad ways was Amory. I didn't know it was your last name until I saw your pendent."

She looked disappointed. I guess it couldn't have been easy knowing that her blood line was dark. It didn't matter though. She was the brightest star amongst a black night sky.

"That makes sense. Sorry for being so suspicious about it, I should've worked that out myself really."

"Don't apologise!"

"I am sorry, though, Asher. I feel responsible for this whole thing. In two weeks, we have to make this massive decision that chooses our future because one of my ancient relatives didn't know how to practise self-control! The pendants wouldn't be a thing and you wouldn't have blanked out of reality consistently throughout your life if it all hadn't happened."

"Brannon, do you know the meaning of Amory?"

She shook her head.

"It means home strength, but the older, more ancient meaning, was of ruler. A strong ruler. Within the supernatural world it came to signify a powerful leader. That's what it stands for now, because, despite what happened, if magic still existed, your family would dominate the supernatural world. You would be the most powerful witch to live. And, my God, you're a leader! The way everyone respects you and admires you without feeling intimidated or scared. It's inspiring. Don't ever feel ashamed of who you are or where you come from. One generation's mistake cannot be blamed on another."

She listened to me intensely and processed every word. She didn't speak, though. So, I carried on, "The power that has built up through the passing of the pendant is unimaginable."

"That's how my father died."

Of course. I hadn't even realised this. Her father would have had to absorb the magic when the pendants met considering he was the last person to own the pendant before Brannon. This made me angry. At myself. She lost her father because I couldn't resist her. Yes, the whole point of the pendants was to allow the universe to decide when magic could be reborn in another world, but it didn't come with a leaflet on the terms and conditions. I was never warned about this. She must've hated me, for weeks. Knowing my father was still alive and breathing, simply because we come from a blood line that wasn't cursed.

I didn't know what to say. But she knew this.

Instead of talking, she gently intertwined her fingers with my own, and let her hand fall into mine. I loved how she never made me feel guilty for our circumstances. She never blamed me. I loved that she cared less about the past and more about the future. I loved how her smile had a thousand meanings, this one telling me it's okay as her dimples appeared beneath the apple of her cheeks. I loved her face. I loved...

Brannon

We walked slowly, hand in hand, back to my cabin. I wore his black jacket, the one he had on at the bonfire, around my shoulders. We got to the door. He was still stuck in his thoughts, and I didn't want to steal him from them. Instead, I said, "Thank you for a lovely evening. Good night, Asher."

I kissed his cheek, let go of his hand and opened my door.

"Goodnight, Brannon," he said in a distant voice.

As I closed the door, I saw his eyes widen as he realised that I was saying goodbye for today. Suddenly, I felt a hand pushing the door back again. His strength was addictive.

He had one hand on the door frame. I could see the firmness of his grip from the way his veins tensed on the back of his hands. Engorged with blood, the blue shining out from beneath his skin as bright as a neon sign.

"Don't do that," he said.

"Do what?"

"Don't say goodbye like that. Ever," he looked serious at me with his ocean blue eyes, and I worried I'd done something wrong.

But then he smirked. I love that smirk. I rolled my eyes at him.

He took his hand from the frame of the door and tenderly gripped my jaw. I allowed myself to be pulled towards him. My eyes closed as I felt the soft touch of his lips. Quick and gentle.

"I'm going to need you to say goodbye like *that* from now on."

I laughed delicately at him. His hands left my face.

"Goodnight, Brannon."

"Goodnight, Asher."

Asher

I jumped onto my bed, back first, and let my mind ponder the evening. She was everything. I've met girls before, just passing by camp and being called to talk to them. They've been pretty, yes, but not nice people. Girls that thought beauty made them deserving of everything they wanted. Who thought good looks were enough to win boys over. Maybe it worked with the small-minded boys, but I always thought to myself, if the whole world was blind, how many people would you impress? Brannon, on the other hand, could impress the world through a brick wall. Her polite nature and contagious optimism. It was everything. Extraordinary.

I was enjoying these thoughts about her, until the colour in my eyes was pulled away and fogged over by white clouds. The room spun, and when my vision re-focused, I was standing in front of a hot planet, paused halfway between the blood orange sky and the still sea, reflecting red light like a mirror.

I hadn't been here for a while. It's hard to imagine I'd miss it because this was the view I'd seen the most in life, but I did.

I turned to see an old lady standing beside me, mesmerised by the sunset. I had a routine that I followed when in the Myst.

"Hey, I'm Asher Curator," I held my hand out to shake hers. "Don't be scared, I'll be here to see you through."

She smiled gratefully and held my hand in both of hers. She must've been reaching her nineties. Her grey hair was clipped up and her cheeks were a blush pink. The lines in her skin were train tracks, symbolising the journey she'd had getting here.

"Well hello Asher," she spoke slowly, and her voice had an aging rasp, "I'm Florence, but you can call me Flo."

She looked around,

"Where are we then, Asher?"

She wasn't surprised to see me because she was here for a reason. She was supernatural and knew that one day she'd be greeted by a Curator or Amory. Lucky for her, she got me. Although also unlucky for her, because she missed out on Brannon.

"This is the Myst. You can stay here until you're ready to cross through and find peace."

"How do I do that?"

"You walk into the sea, don't worry, it's nice and warm. Eventually, you will not have to walk any further."

"I can't swim," she laughed. Old people were always concerned about how to die completely rather than the dying itself.

I reassured her, "You don't have to swim. It's shallow water. When you pass the light of the sun, you'll be fine."

I smiled at her. She looked frightened.

"Tell me, Flo, what's one bit of advice you could give a boy like me."

This normally made them feel better. Reminded them that they've lived a fulfilled life. It also gave them one last reward. Educating a youngster on mistakes that they once made. I asked this of everyone who passed through me. She smiled and gave me the piercing eye contact that the older generation like to do.

"I'll tell you one thing, Mr Curator. Behind every good man, is an even better woman," she paused, waiting for me to acknowledge that I'd listened.

"Is that right, Flo?" I said, trying to encourage her to continue.

"Oh yes, boy. If you don't believe me, ask my husband! The lucky git managed to live longer than me, but he'll tell you."

I laughed, "How long have you been married?"

It's always best to speak in the present tense. They didn't need reminding.

"Seventy-two years."

I watched her eyes glisten as her mind raced through memories.

"Oh, he'll be joining me here very soon."

She saw my concerned face, "No, don't worry, he's not ill! He just doesn't know how to cook!" She burst into laughter, clapping her hands, making me crack up with her. "He's a good man, he really is. Kept us going for all them years, working hard to give us a pleasant life."

"He sounds like a hard worker."

"He most definitely was."

"But what would he have done if you weren't there to keep him going, hey!"

"You're right about that, Asher! It's a man's world, but it wouldn't be nothing without us women!"

We both smiled for a while, and admired the setting, until she was ready.

"My advice to you is to find an amazing girl and let her make you a better man."

My heart warmed as I knew I had already found my girl and she had already made me a better man.

"I don't think you'll struggle with that. Such a handsome boy." She turned to me, "I'm ready now."

I held out my arm, and she held it with her small hand. We walked together, slowly, into the sea. When we got close to the sun's blinding glow, I let her grip fall away and watched the sunlight capture her, surrounding her in the peace she deserved.

Flo. A strong woman. An incredible wife. A pleasure to meet, and an honour to spend her last minutes with.

Brannon

I was quick into bed when I got in. I threw on an oversized t-shirt and got comfy in the quilt. I let my head submerge into the pillow, shut my eyes and imagined myself sitting next to my dad. When I opened my eyes, I was shocked. A chest of oak wood drawers. The yellow glow of a corner lamp. Walls made of old tree trunk. No sunset. I hadn't gone anywhere.

I told my dad I'd be visiting later today, so I knew he'd be there waiting. Why couldn't I reach him?

I tried hard for an hour. Nothing was working. I had so much to tell him. Now he'd be waiting there, alone, expecting me. Feeling disappointed that I didn't show up.

I couldn't think of any reason why this wasn't working. I'm the anchor for the Myst, the very place I needed to be. Although, I'm not the only anchor and only one of us could be there at a time. It was Asher. But why was he taking so long?

Asher

I got back to shore, pushing my ankles through the water and feeling the force of it against me. I stood there, waiting, expecting to be taken back to my bed. But nothing was happening. Why? Was someone else passing through?

I kept holding my eyes shut but opening them to the very same view I had when I arrived. I sat down, legs in front of me, knees up like a bridge. I decided to wait. There must've been a reason for this.

I was right. The reason sat beside me, mirroring my position. He had beige shorts on and a white shirt. His hair was a similar colour to Brannon's. Then I remembered. Brannon got her hair from her dad. Her dad, sitting beside me. Suddenly, my hands became clammy, and my throat tightened.

I immediately stopped looking at him. She didn't mention that her dad was only middle aged and looked like he'd spent a good proportion of his life in a gym. I didn't know what to say. What does one say to the father of the girl he hoped to spend forever with? I didn't expect to ever meet him. Now I was sat here, I felt an immense pressure. He had to approve of me. After all, he wasn't going to be there to look out for her anymore.

"Hello Asher, it's nice to finally meet you," he said and shook my hand. His voice was stern. My voice was shaking.

"Hi Mr Amory, it's nice to meet you too."

"Call me Dave."

I did not call him Dave.

"I've heard good things about you, Asher. She admires you."

This made me ecstatic. To know she had mentioned me to her dad, her greatest protector, was an honour.

"How is she?" he asked.

"She's doing okay, I think."

"Of course she is." He smiled, proudly.

"I think she is doing it to make you happy, thank you for encouraging her to leave her room."

"I know she is. That's fine, for now. But eventually she's going to need to do it for herself," he was half in conversation with me, half in his own head, thinking about his daughter, "Tell me Asher, is this going to be the last time she feels hurt for a while?"

He knew our birthday was coming up and we'd have to decide on what to do with the pendants. Easy for me. For her, I'm not too sure.

"Yes, Mr Amory. I intend on keeping her happy for as long as I can. And when I can't, I'll be sad with her."

"She's fragile. Very strong, don't mistake me, but fragile," he looked at me, "She likes to deal with things on her own. But I don't want her to."

His voice was walking a tightrope. It was balancing on a firm tone, nearly falling into the sound of sadness and heartbreak.

"She will never be alone again, I promise."

"Good."

He was protecting her in a way that didn't intimidate me. He was trusting me to try my best with her. To do right by her. Promise is a big word, and I meant it.

"Has she decided what she's doing with that pendant yet?"

"No. I don't think so. I say this because I know exactly what I'm going to do, she seems unsure."

"She's a clever girl, our Brannon. She knows that getting rid of the pendant means..."

He couldn't finish it. It means she wouldn't have access to the Myst anymore. Meaning she wouldn't be able to see her dad anymore.

"I know," I assured him, allowing him to steady his voice, "She isn't going to get rid of it. You're her Dad, she loves you more than anything. She'd never get rid of it when she knows you're here and that's okay. If it was my Dad, I wouldn't either."

"But I don't want that for her."

I could see the pain in his chest through the strain on his face.

He coughed to loosen the tightness in his throat, "I want her to choose with nothing swaying her. She's always wanted a normal life, away from this. The pain she goes through every day, the migraines and collapsing, it's draining. She's cried into my arms on some of the worst nights, telling me how badly she wanted the pain to stop. I told her to just wait a few more years and she could get rid of it. That's what I did when I turned 18. That's why I made the choice to have children, because I knew they'd be able to get rid of it. She's not going to do that if I'm here."

He was blaming himself. He was right, though. Brannon would keep the pendant because she could still talk to her dad anytime she pleased. It might have sounded like a gift, but in reality, she would be going through pain, pain that I never have to go through, in order to do this. The more times she visited him, the more painful it would get. That's how revisiting someone works in the Myst. The pain is punishment, for preventing someone from their peace. The decision over the pendants was meant to be about me and her. She should only keep it with the intention of staying with me forever. But this was not her intention right now. I wouldn't know her intention for as long as her dad was in the Myst.

"I don't know how she feels about me, to be honest. I'd love to think that she'd keep the pendant to be with me."

"You'll never know that as long as I'm a closed eye away," he shook his head, "You are both the strongest kids I know. Going through this."

"She's made it easy," I told him.

"She always does. You're very mature, Asher. I'm impressed with how you handle the situation, and how you care about her enough to let her do what's best for her. That's what love is all about."

The 'L' word again.

"Thank you, Mr Amory."

He stood up, so I stood up too. He looked out to the tropical horizon, then back at me. He placed his hand on the top of my arm, in a kind way.

"Look after her, won't you?"

He needed me to reassure him that I'd protect her like he did, not that she needed it. She was very capable on her own, but he wanted to know that I was there for her if she wanted me. Why was this my job? Was he going somewhere?

"I will, always."

He nodded his head at me, lips sealed but smiling slightly. Then he let go of my arm and sat back down. He wasn't going anywhere. Yet. It was finally time for me to return home.

I arrived in bed, staring at the ceiling. I wasn't sure if I was going to tell Brannon about this, but I didn't want to give it a thought right now. If I started to analyse what had just happened, I'd be up all night. And I couldn't be tired when I saw her tomorrow, I had to show up as the best version of myself.

I knew that I wasn't going to meet her dad again. That was the first and last time. But it was enough. Enough to assure him that trusting me wasn't a mistake. I shut my eyes.

Dave Amory. A brave man. A respectable person. And an amazing father to an amazing girl.

Brannon

"I cannot explain how excited I am!" Blain said whilst I was still half asleep in my bed.

I didn't reply to his comments. It was too early to talk.

Honestly, it was about one in the afternoon, but I'd just woken up.

He started shaking my shoulders, quite aggressively.

"Brannon, get up!"

"I'm getting up!" I shouted back.

Blain was excited for tonight. There was a basement party under one of the canteen seating areas. If this land once belonged to the Curator Ancestors, then the basement would have been a safe space to practise spells and store books, but that was then. Now, it is a perfect place for a rave. And me and Blain loved that sort of thing.

After pressing an invisible snooze button for several more minutes, I carried myself to the shower and washed away the tired and miserable morning attitude, which was actually early afternoon.

I threw on a robe and sat with Blain on my bed. We chose moisturisers and did each other's hair. He had jet black hair, easy to disguise a bottle of hairspray in when creating the flick at the front of his head. He curled my hair for me. Then he did my makeup, because my cosmetic skills were not up to his standards.

"You know it finishes at 12, don't you?" he told me.

"That's fine, I have plans for after," I smiled at him, and his excitement returned.

For the last couple of hours, we did best friend sort of things. Talk. Take pictures. Pick outfits. Sing to music from the 2000's. Jessy joined in when she returned from the beach. And then Red knocked on the door, with a bottle of Apple Sours and four shot glasses. Red had blonde curtains and emerald green eyes that lit up with the idea of pre-drinks. We couldn't drink at the rave, but there were no rules for before or after.

Being around them made me forget. About my dad. About missing Asher. About my birthday in just over a week. They were fun and freedom and youth. Normal.

As we all got ready, defying the view of having to segregate genders when skin was revealed due to the dreaded fear of inappropriateness, the room became rich in perfume and aftershave. I felt privileged to be surrounded by the purest people I knew, all beautiful as well. When we were all finished getting ready, an hour after we'd hoped, we decided to spare another few moments to set up a timer camera and have a group picture.

Jessy's maroon hair fell in waves, parted down her shoulders, covering the straps of her deep purple bodycon dress. She didn't fit into the societal mould of body expectations, she completely owned her own skin and looked powerful in doing so. Her confidence was something I aspired to have.

She tilted her head close to Red's Hawaiian patterned shirt. One of those shirts that had repetitive palm trees on a blue background with the odd parrot flying amongst the tackiness. He left it unbuttoned, showing off his gym-bod, the untucked shirt flowing over his tight black denim shorts. His shoes were a bright white, because he was also the type of boy to cry if a spec of dirt touched his trainers. He had one arm around Jessy and the other around me.

I tilted my head the other way to Jessy's, accidentally making symmetry for the picture. I bent my knee a little, the cliché pose. My hair was pulled up into a high pony tail, cemented in hairspray on the top and puffed with silver curls down the back. Blain was the best at doing this hair style, I could never do it to myself. My dress was a silky black that hugged my body and had several straps at the back which look good now but were a struggle to figure out. I was scared it would be loose due to my lack of food recently, but it was okay. I felt insecure about the sight of my collarbone and bony shoulders, but Blain comforted me whilst dazzling my décolletage in body glitter that I didn't ask for.

Then there was Blain. Balancing on one leg, the other stretched in front of us all, us holding it up. He held his right arm out like a jazz hand. He kept slipping which made us all laugh. The picture captured this moment of happiness and love.

But that's all it did. It took a shot of the moment. Still. This was good. But what was better was what I'd remember. The smell of metal hairspray and burnt hair from the curling wand. Men's cologne and expensive perfume. The sound of deep laughs and innocent giggling. The feeling of Blain's grip on my arm and the weight of his leg in my hand. Red's arm digging into my neck. Jessy's blueberry shampoo and list of compliments. This would resonate within me like burning firewood and melting marshmallows, and salty ocean water next to warm golden sands. And a view that would leave one speechless. In this moment, I was happy. In this moment, coming to camp was a good idea.

Before we left, I rang my mum, wanting to talk to her whilst my flame of happiness stayed lit.

"How are you, Mum?"

She could tell I was doing better, and this had a domino effect on her, "I'm fine thank you sweetie, missing you lots. You have fun tonight, okay?"

"I miss you lots too. I will!"

"I love you, Bran."

"I love you too, Mum."

I put the phone down and was spritzed by Blain's body shimmer one last time. He hugged me, tightly.

"I'm so proud of you, Brannon."

I hugged him back.

"Come on, we are already an hour late!"

Asher

The music was so loud my chest was pounding against my skin. Neon lasers traced the room along with the smell of the smoke machine and 'hidden' vodka in people's drinks. I was standing in my group of friends, some old, some new, waiting for her. The DJ was remixing dated and modern songs, creating a familiar vibe amongst the crowded dance floor. It was muggy in here. The basement had air-conditioning, though it couldn't combat the number of people in the room. The girls danced together whilst the boys did a sort of bop to the beat of the music. Someone offered me a drop of secret alcohol, and I chose to accept in the hope that I'd loosen up and have fun. After an hour of waiting for Brannon and gratefully accepting my friends offer, it began to work, and I felt my confidence bubbling. I unbuttoned my black ironed shirt halfway down my stomach and danced with the crowd. This was fun. And freedom. And youth.

Although I was letting off steam in a group of amazing people, I was still unconsciously glancing back at the bottom of the basement's staircase, waiting to catch a glimpse of her contagious smile lit up by a blue beam of light.

"Mate, she has got you right where she wants you," unnecessarily spoke Dylan, a boy in the group who believed he was bigger than life, in a harmless way.

I laughed. Not because it was funny. But because he couldn't be more wrong. She didn't want me anywhere. I wanted her.

"Can you blame me?" I replied, making light of the comment.

His reply was unwelcome. "No mate, she is fit!"

Typical for a boy like him. I'd like to say I'm not judging, but I am. It didn't bother me that someone else found her attractive. That was inevitable. But 'fit' is the type of word you use to describe a one-time interest, and she would never be that for anyone. If only he knew her, he'd use a different word. Like stunning, or beautiful, or gorgeous. Shame for him that he'll never get to find out.

The growing desire to take his unwanted answer and reinvent it in a burning rage dissolved suddenly, as I saw her face lit up by a spiralling white light.

Her golden skin glittered more than usual. I'd never seen her hair like that. It made her face look smaller and her jawline sharper. Everyone in the room disappeared. Instead of the thumping music, I heard my thumping heart. Would I always feel this way when I saw her? Lost for words. Thanking the universe for this blessing. She moved in an atmosphere of happiness tonight. I wanted in.

She knew the majority of the people here. In the first week of camp, she became a favourite of everyone's. She didn't realise how much fun she brought with her, everywhere. Her and Blain and Jessy and Red were people that you wanted to be your friends. To be a part of. Despite the attention she received walking in, she came to me first.

She threw her arms around me and I squeezed her lower back, pulling her into me. Her perfume was rich and exotic. Her hair added some height to her, but I still had to look down to find her eyes. The roaring music made it hard to talk.

"You look unreal!" I leant in and shouted in her ear.

"So do you!" she shouted back, her voice drowned out by the volume.

I noticed Blain walking over. I assumed he'd have most of her attention for tonight, which was fine. I held my hand out to shake his. He rejected it and threw his arms around me. I tried to balance my drink to stop it spilling, noticing the smile on Brannon's face as he hugged me. I hugged him back. He moved his eyes between me and Brannon.

"Let's dance!" he yelled with excitement.

For the following few hours, we did just that. Danced. Partied. I watched Brannon's body move to the rhythm of the music. Blain broke into street dance, making a bigger space for us all, which I believe was a calculated move from him. Dylan, annoyingly, kept coming round offering out alcoholic drinks.

Sometimes Brannon danced with Jessy, or Blain. Her other friend, Red, was more interested in dancing with other girls. Sometimes Brannon danced with me, hand in my hand, but not romantically, throwing ourselves about, enjoying the moment. Sometimes she danced by herself.

I watched her as she did this, like she was under a spotlight amongst a crowd of teenagers. She'd move her arms and head to the beat, not taking life seriously. I loved this about her. Then she'd take her hands and tighten her ponytail, scrunching it up, tilting her head back. She was in slow motion. Hips swaying, voice singing.

The chaos from the frantic lights and increasingly loud music was addictive. I immersed myself into the night, embracing the sense of escape. The alcohol built up, making my skin tingle and bravery grow. I was starting to feel like tonight was a good opportunity to talk to Brannon, about anything. But it would be honest, because she was drunk too.

For now, though, we danced. We celebrated friendship and a good DJ. We got so caught up in normal teenage life, that we forgot who we were. It worked in our favour that no supernatural being died tonight. For the first time, I understood why she wanted normal.

I noticed her and Blain jump like kids, holding each other's hands and smiling effortlessly. She turned her head to smile at me and scrunched her nose up, the happiest I'd seen her.

I'm sorry Dad, but you were wrong. This does have to be a love story.

Brannon

Dylan was getting closer after every song. Blain was blocking me from him. Asher kept him in his eyesight. At first, I didn't mind. But now it was uncomfortable. He was trying to grab my hand and touch my skin. My face was telling him to stop, but being the arrogant boy that he was, he found it impossible to be rejected.

He tried to pour some more vodka into my cup.

"I'm good, thanks though," I moved the cup away.

"Don't be silly, have some more," he started to pour the bottle.

"No, really, I'm fine."

He grabbed my wrist, harmlessly but harmfully.

"Brannon, you're having some more."

"She said no," Asher took a stance in front of me, eyeing Dylan.

The business of the room went from a welcomed chaos to an electric tension. I took Asher's hand, noticing the fire in his stare.

"Come on, let's get some air."

I had to drag him to move him and his anger. We walked past one of the activity leaders who was monitoring the party. Asher must've known him. They did a laddish handshake, Asher still distracted by Dylan's disrespect.

"You alright mate? There's a boy over there giving out alcohol. Everyone's said no, he shouldn't have that."

Asher lied to keep Blain, Jessy and Red out of trouble. Or to pin it all on Dylan, which at this point was understandable. When he spoke, he kept a distance so the man wouldn't smell the liquor on his breath.

"Cheers for telling me Ash, let your Dad know I said hi," the man nodded and walked to Dylan.

I led Asher up the stairs of the basement, having to pull him a little. Once we were outside, the fresh air surrounded my skin. The lack of rave music left my ears ringing and the quiet of outside felt so much quieter. I guided us past the cabins, at what seemed like a rapid speed, past the staff rooms and canteens and stopped at the start of the pier. The ocean scent wafted through the air, refreshing our lungs. I looked up. The night's black canvas was dotted with specks of light. The water splashed against the shore softly.

I took a deep breath in, appreciating the total change of scenery. Next to me, Asher did the same. The cool breeze extinguished the rage that had started in him. He shut his eyes and ran his fingers through his curls. As he swallowed, the ball in his throat moved. His black shirt flapped in the gentle wind. He must have unbuttoned it in the heat of the basement It revealed his toned stomach and the button of his dark denim shorts.

His grip on my hand released as he noticed, and he did his buttons back up. His rosy lips parted as he inhaled.

"You good?" I asked him.

He looked at me slowly and grinned, "Am now."

I smiled back, he took my hand and we walked with a spring in our step to the end of the pier.

My black slip-on Vans hung above the clear sea, lit by the glow of the full moon.

"Do you enjoy things like that?" he asked me.

"Yeah, me and Blain love it."

I didn't want to ask him back. Partly because I knew he wouldn't have been to many. Also, because I knew after what just happened, his answer would be no.

The alcohol raced to my head as the air rushed over my pulled back hair. I felt the confidence that I only feel when I'm slightly intoxicated.

"Not long now Bran, we'll officially be adults," he nudged my shoulder with his elbow.

I decided it was time to acknowledge it, to an extent.

"It's a big one. And even better, we get to make a life changing decision to celebrate!"

His mouth lifted softly but certainly. I feared he knew what choice he was making. I'd feared this for a while. I knew what I was doing too, but it had nothing to do with him and everything to do with my dad.

"Are you scared?" he asked me, concern in his voice.

"A little."

"Why?"

"Well, because we don't really know what's going to happen. We have some calculated guesses, but no one is really sure. What about you? Are you scared?" I asked him back, interested in what his answer would be.

"Kind of."

I looked at him, waiting for a better reply.

"What you just said plays on my mind but there's more than that. I'm scared that your decision might mean I lose you, and if I don't lose you then I fear your decision will have the wrong motives."

He sounded more serious than ever before. I was under the spotlight.

"That works both ways Ash."

Asher

She was wrong. It didn't work both ways. She wouldn't lose me on my accord. I had no intentions of hurting her. Not now. Not then. Not ever.

It was frowned upon to tell each other our decisions before the day. Instead, I hinted. In the most obvious way possible.

"You won't be without me if that's what you choose. I promised I'd never hurt you."

I hadn't actually made this promise to her, which is probably why her face was momentarily painted with confusion. However, she didn't question it. I made this promise to someone else. Mr Amory. But I didn't feel as though she needed to know that. It only mattered that he did.

"Well, you won't lose me either."

"I won't lose you?" I paused, "Or your Dad won't lose you?"

This came out harsher than anticipated. She looked annoyed. Disappointed in my words. Her stare shot me in the heart. It was no longer me and her. It was her *against* me.

"Does it matter?" she asked with an attitude I didn't recognise.

I had to tell her how I felt about this because it wouldn't be fair. I didn't want to be with her if she didn't want to be with me.

"Well, yes. It does."

"Why?" she snapped.

I felt cruel, challenging her on this, and slightly scared.

"Because you should only keep it if you want to be with me."

"That rule stopped applying to me when my dad died."

She wasn't even looking for pity. This was a trigger for her anger. She was a perfect storm.

"I'm sorry Brannon, I really am, but I can't be with you for however long that may be if you are doing it to see your dad. I understand, but it shouldn't be that way," I sounded like my father.

"No, you don't understand Asher. Your Dad is still alive! Because your blood line is pure and clean and good," she sounded mocking. "Maybe if your Dad was dead, you would feel the same. But he's not, so stop telling me what is right and wrong. It's my choice and you'd do a good job to remember that."

Her voice in the last sentence was calm. Intimidating. She was right, my dad was still alive, and I didn't understand that part. Couldn't. She stood up to leave. I jumped to my feet.

"Don't go."

She started walking.

"Brannon."

"What?"

She turned to me with vigour. Her eyes watered on the burning rage casting shadows over lilac pools.

"I'm sorry, I didn't mean it like that."

"Yeah, me too Asher," her voice didn't sound very sorry.

"Why are you apologising?"

"Because if you choose to keep the pendant then you'll be stuck with me," her words were sharp and viscous. "Because I will not choose to say goodbye to him. Trust me."

She left, in more of a run than a walk. I'd hit a nerve. A few nerves. I let her go. She needed to calm down, I thought. I held my hands at my head, eyes shut, squinting. Angry at myself.

I sat back down, looking for comfort in the movement of the sea. The collision between the ocean and the sand made a delicate yet certain splash.

I missed her already.

Brannon

I had to get away from him out of fear that my words would cause irreversible wounds. Blain was still at the basement with everyone else. I didn't want to ruin their night. I went back to my cabin, shut the door and stared at nothing.

Suddenly, rage ran through my veins. I grabbed my hairbrush and launched it at the wall. My eyes tight shut, water escaping the seam. It was a lot. The drastic change in setting. The tension. The decision. The argument. The pain from missing. Everything. It was too much.

Weakness won as I let my legs collapse and my back slide down the door. I sat in sadness for a while.

It must've been an hour. The anger had drowned in the sorrow. I heard a knock at the door. Jessy must be home.

I forced myself up, quickly wiped under my eyes, took a deep breath and opened the door.

"Asher?"

He stood with one hand against the door frame, the other on his hip, looking down at the wooden panels beneath him. I wasn't angry to see him. I was safe.

I stepped outside, desperate to breathe fresh air. He didn't move his hand, despite me being at his chest. Instead, I felt his strength wrap me up in him. The coconut smell in his hair wax was noticeable. I hugged him back. I love—

We paused in this position for a while before taking a seat on the steps. My arms were crossed, trapping as much heat as possible. It got colder as the night went on.

I could see he was struggling to find words, so I started for him. Us. "I have a bad temper. I'm sorry. I shouldn't have reacted like that."

His head leant against the side of the cabin. His jaw was set like steel. He looked at me with regret and understanding and warmth, though he didn't reply.

I continued, "It's always been like that. I struggle coping sometimes. Well, a lot of the time. I know you think that my desire for a normal life is strange. But normal isn't always a bad thing, Asher. It represents peace and tranquillity and answers. Opportunity. I have always wanted that. I don't enjoy the pain or the blanking out of existence. I don't find it rewarding."

"I know, I don't blame you," he replied, bluntly.

"I'm trying to be happy, but it's still there. The feeling of loneliness. Don't get me wrong, I have plenty of people. But a dad is someone you can't replace. Or even find a familiar feeling. No one sounds like him or smells like him or feels like him, other than him. Now he's gone," I swallowed the thick emotion clogging my throat, "I can't say goodbye to him. It's not a choice I'll make. I'm sorry."

My body was trembling, shivering. He moved next to me, arms supporting me. He rested his head on top of mine.

"You don't have to say sorry. You shouldn't have to make that choice."

A tear trickled through my barrier of denial.

His voice was homely. "I've got you. Always."

Asher

She fell asleep in my arms. I left her tucked in her duvet. I had to go home because I had something to do before having somewhere to be the next day.

My family and I were to be gone for the next few days. We'd be back before our birthday. We were visiting family and celebrating my milestone with them.

From the moment I left her cabin, I started to countdown the hours until I could see her pretty face again and feel the excitement that only she brought me. A few days and I'd be home. To her. With her. For her.

I left a note under the lamp beside her bed, 'I'll be home in a few days, before our birthday, seeing some family. I've left you an early present, but you'll have to find it. First clue, check the first place we met. Miss you already, your Ash x"

Brannon

I headed to the place in the woods where we had the bonfire.

I was mapping the timeline of the next few days. Today is the 28th of June – Asher left yesterday. He'd be home on the 1st of July; the Summer Ball is on the 3rd and our birthday on the 4th. My life had gone from mourning alone in bed to having plans and being happy, distracting myself from the decision my birthday gifted me.

On my walk to the woods, I pondered on thoughts. I only came to camp because mum forced me. She forced me to leave my hometown of Heston, where I lived the same day over and over again. Admittedly, I was fed up. I woke up, went to school, came home and had a few adventures to the Myst every now and then. I could predict the day before it started, which is what I loved about camp. It was unpredictable. And exciting. Memories. And Asher was here.

I stepped over a fallen trunk and then sat on it. This was where I was called to help Asher collect firewood from the shed. And where my dad informed me of why I am who I am. The descendant of the sad one, paired with the fortunate Asher. It sounded more like a journey of redemption than a love story.

The air was tinted with the scent of old burning wood and laughter. Both hands against the bark, indenting my hands with traces of tree, head tilted towards the sky, inhaling that night all over again. I looked at the fire pit where we roasted marshmallows, and I felt the butterflies that he gave me for the first time. Then I noticed a picture. I leant forward and picked it up, remembering that I was here for a reason. Because Asher had told me to be here. I recognised the picture. Blain took it of me and Asher later in the night, after the cliché group picture. Asher had his arm comfortably around me, in his jet-black hoodie and ripped jeans. Me, in my flowery navy dress, smiling comfortably beneath his arm. I had always felt like this around him. Comfortable, but giddy.

He must've printed this himself. I stared at it for a while, admiring the happiness that had outlived the photo. I'd had relationships before with boys. One of them cared, but we were too young. One of them didn't, and he's now a stranger. The typical first loves of a teenage girl. But this one was different. It was real. I know this because I can't find the words to describe it. And if you can describe it, it isn't real.

I turned over the picture, mindful not to leave fingerprints on the shiny finish.

To my Brannon,

I'm taking you on a trip down memory lane.

We are starting here because this was the first place that I heard your name. You rushed into the woods and I followed you like a map, to the happiest destination I have visited yet.

I hope to follow you anywhere. Everywhere.

Yours always, Asher.

Next place – the mountain top that we hiked up.

142

I smiled, suddenly missing him like never before. For some reason, I felt tearful. He'd done this for me, and effort was the only present I'd ever ask for.

The hike to the top of the mountain felt quicker on my own. Asher was a slow walker. When I reached the top, I was tired, and full of anticipation.

It was about 5pm . Birds flew over the sparkling water, blurred by the glow of the sun that would soon be setting, but not yet. When we went on the hike, we stopped to sit on a large rock at the top. So, I headed for that very spot, where I found a letter folded up and held down by many smaller rocks.

Brannon,
   I'd like you to look at the view right now and describe it.'

I couldn't. But he knew this.

   I bet you couldn't. A wise, and beautiful, girl once told me that this view would leave me speechless. It did.
   She also asked me where my favourite place was on our way up here. I told her I hadn't found it yet. Really, this is because my favourite place is not a place at all, but a person.
   The next thing we did together, that was forced on me, was the zip line.
   You'll find your next message on the other side.'

This time, a tear trickled down my glowing cheek. I couldn't wait for him to get home, so I could tell him the thing I'd been waiting to tell him.

When I got to the start of the zip line, I waited for the man to buckle me in. He was miserable, something that hadn't changed since the last time I was here.

My mind was flashing between the past and the present. He was so scared to jump. To fall to his death, which was dramatic for Asher. I told him it would be worse if he had to regret not jumping, which I still believe to be true. I pictured his face as his feet left the ground. He looked terrified yet free. He was also watching me intensely as I released my hand from the rope and held myself back.

I'd let my feet jump without realising, and I was now gliding through the air. I let my hands go and spread them like a bird. The air brushed through my hair which was waving behind me. I let the rope swirl me through the breeze until I reached the other side, let my feet find the ground and unbuckled myself. There was another note, similarly, wedged under rocks, on the other side.

I read it, catching my breath still.

I'm glad you made it.'

I laughed.

The next note is at our place.'

I headed to our place.

Asher

My grandparents fussed over me and I told them all about her. My Brannon. They were intrigued that we'd met. My mum insisted on showing them pictures of her. They responded by telling me how beautiful she was, which I know already.

I was hoping she'd be enjoying the trail I set up for her. Our birthday wouldn't feel much like a birthday with the pressure on our shoulders. I decided to give her this gift without me there, so she could react how she felt was right, rather than how I'd have wanted her to.

Whilst leaving the pictures and notes, I reminisced on the amazing couple of months I'd had with her. Although she wasn't present for three weeks of it, camp had been unforgettable. And, despite the decision made on our birthdays, I would not forget her.

Brannon

The sea was a blanket of Prussian blue fading into overlapping waves of azure. The flamingo pink sky reflected in the distance, blending into the apricot sun. Colours are not as simple as blue, pink or orange. They are much like people in this way. There are different shades, cooler and warmer tones, vibrant and less vibrant. All beautiful, but different.

I sat on the warm wooden pier, feeling like something was missing. Someone. We'd solved problems here. And had our first kiss. And argued. And my dad died. It was our place. I was reassured by this when I noticed the piece of lined paper tied to the pole beside me by a cut of string.

Brannon,

I have lived here my whole life. I have often found myself sat with my legs dangling above the ocean, thinking about my day. It wasn't anything but a place to me, until I met you. We have shared moments here that have changed our life. I kissed you. We fell out. The Myst welcomed a respectable man, your father, Dave Amory.

I'd never told him my Father's name, but at this point I assumed he was just good at knowing these things.

Every one of these moments made me realise something. The pier is my favourite place. Although, I've been here many times without you and have never felt this way towards it. This told me I was right in my answer to your question many sunsets ago. It is only my favourite place when you are in it. You are my favourite place.

Your final location is the basement.'

My cheek bones ached now. This was the most thoughtful thing anyone had done for me. My mind was full of happy memories of us.

I was less excited to venture into the dusty, dark basement alone. But I wanted to see the final note.

I noticed Blain waiting at the door of the room that led to the basement. His feet were almost leaving the floor with what looked like excitement.

"What's wrong with you, happy?" I nudged his shoulder with the palm of my hand.

"Nothing," he replied, dragging out the last syllable of the word, "Asher asked me to help him with your gift. He couldn't be here to do it himself. And it's so much more fun that he isn't here!"

I disagreed with him silently, "Well, I've been told to go to the basement. Are you coming?"

"No, no I'm just waiting for it to be ready. You can't go in yet."

"Oh, right."

He smiled at me, eagerly.

"What?" I laughed at him.

"Nothing! But just so you know, I really do approve of Asher. And you really do deserve this."

"Thank you, and I'm glad."

I didn't say much as I was begging my emotions to settle.

Suddenly, a red-haired Jessy came galloping to the glass door of the seating area, similarly smiling like a Cheshire cat.

"Ready!" she announced.

We all paused. They'd made this a bigger deal than necessary.

"Can you two wait for me please?"

They both nodded, pushing me through the door.

I began walking down the stairs, feeling nervous and excited and overwhelmed. These feelings heightened when I saw the room, lit up by dots of gold light from the lasers, spreading from the floor to the ceiling of every wall. Gentle music was playing in the background through a quiet speaker. On the stage, next to where the DJ would have set up, was a small box with a ribbon on it. I sat down next to it, legs dangling off, nearly reaching the ground.

Asher set this all up, for me. For my birthday, that wasn't for another few days. All I wanted to do was throw my arms around him and hold him until the words 'thank you' were deeply embedded in his skin.

I unrolled the paper and began to read it, vision slightly blurred by the wetness of my eye.

Brannon.

I chose to give you your present here, firstly, because it made the wait longer, and secondly because we shared another important night here together. I watched you dance with your friends and sing loudly to songs. I watched your gorgeous eyes be struck by green laser beams. I watched your ponytail swinging and bouncing as you moved. I watched you laugh and smile, surrounded by people you love. I watched you be normal.

You watched me get angry. And then you took me away and calmed me down, effortlessly. You extinguished my rage quicker than it had got there in the first place. You simply make everything better.

This is not my favourite place that I have been with you. But it is one of my favourite images of you, and a moment that I realised the effect you have on me. You are important, to everyone, but especially me.

Thank you for this version of life that you have shown me. It is truly extraordinary.

One last thing, be my date to the Summer Ball?'

The final words were blurred by a droplet of water that fell, happily, down my face.

I picked up the box. What I saw inside sent a warm buzz through my veins. A bracelet, gold like the necklace permanently attached to my neck. It was a firm circle of gold, with a symbol on top. It was two halves of a semi-circle, connecting. The symbols that me and Asher had carried with us since birth. The pendant, together. As a whole, like us. I took it out and gently forced my hand through the centre.

I looked around at the lit-up room. The pendant had always represented a sense of isolation, and pain, and the feeling of being incomplete. Now, looking at the bracelet, it represented something totally different. Something indescribable.

But this time, complete.

Asher

Two days until I see her.

Brannon

The effort, care and extent that Asher had gone through to make me feel special left me feeling high all night. But the next day wasn't the same. I was in and out of the Myst all day. The supernatural population must've decreased by at least 20 people. Most of them were old and all of them were above 50. They all found peace fairly quickly. No one was scared or confused either, which surprised me. My constant involvement in supernatural activity that day had me questioning whether it was purposeful. This many deaths in one day were not normal. By the evening I felt a painful pulse behind my eyes and a sharp sensation piercing my skull.

I decided to stay in the Myst with my dad after a late night passing of an old man who told me that he was a retired vampire. I wanted to ask him how a vampire can retire but I was tired and in pain. I just wanted to see my dad.

"It's late sweetie, get some sleep," he greeted me with a hug.

"I have a headache; I won't be able to get to sleep yet."

"Long day?"

"That would be an understatement. Dad, is there any reason why so many supernatural beings died today? Surely that's not a coincidence," I asked him, feeling more knowledgeable on this than ever before.

"Nothing certain. There are so many myths and suggestions and 'maybes' passed through family books. I've read a passage from a witch once, she was known to be very wise, and she said that relatives of the Ancestors, aside from the most powerful two, agreed to their elderly relatives dying when the pendants were to meet again, and a decision was close by."

"Why?"

"To grant the pendants with more power. To recreate the events that took place on the night those pendants were created."

"Do you think Asher had a day of it too?"

"Unfortunately, no. She suggested that this would be a formal reminder to the descendant of the bad Ancestor. Reminding them, or you in this case, of why the pendants were separated in the first place. They couldn't assume that the same thing wouldn't happen again."

"That's not unfortunate, Dad. I'd rather me go through it than him."

"I know you would."

We sat and thought for a few moments, gazing into the glowing ball of tangerine.

He started talking again, "There's a lot of things that we aren't sure on, Brannon. This is the first time the pendants have met. No one knows what will happen. Whether you both keep them or not, it's not been seen before. I want you to think about that before making your decision."

"I've made it. I'm hardly going to get rid of it when it's the one thing keeping you here."

I was sure on this. He wasn't going to change my mind. The only thing that scared me more than not knowing what would happen, was knowing my dad was gone for good. It wasn't an option.

He looked down sadly, "I'm worried that you will be punished with these reminders of our Ancestor in harsh ways if you keep the pendant. I'm worried that you'll suffer for not keeping it either."

"Exactly. You are worried either way, so there's no point in getting rid of it."

"There is a point, Bran. You won't be in pain anymore. You'll be normal."

This was one of the few things powerful enough to sway my decision. Something that Asher wouldn't understand in his pain free life.

My dad knew this was something I'd love. To only get headaches from looking at a screen for too long instead of seeing dead people into peace.

"If I keep it, I can see you, Asher, and magic can be practised in peace again. Supernatural creatures will have a chance to be themselves, knowing that when they die, they will be able to embrace their abilities."

"At the cost of your health."

He sounded angry now.

"So what? I'll have some more headaches. I'm used to it."

"No Brannon," he shook his head, "The pain will be much worse. You and Asher will be bearing the power of the Myst. If all supernatural magic is in use, you'll be bearing that as well. Asher won't feel anything, just you. It will have its side effects, I'm sure."

"It will be beautiful for them to have that opportunity," I said, realising that it sounded like we were beginning to argue.

"That's not beautiful Brannon, that's tragic. Don't glorify something that will bring you nothing but suffering."

"You know what Dad, you're right. It's not beautiful or poetic. But the supernatural population have gone centuries without exploring their limits. The spells, the heightened abilities, the power of the full moon – they don't know it. And it's not fair."

"It's not fair on you either. I raised you to look out for other people but also to look out for yourself."

"Trust me, Dad, if I keep the pendant, it will probably be the most selfish thing I've done because it won't be for Asher, or even the supernatural people, to be honest. It will be for me. So, I can see you, my dead Dad. Is that too much to ask for?"

I began to cry, of course. I do that a lot at the moment. He wrapped his arms around me and suddenly I felt calm. I rested my head on his shoulder. No more words were spoken. I woke up in bed, in the cabin, my mind conflicted with what to do in three days.

Today is the 1st of July, and Asher will be home tonight. Focus on that.

Asher

The journey home was a six-hour drive. I listened to music, thinking about the 4th of July. I was pretty confident that Brannon would keep the pendant until I replayed some of our moments together. The first day I met her, I mentioned how normal was boring and she hated it. She rejected it. When she found out I had pain free episodes, the hurt in her eyes paid for it. When I questioned her motives behind keeping the pendant, she walked away from me. A burning flame. I was confident she'd keep it until I spoke to her father. It sounded like he was going to make a decision to ensure that her decision was not motivated by his existence. Then, all she'd have to benefit from keeping the pendant would be...me.

My mind circled around these thoughts for the whole drive home. When we arrived it was midnight, and I was distracted by unloading the bags from the car.

I didn't expect Brannon to be awake and it had only been a few days. She wouldn't be missing me too much. But I went for a walk around the camp anyway.

When I got to the cabins, I was pleasantly surprised by the sound of laughter and chatting. I noticed Brannon's voice. I think I'd notice her voice anywhere. Then I saw

Blain, Jessy and Red. They were sitting on the grass in the middle of the surrounding cabins, playing cards.

I heard Blain gasp, "Bran, Asher's home!"

She flicked her pearly hair aside and looked at me, with a smile that looked like exploding fireworks and a dancing flame of a bonfire, warming up the world. I took my hand out my jean pocket and waved. I don't know why I did that. It must've looked strange actually. I put it back in my pocket and let her walk to me.

"Hey, you," she greeted me, "Shall we go catch up?"

I followed her into the jungle of trees, and we sat on a fallen tree trunk near the fire pit. She was wrapped up in a knitted blue blanket, covering her shorts and bare legs.

"Thank you for the bracelet," I saw it fit on her wrist, "I had a lot of fun finding it."

"You're more than welcome. It's only something small, I just wanted you to look at the pendant in a different way, maybe."

"It worked," she grinned.

I'd been gone for only a few days, but that was enough. I didn't want to leave her ever again.

"How was your trip away?" she asked me, wanting to listen, though I didn't have much to tell her.

"It was good to see my grandparents and the rest of my family. They were very interested in you. How have you been?"

"I've been okay, thank you."

"Just okay?" Something was on her mind.

"Yesterday and today haven't been great. There's been supernatural deaths, consistently. I haven't slept much."

"What? I haven't had any episodes. Why didn't I have to do some?"

"My Dad thinks it's something to do with the pendants meeting and the decision approaching. It's my punishment for being her descendant."

"Oh, I'm sorry. Have they stopped now?"

"They seemed to stop a couple of hours ago. Blain begged me to play cards with them to have a break."

"You should be catching up on some sleep."

"I've been waiting for you," she smiled, softly and painfully.

"How's your head?"

"It's hurting, but I'm fine."

I moved next to her and held her hand in my lap. She rested her head on my shoulder. She was tired. Tired of this life. I could tell. I didn't want this for her. But I could make it easier for her if she gave me the chance to.

"All this mystical stuff, it sounds silly doesn't it? It's hard to believe, even for me," I told her, letting my thoughts translate into speech.

She lifted her head. "Do you ever feel like there should be more to life than this?" she asked, staring up at the twinkling star light.

"Sometimes, I guess."

"The supernatural world that we are yet to know, maybe that's it."

I walked her back to her cabin. The others had gone to bed and she wanted to as well. I headed back to my house, contemplating what she had said. She has the ability to change one's mind, on anything. I thought the mystical rules and predictions could be nonsense. Now, I'm starting to think they could be an opportunity. An opportunity for life to be more. With her.

Brannon

I got to bed, feeling better now I'd seen him. His chestnut curls, swimming pool eyes and copper skin.

I thought my episodes had stopped. That I'd been punished enough. As soon as I let my head hit the pillow, my vision blurred. At first, I thought I was falling asleep. I wasn't. I was falling into the middle ground between life and death. Then the shooting pain in my head became harsher. I'll sleep after this, I thought to myself. It's my job to ensure they find peace, that's all that is important.

What I didn't expect was to see my dad, sitting with his knees up, shoes buried in sand, staring at the setting sun, still. I didn't think he'd call me to the Myst this late at night, knowing the past couple of days I'd had. I was intrigued to know why.

"Hey Dad," I said, sitting beside him and letting my tired head fall on his shoulder. He was probably just checking that I was okay. He did that sometimes.

"Hey sweetie," he sounded different. Sad, perhaps. I sensed a hint of fear, I thought.

"Are you okay?" I asked him, not certain I wanted to know the answer.

"I'm good, how are you?"

"I'm tired, but fine."

He still hadn't looked at me. I was concerned.

"You're probably wondering why I've dragged you here?"

I nodded. My head was pounding, but had I known what was about to come, the deaths of a hundred supernatural beings would have been an easier option. Compared to this.

He began to explain why I was pulled over here, hesitating to speak every word. "I've been thinking about the decision you're making in a couple of days."

"Yeah, I'm keeping it."

He struggled to form his sentences. "The thing is, I can't let you do that, not whilst I'm still here."

"What do you mean?"

"I can't let you make that decision. You're only making it to see me. That's not how the universe wanted this to go."

"That's not true, there are worst things than spending a life with Asher."

This was true.

"But it's mostly to keep me here."

This was also true. I didn't reply.

"From the moment you understood that pendant," he looked at me for the first time, "All you've wanted is to be normal. To not have the pain anymore. You won't have to ask questions about our history. You won't have to risk your future. You won't be punished anymore. You deserve to be free from it, Brannon. And I know you won't make that decision whilst I'm still here, in the space between," his voice was firm but breaking and a tear rolled down his face. He was serious. He was actually being serious.

"But Dad, you'll be gone. For good."

"Isn't that how deaths supposed to work? We are playing a game with it right now, and it shouldn't be that way."

"I don't care," I was also serious. And stubborn.

"It's not fair on Asher. He will never have your heart because you're sparing it for me."

"He will understand."

"Yes, he will. But he shouldn't have to."

I was running out of arguments. I couldn't disagree with him. "But I can't lose you. I don't know what to do without you," my voice was trembling and aching.

"You won't be without me. I'll be here." He pointed to my head. My headaches, I guess, were a representation of the Myst. I'd be keeping him in peace.

"And here." He pointed to my heart.

I looked at him, eyes full, breathing restricted. Catching on my emotions. "What can I do?" I was looking for answers, about anything.

"You can go back and make this decision, for yourself. Not for Asher, or for the potential of the Myst. For you. You remember every touch of pain this pendant has given you and remember that I'd do anything to keep you from pain. And remember that you have my support in everything you do."

I was bawling into my hands. "I'll miss you so much, Dad."

"I'll miss you too, sweetie," he was also crying.

We sat, drowning in tears, hugging each other, for a while. I felt the pace of his breathing steady.

"This place is so beautiful," he said, half an orange and red sun reflecting in the sparkle of his eyes.

"It's just a sunset," I bluntly replied.

"No, it's not. It's a lesson," he stopped and made sure I was looking at it, which I wasn't, until I felt I had to. "It's telling you, me and everyone who comes to find peace a very important message. That endings can be beautiful, too."

His words calmed me in an instant. He was never wrong. And this ending was beautiful.

"Tell Mum I love her and tell Marley that I'm proud of him."

"I will," I assured him, tasting the sweetness of my tears on my lips.

He smiled at the sea.

"Thank you for everything, Dad."

"Thank *you*, actually," he looked at me, two sets of purple and grey rock pools meeting for the last time, "Brannon, I'm ready. Because of you, I'm going to rest, in peace."

I hugged him tighter. "Can I sleep on your shoulder?" I asked him, avoiding having to watch him leave, and seeing the rays of sun take him from me.

"Of course, you can," his arm reached around me, and I buried myself in him and the smell of home.

"Sleep well," I tried to say, voice collapsing. I held my breath, so he didn't have to hear me cry anymore.

"Goodnight, Bran."

"I love you, Dad."

"I love you more, sweetie."

Asher

I didn't see her the next day. Everyone was at the beach, laughing at each other failing to surf on a perfectly calm blanket of water. She was tired from the past couple of days. I assumed she was catching up on sleep, and I didn't want to disturb her.

Jessy told me later in the day that Brannon was still in bed when she'd left, so I carried on with my day. The sun was scorching and the sky was crystal clear. It would be a perfect night to see the stars and watch Japanese lanterns float away.

The camp leaders agreed to let us do this. We'd planned it a few weeks back. It was to be an informal celebration of an amazing summer before the formal Ball tomorrow night. We planned to push surf boards and a couple of paddle boats out to sea, sit on them and release the lanterns, dedicating them to a person or memory that impacted our summer.

The person I planned to dedicate my lantern to was obvious. Blain. He'd become one of my few friends. And one of the only people I could rely on. Camp only happened once a year. Other than that, this site is full of dog walkers and visitors hiring the cabins. Never people my own age. The only people I'd met my own age had been stuck in a mobile phone or rude. Blain proved to be different, and I respected him.

The day went quicker than normal. We played beach volleyball, had water fights, laid in the heat and bobbed up and down on floats in the ocean. After dinner, we all headed back to our cabins to wait for the sun to go down and to meet when the sky was dark.

When I got home, my mum showed me the suit she'd brought me for the Summer Ball. It was black like ink and ironed so there were no creases. I enjoyed black clothes more than colourful ones because they complemented my skin colour and highlighted the blue in my eyes. It is also hard to tell if I've spilled anything on it.

I couldn't wait to see Brannon. She'd look beautiful.

Brannon

I spent the day alone, to be sad. I couldn't be sad for longer than this because everyone other than Asher and Blain thought my dad died weeks ago. They wouldn't understand my overwhelming sadness for a second time.

When I woke up, I couldn't help but revisit the Myst. Just to be sure. Emptiness. He was gone. He must've left when I'd fallen asleep and slipped back into the real world.

One thing he had done was left me with an even harder decision. It was no longer between a life with my dad or a life without him. Now, it was a life with Asher versus a life of pain free normality. I knew the pain would grow forever but this was Asher. He might be worth that.

Jessy reminded me of the lantern festival I had to attend tonight. She was in a swimsuit, ready to walk into the sea and sit on surfboards. I didn't feel like doing that tonight. Instead, I threw on a white hoodless jumper and some black jean shorts. I'd take part on my own.

I walked past the camp leader who was handing out lanterns on the field. I took one and walked to our spot. I sat, feet resting over the calm sea. The sky was so clear. The stars were dotted everywhere, surrounding the giant white ball of light that reflected over the sea, casting a romantic glow on the gathered teenagers, celebrating an amazing summer.

They were laughing and splashing each other. I had no desire to join them. Not even when I saw Blain, Jessy and Red. They were probably waiting for me, but if I sat with them, they'd notice something was wrong. I thought I spotted Asher with them but, after glancing at every one in front of me, he was gone again.

The air was cool and fresh. I breathed it in and let it fill my lungs. Everyone was opening out their lanterns, so I did the same.

"How are you planning on lighting that without one of these?"

It was Asher, waving a lighter in his hand behind me. I smiled, hoping he'd stay. Which he did.

He sat next to me and started to open his own lantern. He could read me like a book. He knew I didn't want to talk, or be down there with everyone else. He didn't try to make me, either. He lit his lantern and it glowed like a mini sun. Then he lit mine.

We looked ahead. A hundred floating candles mirrored in the water. People watching them head for the moon. Every other second, another was lit and released. Everyone became silhouettes against the flying lanterns, giving off a warm golden light. The air smelt of distant burning, like when you blow out a candle. And youth. Freedom. Togetherness.

"Who are you dedicating yours too?" I asked him.

"Well, I hope you don't take offence, but I told Blain I would dedicate it to him for being such a good friend to me this summer."

I giggled a little bit, knowing the power of persuasion that Blain held.

"What about you?"

I looked at the crowd of flickering lights. "To my Dad, who is now resting. In memories. In love. And in peace."

I felt a tear trickle down my cheek and noticed Asher's eyes widen as he realised what I was saying. He smiled at me, warmly.

"To Mr Amory." He took my hand and let go of his lantern. I did the same, and we watched them join the others, in harmony.

I felt his eyes on me, now. I noticed a star, brighter than all the rest, and smiled. Then I let my head fall onto Asher's shoulder. He kissed my head, and we sat in silence, until the last dancing lantern drifted away into nowhere.

***

I woke up late, again, and missed breakfast. Jessy roused me by informing me that my mum had sent me a parcel. It was quite a large brown box. Wide but flat, with a royal blue ribbon tied into a bow.

There was a tag tied to it that read, 'Happy Birthday Brannon, love Mum and Marley'.

I opened the lid and lifted the material that was inside. It was perfect. A royal blue gown. It looked like it would be tight to my body until it reached the bottom, where it flared out slightly. There was a glittering silver strap that went around the neck and traced under the chest area. She'd also sent matching shoes. I hadn't even remembered to buy myself a dress for this Ball. She was a life saver. I decided to call her.

"Hey Mum. Thank you so much for the dress!"

"Hey sweetie! Do you like it?"

"It's perfect! How are you and Marley?"

"We are good, everything is fine here. How are you?"

"I'm fine, thanks. I woke up late though, so I need to start getting ready soon."

"Yes, you'd better. We are missing you lots Bran, can't wait to see you."

"Not long now, Mum. I'll see you later. Love you."

"Love you, send pictures!"

Jessy smiled at me, "Let's get ready!"

The afternoon went quickly as we did each other's hair and makeup. We zipped up each other's dresses gently. She wore a metallic grey princess gown. Of course, Blain and Red joined us halfway through so that we could help them with their suits and ties.

"You girls look gorgeous!" Red complimented.

"Thanks, Red!" Jessy replied.

Blain sat next to me on the bed as I brushed out my curls.

"You good?" he asked.

"I think so. Are you?"

"Of course!"

We laughed, and then spoke quieter whilst the other two practised their slow dancing.

"Thank you for forcing me to come to this summer camp, Blain. It really has been an adventure."

"You needed it, Brannon," he looked me up and down, then started spraying me with perfume that he found on the bedside table, "Red was right, you do look gorgeous!"

"As do you!" I said back.

"Picture time!" he shouted.

We set up the camera and posed. This time, with no legs in the air or silly faces. It was the four of us, linked, and smiling. We then spent the last 40 minutes taking fun pictures and individual pictures for our family.

Blain pulled me to the side before he left.

"Your Dad is looking down on you right now thinking exactly what I'm thinking. You look beautiful. And I'm so proud of you."

I hugged him. Enough was said already.

Red, Jessy and Blain left at around 6pm. I stayed and waited for Asher, surprisingly nervous.

He'd never seen me dressed up like this. I felt uncomfortable as it was. But I was excited to see him, suited up.

Tonight, we could forget about everything and dance till the clock struck midnight, signalling our birthdays.

Asher

I knocked on her door, feeling ready. When she opened the door, my jaw dropped and I couldn't stop from saying, "Wow."

She laughed, and I continued to stare. Mesmerised. Her hair fell in natural, purple waves - my favourite. Her body was an hourglass, covered in a perfect blue shade that trailed to the floor. The sparkling strap stood out on her glittery skin, which must be the body glitter that Blain likes to cover people in.

"You smell nice," she told me.

I'm glad she noticed.

"Do you like the suit?" I asked, modelling the jacket for her.

She pulled a face, "It's okay."

My heart sunk a little before I saw the smile spread across her face. I nudged her, "Come on, let's go."

I held my arm out for her to take, much like I'd done with my heart. I guided her to the hall where the Summer Ball had been set up.

We stood at the doorway, admiring the look of the old, rustic hall. The ceiling was hidden by fairy lights that lit the room up. They were the only lights, a bright white that could be reduced to a dim flicker. There were tables with chairs lining the edges of the room and a dance floor in the centre, with a DJ deck at the top. There was a carriage with a variety of sweets near one of the walls. That's where I first saw Blain, nibbling on cola-bottles.

"Shall we?" I asked her, in a posh voice.

She matched my impression, "We shall."

We didn't sit down all night. For a while, it was just the five of us dancing, until the old songs came on and everyone joined in. This time, Brannon danced with me more than by herself. I had the most fun when I was with her and I couldn't wait for a future of this. She looked like she felt the same. When her hand gripped mine, I felt her relying on me. Not for support but for excitement and happiness. The smile on her face lasted hours. Her beauty was indescribable, much like the way I felt about her.

I was just getting comfortable with the dancing and the crowd of teenagers until the slow songs came on. About four in a row. I felt pressure to pull off some ballroom dance. In this moment, she was relying on me for that.

I took her hand and pulled her close, placing my hand on her hip. I exuded confidence and she liked it. Then we danced, slowly. The pressure dissolved as my eyes met hers. We were in our own bubble. No one else was here. Just us.

Brannon

The feeling of his hand firm on my hip sent goosebumps over my body. He had this effect on me and I liked it. Simply because no one else could.

The music was elegant and gentle. The type that forces you into your own feelings. It makes your emotions twice as strong and your stomach warm.

This would be the last time I saw Asher until tomorrow evening, at sunset. We'd been dancing for hours. The clock was reaching 11pm. One hour to go.

He spoke softly in my ear.

"You know, my whole life has been a build-up to this. An hour before our 18th birthday."

"Trust me, I know."

He laughed, slightly. "Have you enjoyed summer camp?" he questioned.

"Overall, yes. Some of it was the hardest time of my life," I told him, honestly.

"You're the strongest person I know, Brannon Amory," he twirled me unexpectedly and caught me back in his hold.

"Have *you* enjoyed summer camp?" I asked him back.

"Very much."

"How come?"

"Because I met you."

We swayed, slowly to the music.

"Let me ask you something Brannon, are you ready for a future with me now?" he smiled, speaking in a sarcastic tone yet sure that forever is what I wanted.

I didn't reply. I smiled back but didn't reply. He knew something wasn't right because his grip became a touch, and his smile became a frown. We kept moving to the music but less connected. He'd never looked at me like this before. Not angry. Not worried. But disappointed... and surprised. He expected more from me. Especially now my dad was gone.

"You're not going to keep it are you?"

I looked to the floor, unable to look him in the eye.

"It's unlucky to tell each other our decisions Asher."

Then he let go of my body, and the hope he'd found in us, and left the room. He walked away rapidly, heading straight for the door. I followed him.

The breeze felt colder, now. He had his back to me, running his hands through his ringlets.

"Asher, please don't be angry."

"I'm not."

I didn't know what to say. He clearly was. "After speaking to my Dad, I realised that this decision was about more than just me and you being together."

He turned quickly. "Maybe, but it's a lot to do with me and you being together. The universe decided that the pendants would meet when the time was right. We are destined to be together, Brannon!"

"The time is right for you! Have you even considered how my life would be if I kept it?"

He was now looking at the ground, too bothered in his own self-pity.

"I'd have to have these excruciating headaches that would probably get worse after every death for however long we are together. I'd be punished forever. If I made one wrong move, I risk becoming the bad Ancestor myself. Do you understand that?"

"Yes, I understand that. But do you understand that if you get rid of it you can't see me ever again? You can't be near me, Brannon. Do you understand that?"

Asher

Of course, she understood that. But she didn't care anyway.

"It's selfish, I know."

Suddenly, a rush of guilt made me swallow the words that were about to come out of my mouth. I was angry, but she was still Brannon. How do you tell someone the reason you're sad is because you love—?

She continued to speak, melting my heart more, "Asher, you showed me something that no one has managed to before," she stepped closer to me as she spoke, "Not that I'm beautiful, or intelligent, or sweet. No. You showed me I was important. And that I had a purpose. You made me feel like the world needed me. Like it was lucky to have me. And I don't know if I'll ever feel that way again." She placed her hand on my cheek. "But I am not strong enough to live this life anymore. Not without my dad. He was the person who taught me how to cope. Now, he's teaching me how to put myself first, and to chase that normal life I've always wanted."

My throat tightened. I was trying to resist eye contact. Her voice forced me to look into hers.

"Please don't be so distracted by the ending that you forget how beautiful the beginning was."

A tear escaped my eye and broke against her hand, still resting on my cheek. This was it. She was leaving me. I could have helped her cope. I could have shown her a life far better than normal.

I placed my hand on hers, removing it from my cheek. She had to see me tomorrow to throw the pendant into the sea. Maybe I could end things better then. But tonight, I couldn't.

I kept her hand in mine for a little while longer.

"You looked beautiful tonight. And I owe you a thank you for some of the best moments of my life," I let go of her hand, "I'll see you tomorrow."

I didn't blame her. I couldn't. I will never understand what she's been through.

I walked away, not looking behind me. I headed to the pier. Just a place, now.

Brannon

I watched his heart shatter in front of me. I felt selfish. It didn't feel right, letting him down. Wasting a summer of memories that I'd have to give up. But this is what I want. To be normal again, and the pain to be a feeling of the past. I'd be able to go home in a few days and be with Mum and Marley. They'd see me in a pain-free way, and I'd never miss a moment with them anymore. That's all I want. I think.

It was 11:45pm. I couldn't go back to the ball, not like this. I'd been sitting on the steps of my cabin for half an hour.

I contemplated going to see him. We shared this moment, whether he liked it or not. I thought he wouldn't want to be near me. But then I decided it was worth a chance.

I knew where he'd be. He wouldn't go home in the state he was in. He would go to our place.

I was right. He was at the end of the pier, staring into the distance. He stood with his hands in his pockets and his suit was a perfect fit to his body, although his shirt was a little tight. I tried to walk over to him quietly, but my heels gave me away. I stood next to him. Not with him.

I should've spoke but the silence was comfortable. It was disrupted by a quiet alarm coming from his watch. I looked. Both hands were pointing at twelve. I stepped closer to him, leant into him slowly and kissed his cheek.

"Happy birthday, Asher."

Then I walked off, as he did not acknowledge me there. However, it only took a couple of steps before I felt him grab my arm and pull me back around. He stepped into me, still angry. And then, he kissed me, grabbing my face and pulling it to his. This kiss lasted longer than others, but it was not loving or gentle. It was raw. And his way of saying goodbye. I felt his emotions through his lips. I questioned everything in this moment. Was I making the right choice? Leaving him.

He pulled away from me, glanced into my eyes and slowly released his grip. He turned around, with his back to me again, and I walked off. Confused and angry and fulfilled, and most importantly, in love.

I love you, Asher.

Asher

I love you, Brannon.

Brannon

The day of my birthday felt like the longest day of my life. I couldn't rest. I was questioning my decision and what I really wanted. My mum rung to say happy birthday, but I wasn't bothered that I was turning 18. My future depended on this day. And I needed to be certain of what I was going to do with it.

I thought back to the bonfire, the day we first met. His ocean blue eyes had been instantly unforgettable, and his voice a recognisable safety. The way he understood me straight away. The first person who I could sort of relate to. I trusted him in an instant, despite my desire not to. He was there when I lost my dad; my best friend. He *became* my best friend. He makes me laugh like no one has before and distracts me from this crazy life as well as making it feel less crazy, and more normal. It was normal for us. Me and Asher.

He took me on adventures. Hiking, zip-lining, rowing a boat to the middle of a lagoon and having a water fight. He showed me youth, freedom and happiness. He is my break from real life. He showed me that there's more to life than my comfortable hometown of Heston.

If I kept it, me and Asher would be powerful together. We would be the descendants of the two most powerful ancestors, and we would harness their power. Maybe. The magic is within us. We've just never had access to it before.

Smoke from a fire use to be my favourite smell. It lingers on your clothes and allows you to hold onto the feeling of togetherness for longer. That's changed now. Now, my favourite smell is musky aftershave, metallic with a hint of washing power. Him.

He was, literally, the other half of me. My purpose is to anchor the Myst. So is his. Therefore, we complete each other. Just like my bracelet demonstrates.

But it's more complicated than that. I don't want to be in pain for the rest of my life. I don't think that's selfish, now that I think about it. Keeping the pendant is a risk, no one knows what will happen. As the descendant of the sad one, I'm in the firing line for punishments beyond my control. We are part of something much bigger than us. It's not a love story.

I liked normal. Ordinary. To do things that wouldn't be affected by episodes. To not have to lie to my friends about who I am. To actually understand who I am. Normal people take normal for granted.

Asher would never see it that way. His experiences with the Myst have been easier. He can focus on ensuring a peaceful ending whilst I can barely construct a sentence whilst battling the feeling of a crushing skull. When he wakes from an episode, he can continue like normal. No lingering pain that may result in having to lie in a pitch-black room until fully recovered.

I paced around my cabin. Then around the field. Then to the beach and back. Thinking of every possible solution. Every 'maybe' that I could think of. Still, it came down to two conclusions. I choose Asher, or I choose normal. And he already knew which.

Asher

I sat on the pier for hours. The sun was falling, casting a tropical mist over the ocean. A beautiful sun, setting on the beautiful story of me and her.

I told myself it would be okay. But there's a difference between telling and knowing. And I knew I was lying. It wouldn't be okay, not without her.

She didn't want this life and I don't blame her. I wanted extraordinary and she wanted normal. Normal isn't a bad thing; it represents peace and tranquillity and answers. Opportunity. Maybe I ask for too much. In this moment that I shared with the ocean and the feeling of an empty, purposeless life, it didn't matter what I wanted anymore. It won't make her want this life and I, still, will not blame her.

I felt this way for the many hours that I sat, dangling my legs off the pier, contemplating the last two months I'd spent at this stupid camp. My thoughts were spiralling through deep episodes of sadness, to a burning rage that even the thought of her no longer extinguished. Not this time, anyway. The words escaped my mouth and the ocean swept them away into nothingness.

"It's funny really, isn't it? A boy gifted with magic, but still not powerful enough to make her stay. What did I do wrong? Maybe I should've told her everything I knew from the start. That way, the truth wouldn't have overwhelmed her as much as it did. She'd have trusted me quicker. Or, maybe, I should've pretended I didn't believe in magic, and that she was silly for bringing it up. Maybe then we could've lived happily ever after, both having secrets, but together."

The ocean became the outlet for my rage, listening to the pain in my voice.

"Together is better than strangers, which is what we'll be now. Happily ever never, that's how this story ends."

I felt my voice growing louder. The rage was dominating me. Anger growing like a wave. I threw my head back, confronting the blazing sun and the tropical sky, yelling at them with a hurting heart and uncontrollable fury.

"She should've kept the pendant!" I shut my eyes and lowered my voice again. "I wish she'd kept the pendant."

It was only after I stopped talking that I realised I wasn't alone anymore.

"Well then," I heard her voice, "it's a good job I'm keeping the pendant."

Slowly, I turned my head, to see her standing behind me, at our place. Her silver hair fell past her face, cascading over her shoulders. I traced my eyes up until they met hers, then I stood. I didn't understand.

"What do you mean? You said you didn't want it. Or to be with me. You said that, Brannon."

She walked closer to me, with a confidence about her that was compelling. "My dad said he'd do anything to keep me from pain. He meant the headaches and episodes. But, to me, that's not the greatest pain I could feel anymore. Keeping this pendant will keep me from pain. Because, without it, I'd be without you. And being without you would be more painful than a thousand headaches."

Happiness lit inside me like a bonfire. I rushed to her, and wrapped my arms around her, squeezing her tighter than ever before. I let go, with another question in mind. "But you said you wanted normal?"

"I do want normal. And, in 60 or 80 or however many years' time, after a million more episodes, it will be normal. And it will also be with you."

She looked down whilst intertwining her fingers with mine, the bracelet on her wrist symbolising a complete pendant. She walked me to the edge of the pier and we both sat down, admiring the burnt orange glow, halfway to sinking beneath the water. The same view that we have in the Myst.

"What if life becomes full of supernatural things that we don't understand?" I asked.

"Then we will figure it out together."

She rested her head on my shoulder. If she was going to get rid of the pendant, she would've done it by now. That means she's not going. She's staying. With me. With us.

"This is a beautiful ending to life as we know it," she said.

"It's a beautiful beginning, too," I told her.

The sun may set, but it rises again every morning. Her gaze was fixed on the distance. I looked where she was looking.

"Well," I asked, "what now?"

"I'm not sure," she smiled at me, with love glistening in her eyes, "Something extraordinary, I hope."

To Be Continued

Acknowledgements

To the reader, thank you for reading this far. Whilst I could fill another book full of acknowledgements for so many people who have thoroughly helped me navigate my way through this journey (the book, and life in general!), there are a few who sprung to mind immediately when I sat down to write this.

Firstly, I want to say a massive thank you to those who have helped me progress this far. To Cetti Long, for her incredible press coverage, as well as her continued support. To Dotty McLeod, for my first radio interview, and then inviting me back again! Without this, I would not have had the chance to work with Ian Hooper at Leschenault Press, who I am also grateful to for this wonderful opportunity.

When I was a child, my Uncle Chris used to tell me to count the bricks on my nan's house. Yes, this was to stop me from annoying him. No, I was not yet old enough to realise this. So, as he advised, I counted the bricks. Or at least tried! I owe him a massive thank you for making me totally hate Maths and love English that much more. Also, thank you to Cool Andy and Uncle Stephen. You can't mention one triplet without mentioning them all!

Thank you to my two best friends, Jamie and Lacey, for the never-ending laughs, the patience you have taught me and the constant sarcasm that will, no doubt, humble me for the rest of my life. But most of all, thank you for inspiring me, supporting me and giving me two people to love and protect, always.

The biggest thank you of all goes to my parents. My wonderful, loving parents, who do nothing but encourage me to chase my dreams every day. To my Dad; the Tough Mudder, Three Peaks, Man versus Mountain, Coast to Coast legend. (It would be wrong to not address you by your full title!) Thank you for always reminding me of my own strength and for sharing my love of sunsets. My favourite place to watch the sun set will always be by your side. Thank you to my Mum, for everything. For guiding me, for educating me, for supporting me and for loving me. Unconditionally. (I love you more, though!)

I wish I could thank everyone without doubling the number of pages in this book. Instead, I will have to hope that you know who you are already. But thank you. Yes, you. The reader. For without whom, this story would only be known between me and my laptop!

Okay...I have one more. Last, but definitely not least, to Sarah Combes, my first teacher. Thank you for teaching me to read and write. I literally would not be in this position without you! I hope to make you and the red group proud forever.

About the Author

Lauren Vinn was born in London, and now lives in Cambridgeshire. She is currently studying A-level English, History and Sociology at Sir Harry Smith Community College, with a place confirmed to study English Literature and Writing at university.

During the first lockdown of 2020, Lauren explored her passion of writing by penning this, her first novella, '*he was the sun*'. Whilst growing up, writing was, and still is, her favourite thing to do. She believes that words are the most invaluable source of power, and that mum is always right... Always.

When she is not writing, she is reading. Or, although aware that this is nothing to be proud of, watching the same few movies and television series on repeat.

Above all, something that Lauren enjoys more than anything is surrounding herself with family and friends. She believes that writing, reading and spending time with her loved ones are the things that keep her happy. However, if all else fails, she finds a sunset. This, in Lauren's eyes, has never failed.

To keep in contact, visit: www.facebook.com/laurenvinn.ink

Lightning Source UK Ltd.
Milton Keynes UK
UKHW010737300521
384607UK00001B/8

'I would say 80 per cent o...
involves reminding Christ...
God's children. Why? Rea...
Krish Kandiah brilliantly ...
experience of adopting wit... ...ight to show
how our adoption as God's children changes
everything.'
**Tim Chester, Pastor of Grace Church
Boroughbridge, faculty member of Crosslands
and author of *Enjoying God***

'This is Krish as we've come to expect him;
inspiring, wise and challenging. But it's also Krish
with his guard down, heart out, pain shared, with a
backstage pass to the wounds and the wonder
surrounding adoption. Krish helps us see what he's
been discovering – that God wants us, loves us,
adopts us and draws us into his heart and home, for
good. Grasping this secret will change everything.
Reading this book will too!'
**Rachel Gardner, President of Girls' Brigade and
author of *The Girl De-Construction Project***

'Not just "an interesting biblical theme" but a life-
changing truth that takes us into the heart of the
gospel; beautifully explained and explored from
Krish's own experience.'
**Paul Harcourt, National Leader of New Wine,
England**

'Krish is someone who has inspired our Church to see the Father's heart of God as more than just an abstract doctrine. Reframing adoption as an invitation into an enfleshed reality; a lived form of discipleship in which the rejected discover a sense of home amongst the people of God.'
Mark Sayers, Senior Leader of Red Church Melbourne, Australia and author of *Strange Days* and *Reappearing Church*

'This book will make you radically rethink what discipleship looks like in light of the greatest privilege that God has given us – the ability to call him our adopted Father.'
Rachel and Tim Hughes, Lead Pastors of Gas Street Church, Birmingham

'In *The Greatest Secret*, Dr Krish Kandiah pulls back the curtain to reveal perhaps the most astounding theme of Scripture: our adoption by God as his daughters and sons. He shows that this is the highest honour humans can experience. This adoption satisfies the cry of the human heart for a family relationship that provides us with unalienable security, identity and hope. It elevates us to a place of dignity and favour that is unattainable through our own efforts. May this

wonderful book inspire multitudes to love and good deeds.'
Dr Rice Broocks, Co-founder of Every Nation Churches and bestselling author of *God's Not Dead*

'In this deeply personal and moving book, Krish Kandiah takes us closer to God's own heart. Why do we speak so little of our adoption as God's children? It took the experience of adopting a child for Krish to grasp the true meaning of the Fatherhood of God. And in the pages of *The Greatest Secret* he shares with us this life-changing revelation.'
Rev Dr Michael P. Jensen, Rector of St Mark's Anglican Church in Darling Point, Australia and author of *My God, My God: Is it Possible to Believe Anymore?*

'I started reading Krish's book and was immediately engrossed – such is the gift of his storytelling. *The Greatest Secret* is as relatable as it is eye-opening; giving fresh insight into a way to view life, the world, God and our relationship with him, through a completely different lens. It is refreshing to read a Christian book that is powerful in its vulnerability, rawness, and ultimately, its hope.'
Chine McDonald, Head of Media at Christian Aid and Thought for the Day presenter

'As followers of Jesus we must understand the implications of our call to receive and give the healing love of God on earth. Both challenging and provocative, Krish Kandiah's exploration of Christian adoption bids us all to consider anew the radical heart of God. Kandiah is right: the deep and abiding love of God changes everything.'

Lisa Sharon Harper, President and Founder of freedomroad.us and author of *The Very Good Gospel: How Everything Wrong Can Be Made Right*

'Krish Kandiah offers a deep invitation to rediscover the radical hospitable nature of God's inclusive love! I believe this truth can lead us towards home together.'

Danielle Strickland, Pastor, Author and Justice Advocate

'This book made me cry. It tapped a wellspring of emotion within me and articulated a profound dimension in my faith that I had suppressed. We are adopted children – adopted by a living, loving Father. In an age riddled with identity anxiety, we keep trying to preach propositional truths. It is authenticity that people crave and Krish has melded a biblical truth with his painful and authentic faith journey.'

Tim Costello, Executive Director of Micah Australia

THE
GREATEST
SECRET

How being God's adopted children changes everything

KRISH KANDIAH

HODDER

First published in Great Britain in 2019 by Hodder & Stoughton
An Hachette UK company

This paperback edition first published in 2020

1

Unless indicated otherwise, Scripture quotations are taken from the Holy
Bible, New International Version (Anglicised edition). Copyright © 1979,
1984, 2011 by Biblica Inc.® Used by permission. All rights reserved.

A CIP catalogue record for this title is available from the British Library

Paperback ISBN 978 1 529 37499 5
eBook ISBN 978 1 529 37500 8

Typeset in Ehrhardt MT by
Palimpsest Book Production Ltd, Falkirk, Stirlingshire

Printed and bound in Great Britain by Clays Ltd, Elcograf S.p.A.

Hodder & Stoughton policy is to use papers that are natural, renewable
and recyclable products and made from wood grown in sustainable forests.
The logging and manufacturing processes are expected to conform
to the environmental regulations of the country of origin.

Hodder & Stoughton Ltd
Carmelite House
50 Victoria Embankment
London EC4Y 0DZ

www.hodderfaith.com

To my adopted daughter

Contents

Introduction

How I lost my love for God –
and the unlikely way I found it again

There are some secrets I am going to share with you
– things I have only ever told a close circle of intimate
friends and family. I will change some names, times
and details to protect the innocent – and the guilty
– because this story is ultimately not about them, or
even about me, but about all of us. I begin with myself
not because I seek your sympathy or because my
experience is unique or in any sense worse than anyone
else's. Actually, it is quite the opposite. I think more
of us struggle to love God than we might realise, or
be willing to admit.

I was perhaps an unlikely candidate to lose love for
God. First of all, I was an 'active' Christian; I had
been a missionary, a youth worker and a pastor before
working as a theologian and church planter. I had
shelves full of Christian books (some of which I had
even written) and many Christian friends on my
contact list (I had even had the privilege of bringing

one or two of them to faith). I was happily married with three beautiful children who, at four, five and six years old, were still full of wonder at the world, still full of respect for their father and still nearly always in bed by 7.30 p.m. On top of that, I had landed a dream job at a prestigious university, which came with a rather wonderful house in a highly desirable post-code.

Despite all of this, suddenly, over the course of a year, I became engulfed by a darkness I could not escape from. I had never experienced a mental health problem at any prior point in my life, but the blackness of those days was so deep that I found myself, on a number of occasions, considering whether ending my life would be a mercy to the rest of the family. I lost my appetite and struggled to get to sleep at night. I woke up many mornings with numb hands having clenched my fists so tightly in my sleep that I had cut off the circulation to my fingers.

Spiritually, emotionally, mentally and physically . . . I was a mess.

A number of things had crept up on me to contribute to this low point in my life. The main one was that the dream job I had landed – the one for which I had uprooted my young family – turned out to be, in fact, the stuff of nightmares. Perhaps I should have seen the warning signs earlier. When my boss started slamming the phone down on me. When my colleagues began lawyering up. When false allegations were made against other staff members. When I walked past a noticeboard and saw my own job being advertised. When I was press-ganged into signing disclaimers against taking legal action against my employer. By the time I realised how serious all this was, I felt acutely aware that if I lost my job, my family would be made – temporarily at least – homeless. But I also knew that if I stuck with the job, the toxic and hostile environment would damage me, my mental health and my family irrevocably. Perhaps you know something about feeling trapped, disempowered, disregarded, intimidated. It eats away at your spirit. It tortures your soul. It changes you.

This was not my first experience of being bullied. When I was a child, I was relentlessly hounded because of the colour of my skin. At that time I found that God's unshakeable love for me, the support of my church family and the encouragement of the Holy Spirit gave me the backbone I needed to walk tall no matter how much spit and spite erupted from the mouths of my fellow comprehensive schoolboys. Nor was it the first time I had been threatened with losing my job and my home. As a young married couple, my wife and I had once found ourselves working in a city where constant deafening machine-gun fire rattled our windows and caused us to sleep fully clothed on the floor under a table, a bag packed in case of the need for sudden evacuation. At that time the words of the Psalms gave me hope, and the Holy Spirit came close, giving me peace to trust God, my shield and refuge.

So what was different this time? There were no bullets flying. There were no fists raised to my face. I had friends. I had my wonderful, wondering children around me. In hindsight, I almost lost my mind and my faith because the root of the evil appeared to come from Christians. They were part of the religious establishment. They were well-known speakers who one moment could tell moving stories from the stage about the grace of God and the next, stab colleagues in the back with disparaging remarks, vicious threats and lawsuits. Some went to the same church as me and sang praise to God in the same room. We ate together the bread that symbolised the death of Christ for all of us, drinking from the same cup that represented Jesus' spilt blood. The next day at work they couldn't even look me in the eye. This behaviour of other Christians felt like it was robbing me of the resources to be able to cope. My faith and my family in faith had always been my rock. Now those foundations were being eroded, undermined by the actions of those who claimed to know – and, worse, teach – about God. My safe place, my source of strength had been compromised.

In the middle of that year my mother called me and asked me to go with her to an appointment with an

4

oncologist. The news was not great. She had stage 4 ovarian cancer and there was very little they could do to treat it. I remember getting home, locking myself in the bathroom and sitting on the edge of the bath feeling upset that my mother had chosen such an inconvenient time to begin to die. I didn't know how I was going to cope, nor how I could be a good father and husband while this was going on. And then I remember being hit by my utter selfishness in being more concerned about how this was going to affect me than about how my mother would cope.

I had a degree in medicinal chemistry, but I couldn't stop the cancer. Instead, I clung to a small tin of aromatherapy balm that promised to help me sleep. I had a PhD in theology, but I couldn't find any sense in what God was trying to teach me. Instead, I stumbled across occasional solace in the bedtime Bible stories I read to my young children. I had years of experience of being a pastor, but all my tried and trusted methods of helping people persevere and hold on to faith in difficult circumstances now seemed pathetic. I found it very difficult even to think about God, let alone love him.

I was too weak to face up effectively to the bullying at work, and I was too weak to be able to trust God. I was too weak to support my family and I was too weak to help my mother. I felt a failure.

I meet many people in these sorts of rock-bottom

places. Bad things have happened to them, and the very people who could be helping them up out of the pit seem to be pushing them back down again. When we are in that position, there seems to be no hope. We begin to believe that God has abandoned us. Our faith weighs us down instead of buoying us up through the storms.

I am writing this book more than ten years after that dreadful time in my life. I couldn't see it at the time, but God had not abandoned me. It's just that he wasn't quite where I expected him to be, and he wasn't doing quite what I expected him to do. God is like that. He is higher, greater, more mysterious than we sometimes like to think. 'For I know the plans I have for you,' he says in Jeremiah 29:11. He knows the plans and we don't. He has plans to give us hope and a way forward, even when we are feeling hopeless and directionless.

God's plan for me was a most unlikely plan, seeded years, maybe generations, earlier. My wife and I had both grown up hearing first-hand stories of orphanages around the world. Both our mothers, for very different reasons, had found themselves living in homes for vulnerable children. And so it had seemed entirely natural for us when we got married and had children of our own to offer our home and family as a safe place for children in need to be loved and cared for. The process to become foster and adoptive parents got off to a terrible start when we failed the initial telephone screening. Our deficiency? Not enough bedrooms in our otherwise sizeable West London home. So that was the end of our fostering and adoption journey. Until, that is, a job came up at a prestigious university with a rather wonderful house thrown in for good measure. Suddenly we sailed through the thorough home assessment, background checks and intense panel interrogation and, before we knew it, we were caring for a beautiful newborn baby girl.

Over the next twelve months, as both my situation at work and my mum's health deteriorated, this little girl grew and thrived. When I couldn't sleep at night, her presence provided a little company. When I was drowning in my sadness, her infectious giggle was a lifeline of brightness. When I couldn't pray, I pushed a buggy round the block and spoon-fed pureed fruit into an appreciative, hungry, toothless mouth, and at least one of us was gently nourished and nurtured.

And then came 11 September. This was the date we went to court to adopt that little girl formally into our family. It is, of course, a date that brings to mind the worst atrocities humankind can wreak against itself. But for me that date will always signify one of the highlights of my life. Perhaps it shines even brighter because of the darkness that surrounded it, the darkness of terrorism wherever and whenever it occurs. The darkness of a world full of cancer, and mental health crises, and children removed by law from parents who had not been protected themselves when they were young. The darkness of a world where workplace bullying is allowed to continue unchecked.

I never did rediscover my previous relationship with God. I say that because I encountered a whole new relationship with him. My family had grown from five to six and then to seven as we fostered another little boy. We had moved house and job and community again, not knowing what the future would hold. There were a lot of strange connections and new relationships unfolding. I always knew that God was my father, and that I was his child, but after 11 September my developing relationship with my adopted daughter opened my eyes to the truth that God was my *adoptive* father, and I was his *adopted* child.

That changed everything.

Imagine you were to attend a family get-together today – perhaps a birthday party or an anniversary. The sort of event where your distant relatives appear – the relations you usually forget you have. The sort of event with lots of food and little expectation, and children running around the crowded rooms. These are the events that end with the leftovers being boxed up for guests to take home and people saying they ought to do this more often. Imagine, at this get-together, that an elderly aunt drinks a little too much champagne and, while she's telling all the old familiar stories, she lets slip a family secret and utters the party-stopping words: 'Didn't you know, dear? You're adopted!'

This has actually happened to friends of mine. When they try to explain what it feels like to hear those words, they liken it to experiencing an earthquake, as though the firm ground beneath their feet had given way. You lose your balance and are sent into mental and emotional freefall. In a heartbeat, those you thought were your family feel like strangers, and strangers are somehow family. The cracks come to the surface and you begin to see or imagine the cover-ups, the conspiracies, the lies. You wonder who you are, where you have come from, and what you are going to do with yourself now. Adoption changes everything.

My daughter will never have that earthquake moment because she has always known she was adopted. That does not mean she will not struggle with seismic issues of identity and belonging, but it does mean she is piecing together her life story with the knowledge that she was once loved and lost, but also loved and found. She was chosen and welcomed unconditionally despite the mysteries of turmoil in her biological ancestry, and regardless of what the future may hold. She both blends in and stands out in her adoptive family. Whether she is learning to sing, or giving blood, or sitting exams, or brushing her hair, she is growing up with an awareness that adoption and its aftershocks somehow impact everything.

When we adopted her, I felt something of the ground-shattering force of suddenly realising my own identity as an adopted child of God and how this affects every aspect of my life and faith. Over time this realisation has substantially shifted the way I view myself, and the way I view people around me. It has made me question what I really know of God. It has exposed some of the cover-ups, conspiracies and lies regarding my faith to which I had previously been blind. It has also revealed some of the untold treasures and mysteries of the gospel that I may otherwise never have discovered.

I wrote this book for two reasons. First, because I meet many people who have similar secrets to me. People who struggle to find God and to love him. Perhaps this struggle is because of difficulties at work or with health or church. Perhaps it is because of the terrible things we see on the news or hear about in our own communities. Perhaps it is because we sense that there is some sort of cover-up going on when it comes to faith. Perhaps it is for totally different reasons. From my experience and from talking to others it seems that many more of us struggle to grasp God's love than we might expect. There are swathes of us who find ourselves feeling that we don't quite fit in, wondering if we have lost out when it comes to faith, to life. I wonder if God wants you to know that you are his adopted child? Exploring some of the implications of this truth could change everything.

I also wrote this book for my daughter and for those like her, forging a way through complex family dynamics, wondering how faith fits into all that. As she approaches her teenage years, I know that for many adopted children this time can be particularly challenging as they grapple with huge questions about their identity and their parentage and with how to make sense of the story of their lives. Whatever happens, I want her to know that she is mine. I will not give up on her. I will not be going anywhere. I love her fiercely. I wonder if God wants you to know a Father like this – perfectly like this? Many of us experience the anxiety of not being sure if we are really good enough, or if we really belong somewhere, or if we are truly loved, or if we can really trust anyone. Many of us struggle to make sense of our life stories – we have unexplained or unresolved episodes in our lives that we long to piece together. Understanding that God is our adoptive Father could begin to change everything.

Adoption has been a dirty secret in the Church for too long. There have, indeed, been cover-ups perpetuated to avoid talking about it. Our pastors and youth leaders have much preferred to preach and talk about forgiveness or rescue, about freedom and redemption, without noticing that without the missing ingredient of adoption even these amazing truths are impoverished. The theme of adoption is neglected in our pulpits, our songs, our programmes and our gospel, even though it is present throughout our Bibles, from Job to Jesus, from Moses to Paul, from the prophets to the epistles. Failing to reflect on or to celebrate our adoption skews our faith, limits our relationship with God and undermines our sense of identity, purpose and confidence. The good news is that everything can change. Instead of a flawed sub-biblical understanding of Christianity, the Spirit of adoption wants to seismically recast the way we understand faith, read Scripture, practise discipleship and experience God's love.

It wasn't my PhD in theology that helped me unlock new depths to my relationship with the God who adopted me, nor was it my role in the divinity faculty at a prestigious university. It was a baby girl who appeared in my life at just the right time. Sometimes, I think she saved my life. I wonder if she can save yours too?

Chapter 1

The secret that changes everything about everything

A claim hidden in plain sight – and a clue to the meaning of life, the universe and everything.

In an uncharacteristic, quavering voice she whispered, 'May I have a word?' The hairdresser had just finished and Jazbinda was adeptly applying her make-up while everyone kept telling her she looked radiant in her wedding dress. But her mother couldn't keep eye contact while she murmured: 'I thought you should know, you know, before . . .' As she walked down the aisle, Jazbinda's legs felt like they would buckle beneath her. When the priest asked her if she, 'Jazbinda Shah', would take Brian Jones to be her husband, she didn't know how to answer, because she didn't know who she was any more. As she paused, everyone in the chapel held their breath.

Bill had been tasked with clearing out the attic. His mother's house needed to be emptied quickly so it could be sold to pay for her care. It was so hard watching her health deteriorate, watching strangers nurse the one who had nursed him, watching the family home slowly declutter and de-personalise. As he moved one box after another, he noticed a half-open envelope with a picture inside he had never seen before. It was him as a toddler, in the arms of a woman of whom he had no recollection. On the back of the photo was his birthdate, but next to a different name. That was the day his world changed.

A dirty secret

Adoption has, for many generations, been a dirty secret, something of which to be ashamed, to be sealed in an envelope, to be boxed in the attic with the dust. It is a word best whispered, if spoken at all. Adoption became, at some point in history, synonymous with failure. Didn't it seem to shout infertility or impotence or illicit relations? Didn't it declare to the world that the adults involved were somehow defective, without the physical capacity to produce offspring and forced to accept someone else's cast-off children? While other people could get pregnant by accident and far too often, it seemed, why, despite their most determined efforts, couldn't certain couples get things to happen and why was it them who had to resort to plan B, the booby-prize option of adoption? Didn't an adoption journey go hand in hand with pain, disappointment, shame and feelings of inadequacy and failure? Didn't it undermine a sense of identity, a sense of masculinity or femininity? Didn't it underline an incompetency to parent? The shadow fell across the children, too. Were they deficient, unwanted kids of birth parents, and plan-B kids of adoptive parents? Talking about adoption only brought these heartaches and questions to the surface, and so it was best to hide it, bury it, silence it. Adoption became the dirty secret that was only revealed by accident or in an emergency.

Adoption, the act of legally taking in a child to raise as your own, never needs to incur or imply such feelings of shame and failure. In fact, films present it in a whole different angle. According to Hollywood, children who come from foster homes can be superheroes saving the world from evil beings such as Voldemort, Darth Vader, Lord Sauron or Dr No. Those adopting such children can be well-respected heroes like Jean Valjean in *Les Misérables* as well as well-meaning villains like *Despicable Me*'s Felonius Gru, or Batman.[1]

But while adoption has been celebrated in fiction and science fiction, it has too often continued to be a dirty secret in real life. Somehow this negative misperception of adoption seems to have infected the Christian faith too, causing generations to have neglected the Bible's teaching on the subject. It has become what some might call a Cinderella subject.

Just like the unwanted stepdaughter in the fairy tale, the doctrine of adoption was deemed to be an embarrassment, locked away from the public eye, not given the attention or honour it deserved, and definitely not permitted to come to the ball. It didn't get invited to the worship parties or the conference main stage. Instead it was banished to the cellar. Perhaps it would be let out when all the endless chores were done.

We know how the story ends. The silenced and forgotten one, downtrodden, unacknowledged and unappreciated, turns out to be more precious and beautiful than anyone could have imagined. Once she is discovered and given her rightful place, due honour is bestowed on her. The whole kingdom celebrates.

A Cinderella revolution

It's time for a Cinderella revolution. The one who is neglected needs to be celebrated. The one who is forgotten needs to be remembered. The one who is suppressed needs to be liberated. It's time for a seismic reversal. We need to pull the doctrine of adoption out of the dust and ashes and display it with all the glory it deserves. And guess what? The shoe fits. We don't have to cut our gospel down or squeeze it awkwardly out of shape to accommodate this strange new doctrine. Quite the opposite – it fits together perfectly with our faith because it was always meant to. Everything we value most about life, faith and the universe makes better sense when we understand God's adoption of us. It does not have to be a dirty secret. It is the key to unlocking untold riches, joys and treasures of the Christian faith.

Perhaps you think that sounds slightly ambitious, dramatic, overblown. Maybe it reminds you of one of the many books that over-promise and under-deliver – the get-rich-quick book, the transform-your-prayer-life book, the everything-you-need-to-know-about-decision-making book, the ultimate-diet bible. I should know as I have read most of them (although I decided not to read the decision-making one). They offer so much, but ultimately fail to deliver. I never want to write a book like that. But here I am saying that understanding our adoption may just be the secret to everything – our true identity, our prayer life, our church life, our family life, our hopes and dreams, our history and our future, the meaning of the universe. I can only make such fantastic claims because this secret has been fully accessible for two millennia. It is written in clear and unmistakable language in the world's best-selling book, in one of its most influential sections in one of its most beloved chapters: Romans, chapter 8.

A momentous revelation

This is the apostle Paul writing. The persecutor-turned-preacher. The man who was on a search-and-destroy mission against the Church, yet who miraculously became its chief architect and agitant. This is the letter to the Roman Church, arguably Paul's finest God-inspired work, that singlehandedly is credited as igniting the Reformation that transformed not just the Church, but the entirety of western culture itself. This is Romans 8, the chapter that millions of Christians around the world treasure because of its soaring prose and stellar promises. This is the chapter that begins with the liberating truth that there is 'now no condemnation for those who are in Christ Jesus',[2] and ends with the stirring conviction that nothing, not anything, can 'separate us from the love of God'.[3] This is the same chapter containing the beautiful promise that assures us that 'in all things God works for the good of those who love him'.[4]

But for all the affection there is for Paul's theological masterpiece, for all the recognition of the emphasis on God's grace, and God's sovereignty, and God's love, too many of us have missed the proverbial wood for the trees. I certainly did, despite years of teaching this passage to congregations, to young people and to students. For at the heart of this passage is a momentous revelation:

We know that the whole creation has been groaning as in the pains of childbirth right up to the present time. Not only so, but we ourselves, who have the firstfruits of the Spirit, groan inwardly as we wait eagerly for our adoption, the redemption of our bodies. For in this hope we were saved.

(Romans 8:22–4)

This passage is immense. It references the creation, touches on the fall of humanity with the resulting pains of childbirth and the frustrations the world now experiences, then homes in on our salvation and the incomparable gift of the Holy Spirit, and ends up with the restoration of all things – a new heaven and earth. This is a cosmic canvas on which the secret to the universe is revealed. Our creation, our destination, our salvation – or, in other words, life, death and the universe – are all awaiting, building up to, straining towards . . . our adoption!

If our adoption truly is the event that all of creation has been waiting for, it should change everything. This truth gives us a new lens through which to understand the whole of our lives and the entirety of our Christian experience. It offers us a new perspective on every facet of our discipleship. The metaphor of adoption can radically alter the way we read and understand the Bible. Our adopted status should impact the way we relate to others around us. The sacrament of adoption transforms how we approach our relationship with our Father God. The doctrine of adoption reframes our understanding of our own salvation. The experience of adoption could even affect who is welcomed into our own families.

Adoption is arguably the Christian faith's greatest secret. Great in its place in God's plan for the universe. Great in its capacity to reform our life and faith. Great in its brilliance and promise and purpose. But also greatly undervalued, greatly underappreciated and greatly underemphasised.

Perhaps one of the reasons we have been missing the vastness of the revelation that adoption is the key to everything is because of Paul's downright honesty. Although the chapter is full of echoes of the origin story of the universe, and full of references to our eternal hope, Paul does not underplay the frustrations of real life in the here and now. From sin to suffering to separation anxiety, from our struggles with prayer to our struggles with relating to God, Paul is not afraid to call it out. Maybe you recognise in yourself a sense of dissatisfaction with even the best things in life, a continual disappointment that things don't deliver what you hope for, the sense that you don't really belong. If you recognise some of these frustrations then you are in good company because, according to the letter to the Romans, frustration, whether we like it or not, is the new normal. The frustration we feel is part of that bigger plan, the secret story woven into the very fabric of the universe itself, a narrative arc that is slowly but steadily working itself out from the very beginning to the very end, a journey towards our adoption.

Paul has found a way to have his feet on the ground and his head in the air. He holds on to the hope of the gospel amid the turmoil of everyday life. How can he do this? He sees that the two are intrinsically linked: the frustrations we experience have a purpose. God has deliberately allowed the captivity of the cosmos – in order eventually to set it free. The universe is not reeling out of control, it is not a gigantic accident or some kind of cosmic juggernaut careering unstoppably towards celestial havoc. We are told that even in the trouble and the tragedy God is doing something. While there is cancer and childlessness, while there are mental health problems and injustice, poverty, betrayal and death, there is also hope. While there is great frustration, there is also great expectation.

When faced with the catalogue of struggles that we experience in the world, it is very easy to fall into thought patterns of fear or hopelessness. If anyone understood this, it was Paul – he was only too familiar with suffering, persecution, betrayal and ongoing excruciating pain. He had seen others die, and he fully expected himself to be killed for his message. But he had a secret weapon against fear and hopelessness. Except it was not so secret – again he gives it away in

Romans 8, showing that he understands not only the purpose of adoption but also the power of adoption.

Paul writes that it is the power of the Spirit of adoption – the one that enables us to trust in our Abba Father – that can help us overcome fear:

> *The Spirit you received does not make you slaves, so that you live in fear again; rather, the Spirit you received brought about your adoption to sonship. And by him we cry, 'Abba, Father.' The Spirit himself testifies with our spirit that we are God's children. Now if we are children, then we are heirs – heirs of God and co-heirs with Christ, if indeed we share in his sufferings in order that we may also share in his glory.*
>
> *(Romans 8:15–17)*

Paul writes that it is the power of the Spirit of adoption – the one who lives in us, representing the first fruits of what is to come, a taster of God's overall plan – that can help us overcome hopelessness:

> *We ourselves, who have the firstfruits of the Spirit, groan inwardly as we wait eagerly for our adoption to sonship, the redemption of our bodies. For in this hope we were saved. But hope that is seen is no hope at all. Who hopes for what they already have? But if we hope for what we do not yet have, we wait for it patiently.*
>
> *(Romans 8:23–5)*

In other words, not only does adoption help us understand the problems of the world, it also helps us handle them. The doctrine of adoption gives us purpose *and* power, perspective *and* peace. It enables us to see the big picture of what life is really all about, and it empowers us to deal with life on a day-to-day basis.

That really should change everything about everything.

A now and a not yet

There is a fundamental reason adoption can be both pragmatic and paramount, both empowering and inspiring, both a premise and a promise, and that is because it is both now and not yet. The paradox is there in Romans 8. In verse 15 it appears our adoption has already happened – we receive the Spirit of sonship when we become Christians and now we can call God our *Abba* Father. However, in verse 23 it seems as though we are waiting for our adoption in the future at the end of time. How can both of these be true at the same time?

My daughter was legally adopted when she was two years old, and after she had lived with us for most of her life to that point. But that was not the end of the story, it was just the beginning. Imagine if I had walked out of the courtroom and left her on the steps of the building, saying that all the fight and work I had put into securing her as my daughter was now complete. You would think that was mad. The whole point of adoption is not about the change of status, it is about the change of relationship. Pursuing the legalities was not the consummation of our efforts, it was the conception of an intimate, committed relationship that is still being worked out and developed today. It is true that had I walked out of the courtroom and straight under a bus, she would have been just as eligible to inherit her share of my estate as if I were to live to be 100 years old. But although she was always 100 per cent adopted, there was – and there still is – so much more about our relationship to discover and develop.

This is how we reconcile the fact that we have both been adopted and long for the fulfilment of it. We have a taste of it, but there is so much more to discover. We may sense some sort of intimacy with God, but it is just the beginning, and it leaves us desperately wanting more. It is a frustrating tension. I know many Christians who throw in the towel because their relationship with God does not feel as significant, real or immediate as they sense it should. When their expectations of intimacy with God are not met they walk away from it. But it can also be a joyful tension. Like our anticipation before a holiday, which builds with the emptying of the fridge and the filling of the suitcases, we can cope with the temporary chaos because there are treasures untold yet to come that will be worth the wait.

An act of grace

But before we begin to look at those tensions and treasures of our faith more closely, we must first ask, *Why?* Why is adoption the destination to which all of human history is heading? Why is the fulfilment of our adoption the moment for which creation holds its breath? Why does it empower us to face hardships? Why is the promise of adoption worth waiting for, worth the frustrations and struggles of day-to-day life?

For many people, adoption is merely considered the third and worst way to have a child. There's natural birth. If that doesn't work, for some there is in vitro fertilisation (IVF), and if that doesn't work, well, there's always adoption. But that is not God's approach to adoption. God was not incapable of having his own children, he was not bored or lonely. God did not adopt us because *he* needed it. God adopted us because *we* needed it. God saw that we were enslaved and vulnerable and he stepped up and became what we need him to be, a Father who would go to the ends of the earth for us, who would die for us, who would give us the world, who would put everything right. God adopted us as a wonderful act of mercy, compassion and altruistic grace.

I began to realise how much I had misunderstood

the doctrine of adoption when we legally adopted our little girl. Our three birth children were all we could ever have wanted or dreamed for. We did not set out on our fostering journey to adopt a fourth child. But when a social worker sat in my front room and said that the baby in my arms could not return to her birth family and might never recover from a move to yet another new family on top of everything else she had been through, I knew I had no choice. This child needed adopting, and she needed adopting by my family, whatever sacrifices and changes that would entail. If God was willing to go to such extraordinary lengths to include me in his family, even allowing his son Jesus to lay down his life for me, then I had to mirror that in this decision. Little did I know then that in seeking to emulate what little I understood of God's love, I would rediscover God's love in a whole new way.

The family we know as God – Father, Son and Holy Spirit – longs to welcome us into the intimacy of God's love. God has gone to incredible lengths to ensure that the way is cleared for us to come home with him. In his letter to the Galatian Church, Paul ties adoption to the heart of the gospel itself:

But when the set time had fully come, God sent his Son, born of a woman, born under the law, to redeem those under the law, that we might receive adoption to sonship.

(Galatians 4:4–5)

God, the Holy Trinity, knows the history, the problems, the potentials for disaster in adopting us, but they want us in their forever family anyway. The journey to adopt us began long before we were born, long before the world was created. As Paul writes again, this time in his letter to the Church in Ephesus:

For he chose us in him before the creation of the world to be holy and blameless in his sight. In love he predestined us for adoption to sonship through Jesus Christ, in accordance with his pleasure and will — to the praise of his glorious grace, which he has freely given us in the One he loves.

(Ephesians 1:4–6)

And why? Because adoption demonstrates the compassion of God as he welcomes lost and vulnerable children into his family. Because adoption manifests the faithfulness of God that has been and will be committed to us for eternity. Because adoption displays the love of God as he is willing to embrace us as his children for ever. Because adoption highlights the grace of God as there is nothing we have done or will do to deserve it or earn it.

We need to get rid of the shame around adoption and see it in all its glory. This may have been easier for Paul because in Roman times adoption was already seen as a high privilege. It was often connected with inheritance, as families deliberately chose heirs they could trust with running their businesses or their families, or even their nations. In the Roman Empire, even Emperor Nero and his four predecessors were all adopted, and in turn adopted sons who would succeed them.[5]

Roman adoption was such an honour that it could be a huge insult to existing members of a family, as it implied that the birth sons of the emperor or the business owner or the head of the family were seen as not being up to the task, as being incapable or not credible enough to take on the role. Paul radicalises and reboots the Roman understanding of adoption because there is no question that Jesus is the best son the universe has seen. God the Father has full confidence in his perfect son Jesus Christ, and yet he still grants us the privilege of being adopted as his sons and daughters. Paul also radicalises and reboots a modern-day understanding of adoption: being part of God's family is indeed a privilege – freely and lovingly bestowed on us, no matter where we've come from, and regardless of what we've done or how unworthy we feel.

Adoption is the secret that changes everything about everything. Once we begin to see it, it is hard to avoid. I wonder what difference it would make if our adoption into God's family became not only more openly discussed and more widely celebrated, but, as in Paul's train of thought, the greatest generative metaphor for understanding the Christian faith and life.

In this book, as we work through the rich theme of adoption portrayed through Scripture, we will see how our lives can be caught up in the divine dynamic storyline that revolves around God bringing his lost children home, safe and sound. The revolution has begun. The dirty secret is no longer dirty, and is no longer a secret. The shame can be shaken off. The glory can be revealed. It is time to marvel as the truth begins to cascade the transforming grace of God throughout our hearts and minds. Nothing will be the same again.

~

Questions for reflection

1. What is your initial reaction to the idea of adoption? Where have these positive and negative views and preconceptions come from?

2. What surprises you most about Paul linking God's adoption of us to the meaning of the universe itself? Why do you think the doctrine of adoption is mentioned so little in our churches?

3. 'The shame can indeed be shaken off, and the glory revealed.' Where is the greatest potential for change in your life? How could a deeper understanding of adoption impact that?

Chapter 2

The secret that changes everything about me

Who am I when everyone is looking –
and who cares anyway?

As my aircraft broke through the cloud barrier I wanted to take a picture, but I was having plane shame. There was no way to capture this moment without including the logo of the budget airline I was flying with, and that would mess up the social media post. It's shallow and ridiculous, I know, but it continued to bug me during those beautiful aerial sunset moments.

Maybe that was why I was sympathetic as I read in the inflight newspaper the story of Anna Sorokin, who arrived in New York City presenting herself as a German heiress with $60m in assets and trying to get a loan of $22m for her foundation. She lived the high life, hiring private jets, attending the most elite parties and handing out $100 tips to bag carriers and Uber drivers. But Anna Sorokin, or rather Anna Delvey, was eventually caught out and found guilty of multiple counts of theft and grand larceny. It had all been a lie, a façade, a false identity.

Sorokin's audacity was shocking, and the reporter seemed to revel in delight that she got her comeuppance. But I felt equally condemned as I saw more of myself in Sorokin's manipulating behaviour than I wanted to admit. It reminded me of the guilt I felt when I read Clive Hamilton's insightful verdict on the challenge of our age in his book *Growth Fetish:* 'People buy things they don't need, with money they don't have, to impress people they don't like.'[1]

I know that my Twitter feed only presents the curated highlights of my life in a vain attempt to impress. The sun-soaked beach photo from a recent Miami trip was shared on my Instagram account rather than a picture of the dreary boardroom where I had spent most of my time. I posted a picture of the ornate dessert from a lunch with a client rather than one of the cheese on toast I made for the kids later that day. It is not just on social media that this manicured projected-self emerges. Sometimes when I check myself in the mirror before a significant meeting I realise that my expensive-looking outfit has been cobbled together from visits to the charity shop. Or as I look at the list of jobs and skills on my CV I know that, behind these headline highlights, there are many struggles and difficulties I choose not to disclose. I work hard to present the best possible version of myself to the world. But who am I really, and who am I trying to impress?

Whether it's me or Anna Sorokin, the desire to present a better version of ourselves than is really the case betrays an internal struggle to come to terms with who we are, or with who we would like to be, or with who we feel we should be. Dissatisfaction with our identity is a challenge for all of us. And things have become more complicated of late. What we might call 'personal identity' has been called into question in ways that our ancestors would never have dreamed possible. There are more things we can now choose about who we are and who we become than ever before. In days gone by, our status, our jobs, our social standing, our marital partners were all predetermined. If you were born a baker you would die a baker; if you were born a serf you would die a serf. But now a supermarket shelf stacker can become a rock star, a market trader can become a business tycoon. Not only that, we are immersed in advertising that tells us that buying the right aftershave, clothes or car can make us the kind of person we dream of becoming. Our identities can be carefully curated and constructed, and yet many of us are plagued with such self-doubt, such self-reproach and such low self-esteem that we struggle to understand who we truly are.[2]

This paradox hits me every time I travel to the house in which I was brought up. I was born in Brighton in the 1970s, and my father still lives in the family home. When I visit him, everything is pretty much the same as it was back then. It has the same geometrically tessellating brown and orange carpet in the hallways. The same avocado bathroom suite. The same yellow paisley sheets and pink chenille bedspreads on the same beds. The same dusty copies of *Reader's Digest* on the same shelves. It also has the same pictures hanging on the walls. They are pictures of a boy in desperate need of a haircut, sporting thick-rimmed glasses with his various school uniforms, or wearing one of the many brown corduroy outfits handed down to him by older cousins, and that knitted tank top his mother claimed he even wore to bed.

Who was that child? And what happened to him? In one sense they are photographs of me, but the 'me' I see myself as now is so very far removed from the 'me' that was that boy. And the 'me' others see or project is totally different again. Ask other people who I am and they may define me in terms of my job or my qualifications, my ethnicity or my faith, or in relation to the books or social media posts I have written. Local friends define me as 'the one with all the kids', or use some less polite way of describing an unusually large family. My children introduce me to their friends with a health warning that I will probably talk too much, ask too many questions, and tell terrible jokes. Who am I really?

The challenge with personal identity is that although it is absolutely fundamental, it is frustratingly difficult to pin down. This dichotomy has led to new levels of fluidity when it comes, for example, to our professional life, our styling and image, and even our sexual and gender identity. The long-term mental health implications of continually renegotiating who we are or how we present ourselves remain to be seen. Moreover, many of us are juggling multiple identities. Who we are in public and in private, at work and at home, in school and on social media is not always the same person.

The Church has had an answer to this for a long time. Our primary identity is our divinely given one – the person God made us to be. When we know that we are God's children, created, loved and chosen by him, belonging to him, shaped and protected by him, everything else becomes subsidiary. Sometimes the Church has been guilty of broadcasting this too loudly, and ignoring or over-simplifying the complexities of the issues involved. The Bible, from the first book to the last, recognises the challenges of our identity and factors that contribute to it. From the fracture lines to our sense of self recognised in the curse in Genesis, to the preservation of culture and language when the new heavens and the new earth are described in

Revelation,[3] Scripture gives us a nuanced and balanced framework to understand the very many factors differentiating one human being from another: race, ethnicity, age, gender, gifting, relationship status, health and vocation, to name but a few. Scripture also gives us clarity on the imperative of showing equal value, honour, dignity, love and respect to all people, whatever our difficulties and differences.[4] And it challenges us to respect the good gifts God gives us in the form of social structures such as government, Church and family that can help different people find the same security.

While nature and nurture, history and heritage may shape our identity – for better or worse – and must be taken into consideration, there is something fundamentally important about grasping the oft-neglected but nevertheless core teaching of the Church that has sustained millions of Christians for two millennia: we are God's children. Perhaps the Church has also been guilty of being too quiet about this. We are told clearly in Scripture that our identity in Christ as the children of God relativises every demographic difference, every social barrier, every class structure, every ethnic, gender and class division that separates and divides our societies:

So in Christ Jesus you are all children of God through faith, for all of you who were baptised into Christ have clothed yourself with Christ. There is neither Jew nor Gentile, neither slave nor free, nor is there male and female, for you are all one in Christ Jesus.

(Galatians 3:26–8)

I meet many Christians who struggle with their identity as God's children, and it is a struggle for which I have great sympathy. Just as I would rather not show you the pictures of me aged six in my father's house, so I would rather not, to be honest, talk about myself as a child of God. I'd rather show you pictures of me speaking to a packed room, or parade the most impressive version of my CV, or tell you about the important people who follow me on social media. When it comes to understanding my spiritual identity, I'd much rather see myself as an ambassador for Christ, an evangelist, a conqueror, an heir; these descriptors seem far more appealing, more heroic, more glorious. Defining myself as God's child can feel infantalising, disempowering, degrading even.

The struggles that come with identifying as a child of God may lead us to the conclusion that embracing our identity as an *adopted* child of God would be even harder. But what if the reverse was true? What if the truth of our spiritual adoption could in fact help us with all the various forms of our identity crises? What if adoption were the secret that changed everything about 'me'?

A day in court

As I stood before the judge with my polished boots squeaking and my heart racing, I felt out of place. I had tried to present myself as a worthy candidate for becoming an adopter and as a good father while the social workers had thoroughly scrutinised every aspect of my family's life. And now, here I was in my best suit trying to convince a judge that I was a well-meaning citizen who intended to give this little girl everything she could ever want or need.

The child wriggling in my arms was oblivious to any façade. She wasn't going to sit still or be quiet however much we had dressed her up for the occasion. She was oblivious to the anxieties racing through my mind: what happens if we fail? What if we are not deemed good enough? What if the judge rejects us as adopters because we are Christians? What if he finds me guilty of being a substandard father or a spiritual fraudster? She was oblivious to the location: a building where people go to be examined, cross-examined, judged, sentenced, punished. She was oblivious to the implications: that a man with a funny wig and a little hammer had the power to redesign her future, reassign her name, and realign her identity. That she would be stuck with us for the rest of her childhood. She was oblivious to the tears of relief and joy and excitement as we were finally declared a family. All she really was interested in was whether it was yet time to go to the ice-cream parlour adjacent to the courthouse, as promised.

I was not oblivious. I was only too aware of the agonising wait for the decision, of the fears and concerns that were making my heart race, of the significance of what was happening and the weight of the legal system, of the implications – that these four children beside me would be equally entitled to everything I could give them. I needn't have worried so much. The judge loved adoptions. He said it was the best part of his job and invited all of my children to come and sit with him and play with his judge's paraphernalia. And as I walked out into the sunlight, a huge weight was lifted. I knew that, unlike many people who walk into that court-room, I had walked out a free man, uncondemned, but, more than that, I had walked out legally and irrevocably connected to the girl in my arms I could now introduce as my daughter. She had a new identity. That meant I had a new identity too – I had become an adoptive father.

Later that night I turned to Romans 8 because I knew I could relate to the part where Paul writes about the agonising wait for adoption. Imagine my surprise when I read again the rest of the chapter. It was as though Paul had been in that courtroom with me:

Therefore, there is now no condemnation for those who are in Christ Jesus, because through Christ Jesus the law of the Spirit who gives life has set you free from the law of sin and death. For what the law was powerless to do because it was weakened by the flesh, God did by sending his own Son in the likeness of sinful flesh to be a sin offering. And so he condemned sin in the flesh, in order that the righteous requirement of the law might be fully met in us, who do not live according to the flesh but according to the Spirit . . .

For those who are led by the Spirit of God are the children of God. The Spirit you received does not make you slaves, so that you live in fear again; rather, the Spirit you received brought about your adoption to sonship. And by him we cry, 'Abba, Father.' The Spirit himself testifies with our spirit that we are God's children. Now if we are children, then we are heirs – heirs of God and co-heirs with Christ, if indeed we share in his sufferings in order that we may also share in his glory.

(Romans 8:1–4, 14–17)

Paul recognises that we are often burdened by self-condemnation, worrying about whether we are measuring up, living in fear, thinking of ourselves as failures, enslaved to the demands and expectations of others, or by our physical appetites and temptations. And he wants us to know that the Spirit of adoption can help us know who we are and celebrate it.

More than justified

The prior seven chapters of Paul's letter to the Romans highlight the fact that all of us are facing charges for which we should be found guilty in God's court of law. We have been caught red-handed. There is incontrovertible evidence against us. There is no excuse and there are no extenuating circumstances. We deserve to feel condemned. But there is a dramatic shift in tone between chapter seven and chapter eight. It is as if the judge has adjourned to the privacy of his chambers to make his deliberations and decide on the sentencing. Then he comes back into the courtroom to declare that, although we are guilty and he has to mete out the full extent of the punishment for our crimes, there is nevertheless to be no condemnation for us, no penalty to pay, no fine to remunerate.

More of us than we might imagine live our Christian lives as though we haven't heard God pronounce us innocent and free to go. Instead we continue to live with a sense of obligation, shame and fear of being caught out. I have seen this insecurity work its way out in very different ways. It makes some of us mean, it makes some of us brash, it makes some of us timid. Being uncertain of our forgiveness and insecure in our identity can have myriad toxic consequences.

Sometimes the fact that God has told us there is

no condemnation ironically seems to induce its own sense of condemnation. Some of us are still trying to earn our way out of that debt as well as attempting to pay back everything else we think we owe for our sins. We may have been convicted, but we are not condemned. We were guilty, but we have been declared righteous. But when that pardon and freedom make us feel guilty, something is terribly wrong. When we punish ourselves even when God is not punishing us, it makes a mockery of God's grace.[5]

Grace is an explosive idea. The unmerited gift of God to humanity has inspired a million songs and much activity. When the Church grasps it, it cannot help but share this incredible gift with the whole world. This amazing truth of justification has been rightly celebrated throughout the history of the Church and around the global Church. It is often regarded as the pinnacle of salvation, the central treasure of the gospel, the end of the story.

But forgiveness is not the end of the story. It is only half the story when it comes to God's amazing grace. The courthouse where God justifies you is the same courtroom where he declares you adopted. When you are declared free, you are also declared family. When you walk out of that building uncondemned and released from guilt and servitude, you also walk out with a new identity. The doctrine of adoption takes the doctrine of justification to a whole deeper level.

When the two are put together, we appreciate both better. It is a double celebration.

J.I. Packer, the world-renowned reformed scholar, agrees:

> *[Adoption] is the highest privilege that the gospel offers: higher even than justification . . . That justification – by which we mean God's forgiveness of the past together with his acceptance for the future – is the primary and fundamental blessing of the gospel is not in question. Justification is the primary blessing, because it meets our primary spiritual need. We all stand by nature under God's judgment; his law condemns us; guilt gnaws at us, making us restless, miserable, and in our lucid moments afraid; we have no peace in ourselves because we have no peace with our Maker . . . In adoption, God takes us into his family and fellowship – he establishes us as his children and heirs. Closeness, affection and generosity are at the heart of the relationship. To be right with God the Judge is a great thing, but to be loved and cared for by God the Father is a greater.*[6]

Imagine a man released from debt. He never wants to see that loan shark again. Imagine a woman reprimanded by the judge for misconduct and sent away to do community service. Despite his kindness, she never wants to cross the judge's path again. Imagine a teenager, caught by a police officer who flushes her drugs down a nearby drain. She knows the officer has risked her job for her, but she still seeks to avoid her for as long as she can. The exchange is complete. The transaction is done. Many of us treat God like this. Our faith may as well be a get-out-of-hell-free card that is stuffed to the back of a drawer or in a subfolder in our email filing system. It is archived and assigned to our history. It is there if we need it, but we are moving on. It becomes a status we can draw on in emergencies rather than the beating heart of who we are. We sense we would do best to avoid God as far as we are able to.

Adoption changes the story and raises the bar. There is not only reprieve, there is also relationship. There is not only freedom from the past, there is also family and a future. There is not only a Judge who makes us right, there is a Father who draws us close, and a Spirit who testifies to our spirit that we are his children, co-heirs with Christ. The family that is the Trinity has included us – legally and irrevocably. There is no condemnation – but there *is* celebration.

Sometimes I think we are like my daughter that day in court. We can be oblivious to what is going on, because someone mentioned ice cream. Our identity, our history, our future, our freedom, our inheritance are all being worked out and we are playing with the gavel. If only we understood the full implications. What God has done means that we are stuck with him forever come what may. By God's grace we are both justified and adopted. Everything has changed.

The trouble is that appropriating our new identity as the forgiven and adopted children of God takes more time than we might realise.

One of my daughter's favourite films is *The Princess Diaries*.[7] It's the story of a teenager living in relative poverty with her single mother. She is a slightly goofy kid and doesn't quite fit in with her peers, and then a limousine turns up at her house and the driver informs her that there's more to her identity than she knows. She is, in fact, the last-surviving heir to the throne of the country of Genovia, a princess who will inherit a magnificent kingdom complete with a picturesque castle, a fortune in wealth and an eligible, handsome prince. The book and the film were wildly popular because this is the dream that many a pre-teen girl harbours. Perhaps this dream taps into a deeper longing, in fact. Perhaps we all secretly long to know that our lives really matter, that we are not just run-of-the-mill clones, that we are more than merely another employee, statistic, or national insurance number. Perhaps we long to know that we are royalty, waiting for our kingdom to appear. And perhaps that longing is not as far-fetched as we might assume.

The bulk of the storyline of the film is dedicated to exploring the culture shock that this young woman from San Francisco finds herself in when she arrives into the European elegance of Genovia. She is the heir to the throne, but she does not know how to live out that identity, and so she must learn what it involves before her coronation takes place. The transition time, between knowing who she is officially and accepting her identity and all it entails, is the interesting part of the story. I feel the same about the Christian life. Christians are a people of great hope. We longingly await our coronation as the sons and daughters – heirs and heiresses – of the King, but how do we live that identity in the meantime, in the time lag? How can we learn the etiquette of the future kingdom, leaving behind the culture and mindset of our past? What if we fail, misunderstand things, and relapse into our old habits? We can be reassured – according to the Spirit of adoption, our destiny is assured. Our performance does not dictate the fulfilment of the promise.

Who am I?

Sometimes people ask my daughter about her biological family. When they refer to them as her 'real family' it can undermine, for her, the reality of her status in my family. Because of adoption she may have to wrestle with the nature-versus-nurture debate to work out who she 'really' is. She may have to work out what it means to belong to two family trees. She may wonder what life would have been like with a different name, different expectations and different values.

Adoption seems to go hand in hand with identity struggles. Adoption forces us to question who we really are, who we really belong to, where we will display our allegiance. This might be good news. For those of us who struggle to embrace our identity as God's children, we can be reassured that, because of our adoption, these internal wrestlings are perfectly normal. So normal, in fact, that God has made a plan to help us. He sends his Spirit of adoption to be a constant help and comfort to us in this. According to Paul in Romans 8, the Spirit of adoption can bring release from the past, encouragement in the present and hope for the future.

I will always feel embarrassed about the photographs of a long-haired bespectacled boy in brown corduroy outfits hanging on the walls in my father's house. I no longer look like the child that I was then. I have changed a lot. But they also give me a peculiar hope. Looking back on the photos reminds me that there is a time lag in my relationship with God too. I still have a long way to go to fully realise my God-given identity. I often get side-tracked by petty insecurities and weighed down by deep, recurring anxieties and feelings of self-condemnation. But all that can change. After all, one day I will have a kingdom to inherit, a celebration to attend, a Family to meet.

As I look forward to that, I take comfort from the words of the courageous Christian martyr Dietrich Bonhoeffer, who was imprisoned and executed for his opposition to the Nazis. He wrote this poem from his prison cell shortly before he was killed:

Who am I? This or the Other?
Am I one person today, and tomorrow another?
Am I both at once? A hypocrite before others,
And before myself a contemptible woebegone weakling?
Or is it something within me still like a beaten
* army*
Fleeing in disorder from victory already achieved?
Who am I? They mock me, these lonely questions of
* mine.*
Whoever I am, Thou knowest, O God, I am thine![8]

~

Questions for reflection

1. What are the different ways in which we might struggle with our identity? Why is it so difficult for us often to accept that we are God's children?

2. Why does J.I. Packer describe adoption as the highest privilege the gospel offers? How might this challenge your appreciation of your salvation and your identity?

3. Read Bonhoeffer's poem. How does it help you to know that the most inspiring of Christians are not immune to the most fundamental struggles of identity and self-understanding? What peace can you find in his conclusion that God knows exactly who we are, and claims us as his own?

Chapter 3

The secret that changes everything about church

Why water is thicker than blood —
and chaos more welcome than order.

A team of scholars and their doctoral students were sitting in the heat of the African sun listening in rapt silence to a wise old Kenyan pastor share his story of how he had become a Christian. With tears running down his face, he explained his Muslim family's reaction to his conversion, and how he was subsequently thrown out of his home. Not only that, but when he refused to recant his confession in Christ he was forced to flee from his village to save his life. Many miles away from home, he sought sanctuary in a church building. The Christian community there welcomed him with open arms. They gave him a corner of the building to live in and a mattress on the floor, together with food generously delivered on a daily basis. The man was extremely grateful for their protection and hospitality.

I sat with the listening students and scholars, feeling deeply moved by his story and how the tragedy had ended so happily. But the story wasn't finished. It was not a happy ending after all. The pastor continued, confiding that life was tough being, in effect, a refugee. Despite the hospitality of the church, the hardest part of his week was on Sunday morning after the service when everyone went home to their families and their Sunday lunches, leaving him alone in the building with a plate of food to eat by himself. That was when it hit him – he had truly lost everything. Although he was welcome to make his home inside the church building, he was not welcome inside the homes of the church family.

This was no small distinction, I realised. During my own difficult period – by comparison, light and minor – when I struggled to sense God's love and presence, I went to church. I shared the bread and the wine, even with those who meant to do me harm. I closed my eyes during the prayers, lifted my voice during the singing and took notes during the sermons. I got there early to help put out chairs and tables and stayed behind to wash up the coffee mugs. Sometimes I preached. Sometimes I organised youth events. A little like the Kenyan pastor, I was seeking refuge in the church. But true refuge can no more be found in an event than it can in a building. What we were both missing were true, secure, intimate relationships. Church is supposed to be more than an event or a building – church is supposed to be family.

There is an account in Luke's Gospel where Jesus explains this. He has just outlined to a rich young upstart the financial cost of being a disciple. Without apology, Jesus instructed him to sell off all his assets and donate the proceeds to the poor. The disciples balked – that was not a good message for their recruitment drive. Who would choose to follow Jesus with a message as hard as that? But instead of backing down and minimising the challenge of discipleship, Jesus pressed the point home even further. Not only should people expect to lose all their possessions, they might, like my Kenyan friend, lose all their family too. But Jesus made a solemn promise to compensate for that costly sacrifice:

> *'Truly I tell you,' Jesus said to them, 'no one who has left home or wife or brothers or sisters or parents or children for the sake of the kingdom of God will fail to receive many times as much in this age, and in the age to come eternal life.'*
>
> *(Luke 18:29–30)*

According to Jesus, those who convert to Christianity at great relational cost will receive many times more brothers, sisters, parents and children in the here and now. How is this possible? It is through the alternative family of the church that we receive relationships that can act as a substitute for those that we have lost.

But that is not what the Kenyan convert running for his life had experienced. The church building provided shelter, the church members provided sustenance, and the church events provided sacraments and spiritual teaching – but none of these were a substitute for the lifelong, intimate commitment of a family.

It is relatively rare that I meet people like the Kenyan pastor, who have lost family because of conversion to Christianity. However, I meet people every day whose families have been torn apart for other reasons: violence, abuse, mental health crises, poverty, conflict, drugs, war, illness, tragedy. I expect you could tell me your own stories of the terrible impact family breakdown has had on those you know and love. How reassuring it is that Jesus affirms the importance of family – both now and after death. How wonderful that family is not restricted to those who share our DNA. How incredible that Jesus proposes that the church could be involved in the creation of a new intimate, supportive, protective family for those who have lost their natural family.

Jesus portrays the church as an alternative family whose members, despite not being genetically connected, are committed to one another with the same intensity that blood relatives might feel for one another. The church is described as a family formed through covenant and commitment despite different ancestry and parenthood. That sounds a lot like adoption to me.

Church is family

So what does it mean to be a family? When is a family a family? That was a question I had to ask myself when I began fostering. Is it the sharing of a building? Was I connected to my fostered and birth children only when we were under the same roof? Is it the sharing of an activity? Were we only family when we were gathered around the dinner table? Or out on a trip to the beach? Or when I was involved in teaching the little ones to tie their shoelaces, or helping my teenagers understand Shakespeare? Family is more than any of this. It is a 'we' that is bigger than the sum of its 'I' parts. It is a unit even though we are many different members. It is a togetherness even when we are scattered. It is a bond that can exist even when we live on opposite sides of the planet or have only just met. It is a covenant for the future whatever happened in the past. It is a relational entity that moves forward without leaving anyone behind.

Too often we explain the gospel in terms of a personal relationship with God. Although partly true, the emphasis can be misleading. When I adopted my daughter it did not only affect the relationship between her and me. A family that goes from five people to six immediately increases the number of individual relationships from ten to fifteen. And then there are new aunts, uncles, cousins, grandparents. Relationships increase exponentially. The doctrine of adoption teaches us that when we become a Christian, God becomes our Father, Jesus our brother, the Spirit our comforter, and the church becomes the family to which we belong, with all the multitude of relationships that that entails. Because of adoption, the church was never supposed to be just a building, or just an event – it was always supposed to be family.

There is something about a newborn that displays that brilliantly. Each foster baby that arrives in our family quickly makes him or herself at home in church too. From the moment they enter the service they are surrounded by children trying to make them gurgle and smile. When they begin to tire, some kind-hearted soul will scoop them up and soothe them before passing them on to their neighbour, who will forego all their natural inhibitions in order to communicate in baby language, helping them feel safe and valued. By the end of the service the baby has been entertained, fed and winded and is sleeping peacefully in somebody's arms. There is a warmth and a goodwill that intuitively goes out from young and old, rich and poor, male and female as the foster child who is between families is effectively adopted by the family that is the church. But the church benefits just as much. I've seen it in even the most formal and impersonal of churches: the boundaries come down and the baby inspires an intimacy that speaks volumes about the fundamental importance of family connection: acceptance, belonging, commitment.

Unfortunately, a lot of our language presents and reinforces the idea that church is simply an event where religious goods and services are dispensed. We talk about 'going to church'. We hear terms like 'shopping around' for a church, or 'church hopping'. Some Christians are willing to commute long distances to 'attend' a 'brand' of church that 'works' for them. You don't have to look too far to find a pastor frustrated about a new church that has turned up close by, lamenting the number of young people or families who have left to join this latest show in town. But sometimes those same pastors admit that this may, at least in part, be a problem of their own making. Look at any church website and you'll see that what are advertised are worship services for us to enjoy, sermons for us to listen to, youth provision for our children and perhaps a small group that can provide for other needs. We post pictures of our smart buildings, of our edgy youth work and our well-designed sermon series; we invest time and money into brilliant branding and a hip visual identity – thereby to some extent buying into a marketing mindset and promulgating the idea that our churches exist primarily as events for consumer Christians to attend.

Part of the reason for the popularity of the idea that church is an event comes from an oft-quoted definition articulated in the sixteenth-century Augsburg Confession: 'The Church is the congregation of saints, in which the Gospel is rightly taught and the Sacraments are rightly administered.'[1]

This definition was originally formulated while the Protestant Reformation was exploding across Europe, and was worded specifically to exclude the Roman Catholic churches of the time from being seen as genuine churches. For that moment in history it was revolutionary, bravely challenging the errors of the day, helping people to differentiate between authentic and failing churches. But it was a bit like the treasury department's advice regarding bank notes: it is helpful to know that the genuine ones have a watermark and a serial number, but those features do not fully define a bank note, let alone indicate anything of the purpose and function of money. Similarly, the Augsburg Confession's definition may have been helpful in the sixteenth century as a litmus test, but it does not define the purpose or function of the church. Yes, it is important that the Word of God is rightly preached and the sacraments are rightly administered, but there is so much more to church. Misapplying the information only leads to the development of a transactional or consumer model of church.

I believe that Bible teaching and sacraments are an important part of church life in the same way that helping my children with their homework and providing food for them are important parts of family life. But if that was the only way I related to my children you would wonder what kind of parent I was. Or if I were to define parenting as remembering to be there to photograph my child's sports day, piano recital or birthday party, you would probably argue I had a reductionist and limited understanding of parenting. In the same way, we misunderstand church if we only turn up to Sunday services, Bible studies and prayer meetings and exclude the Bible's clear teaching to 'love one another',[2] 'carry each other's burdens',[3] 'encourag[e] one another'[4] and 'spur one another on toward love and good deeds'.[5] These ongoing commitments to the members of our church family don't fit neatly into the confines of a Sunday worship service. Adoption provides us with a new definition of church which locks into our approach to church life commitments of love and belonging, intimacy and family.

Water is thicker than blood

The children in my home, whether mine by birth, fostering or adoption, are all genuinely part of the family as far as I am concerned. They are included in every meal, every family conversation, every holiday, every festival. In my eyes they have equal value, dignity and worth. It does not matter whether they are with us for a few weeks or a few decades; relationally, they all get the same rights and treatment because blood is not thicker than water according to my understanding of the gospel. The water of baptism unites us together as a family in a way that even relativises genetic relationships.

This is what Jesus wanted the world to know when he refused, on one occasion, to speak to his mother Mary and his brothers. He had been interrupted from preaching to the crowd to be told they were standing outside waiting to speak to him, and he replied:

> *'Who is my mother, and who are my brothers?'*
> *Pointing to his disciples, he said, 'Here are my mother*
> *and my brothers. For whoever does the will of my*
> *Father in heaven is my brother and sister and mother.'*
> (Matthew 12:48–50)

Jesus, who loved his mother so much that he made provision for her care even on the cross,[6] claims that those who serve God are as important to him as the family who raised him. Jesus, who affirms the Mosaic Law that argued that failing to care for your parents is a crime against the God-given value of family,[7] demonstrates that walking away from those who do the will of God the Father is also a crime against the God-given value of family. Jesus, who promised that we would face persecution, even from family, for our faith, also promises that the church can be a substitute family. Being adopted into the family of God gives us the same rights to access Jesus as the brothers and mother who shared some of his DNA. It also gives us the right to expect the same sense of acceptance, belonging and commitment we should expect to find in a biological family.

The Bible depicts a church community whose members are so committed to one another that it could, if required to do so, replace a genetic family. For example, Paul instructs Timothy that he should treat older women as mothers, younger women as sisters, older men as fathers and younger men as brothers.[8] This is typical of Paul's teaching and example. At the end of the letter to the Romans, Paul sends greetings to the church, asking to be remembered to his 'sister Phoebe' and Rufus's mother, 'who has been a mother to me, too'.[9] There is a depth of intimacy indicated in these greetings that may well have been forged during times of common persecution, as a result of separation from wider biological family, and also out of common courageous service to God in difficult and dangerous times.

We also have common ground with our church family because of our common connection with Christ, and because of our common foundation on God's Word. In Ephesians, Paul declares that there is a transformation that comes from being adopted into God's family:

> *Consequently, you are no longer foreigners and strangers,*
> *but fellow citizens with God's people and also members*
> *of his household, built on the foundation of the apostles*
> *and prophets, with Christ Jesus himself as the chief*
> *cornerstone.*
>
> *(Ephesians 2:19–20)*

If we allow adoption to inform our understanding of church, we will recognise that some of the criteria we use for choosing whether to join or stay at a church are not always informed by Scripture. When I go to family gatherings, I don't expect my sister to provide restaurant-standard food, and I don't expect my son to choose a playlist that I would enjoy. I do expect there to be a bit of tension between the crabby uncle and anyone who crosses his path. It will doubtless feel a bit cramped, one of the kids will have a meltdown and we won't have as much fun as the family next door – but there's no way I'd consider leaving my family because of these things, yet I have met many people who use exactly these criteria for leaving churches. I have met people who have left their local church over the diet of teaching provided, over the quality of music on offer, or in favour of the more happening church down the road. This may demonstrate that the bonds of love that tie us together have been disintegrated by the acid of consumerism. If we see the church as our adopted family it will help us to resist that, and re-envision our approach to our communal life as Christians.

The church-as-family metaphor offers a healthy counterbalance to the church-as-event mindset. It can be an antidote to the more individualistic – sadly, even consumptive – models of church participation. Families look out for one another, families are committed to each other for the long haul. Families' bonds are strong and, wherever possible, permanent. They support one another through tragedy and triumph. Families are not making economic calculations about cost and benefit. They are committed for better or worse, for richer and poorer.

Chaos is normal

When I say these sorts of things from the stage at conferences, there will always be a queue of people waiting to speak to me afterwards, and they all say the same thing: 'But you haven't seen *my* church!' I then go on to hear horror stories of churches where the leaders are involved in affairs, where divisions have occurred over the coffee rota, or where satanic forces are allegedly at work against the technology or in the lack of syncopation in the worship band. My heart goes out to them. They remind me of a church I once attended, when I was most in need of the love and support of a church family, but when I saw more conflict, hypocrisy and dissension than I dared believe was possible among those who called themselves God's people.

Adopting my little girl helped me refresh my understanding of church in two ways. First of all, it helped me grasp that because I was adopted by God, the church was automatically my new family. Therefore, our corporate life together is supposed to be marked by a radical and supernatural hospitality, by intimacy, and by a covenant commitment to one another. Second, it helped me understand that just as family is hardly ever straightforward, so in the church, too, there will be complexities, histories and personalities that will necessarily be difficult to work through.

The dynamics of my family when I had two young birth sons is very different to what it is today. Back then, it was relatively simple to make decisions, to take holidays, to manage discipline strategies and treat days. Now I have children in my family who have faced significant amounts of trauma, neglect and abuse. I have children in my family who have disabilities and learning difficulties. One goes into meltdown if something gets dropped. Another can't easily hold a knife and fork or a pen or a toothbrush. One can't cope with noise and crowds. Another can't cope with quiet and predictability. One wants to watch the same cartoons over and over while the other wants to watch new politics documentaries. One wants to do her homework in peace, and another wants to sing at the top of her voice. Our preferences, our needs, our personalities, our talents, our ages are so different that it can make family life pretty chaotic and complicated.

Some adopters don't get this. Many set out to find an easy baby, as close as possible to a perfect child with no baggage, no strings and no complications. Perhaps this baby is supposed to replace the child that they were hoping to have through natural birth. Because of this, both locally and around the world, older children, sibling groups, children from minority ethnic families and those with additional needs or additional trauma wait the longest to find adoptive families. God's adoption of us was very different. God seems to delight in welcoming the most diverse, the most vulnerable, the most chaotic and the most complicated people.

The requirements for being adopted into God's family do not involve power, prestige, perfection, personality or performance. When Paul is reviewing the membership of the Corinthian church, he first acknowledges those who belong to it as his siblings and then notes how God brought them together as family despite their natural disadvantages:

> *Brothers and sisters, think of what you were when you were called. Not many of you were wise by human standards; not many were influential; not many were of noble birth. But God chose the foolish things of the world to shame the wise; God chose the weak things of the world to shame the strong. God chose the lowly things of this world and the despised things – and the things that are not – to nullify the things that are, so that no one may boast before him.*
>
> *(1 Corinthians 1:26–9)*

Because God has offered us welcome and hospitality despite our history, backgrounds and ongoing behaviours, we can expect a degree of chaos and complexity in our churches. Not only should we expect it, we should welcome it. By grace our church families are formed, and grace is to be modelled to one another and to outsiders. The trickier the context, the greater the grace that may be required. But the more conscious we are of our own adoption story, the more likely we are to be patient and hospitable and forbearing with our local church.

Adoption is the secret that changes everything about church. Church is not an event or a transaction or a building or even a community or a religious duty – it is family. As with any adoptive family, we can expect to find not only radical hospitality that is prepared to cross boundaries and overcome obstacles, but a certain amount of chaos. And just as we see time and again on the pages of our Bible, it is in the middle of family chaos that God does the most incredible and beautiful things.

~

Questions for reflection

1. Consider your church: in what ways does it present itself as an event, as a service provider, as a business and as a family?

2. To what extent are you extended family to people in your church? What practical things can you do to invest more deeply into the relationships in your church?

3. 'The more conscious we are of our own adoption story, the more likely we are to be patient and hospitable and forbearing with our local church.' In what ways can you experience this link between God's adoption of you and your involvement in God's family?

Chapter 4

The secret that changes everything about prayer

*Fixing broken attachments –
and finding new connections.*

Aged five months, the little girl we would go on to adopt would smile when I walked into the room, loudly shout or cry when she needed something and babble happily at her foster brothers and sisters. Three months later, those instincts had suddenly gone. It was heartbreaking to see our once-bubbly little bundle of energy sit expressionless on my lap, eyes glazed over, silent and apparently lost. In the intervening weeks she had gone to stay with a birth relative in an institution in London, which social services and the legal team thought might help the family get the necessary help for them to stay together. I do not know exactly what happened there. I expect she experienced multiple carers. Maybe she took part in experimental therapies. I have no doubt that the damp old building with its leaking ceilings caused her to physically suffer. I assume she felt we had abandoned her. Instead of familiar faces and predictable routine, chaos and anxiety took over and caused something inside of her to shut down. The social worker thought she might never recover.

From the moment we are born we have an instinct to seek the proximity and protection of an adult for survival. We are dependent on the physical and emotional availability of a predictable caregiver to look after us. If that care is not given, particularly when we are under stress, it has a huge influence on how we see ourselves, our world, and the people around us. This idea, now universally accepted, is called 'attachment theory', and it was first recorded by psychologists John Bowlby and Mary Ainsworth as they studied disturbed children in the 1970s.[1] Attachment theory explains something of the distress my adopted daughter experienced in her first year of life, and some of the knock-on effects that has had. Perhaps it seems obvious, but the implications of attachment issues for babies in terms of a lifetime of human relationships and flourishing are profound. As a foster carer, I have seen many times the way that broken and disordered attachment radically impacts the way that children in our care react when we seek to offer them stability and security, love and affection, discipline and comfort.

As a Christian, I have seen the way that broken and disordered attachment can impact our relationship with God, too.[2] Our spiritual life story begins with the chaotic temptations, abuses and consequences of sin, which sometimes seem so appealing and addictive, yet at other times we sense something of how cruel and destructive they are. Then God in his grace and mercy steps in and offers us freedom and a welcome into a new family. This transition from strangers to children, from slaves to heirs, from enemies to family is not a natural one. That is why one of the Holy Spirit's primary tasks is continually to assure our hearts and minds that we really do have the right to address God as Father.

A sacred synergy

Issues stemming from broken attachments take a long time to work through and, for this reason, those considering adopting a child are usually sent for attachment training. The knowledge you get from studying attachment theory can transform your relationship with your adopted child in both the short and the long term. The insights I have gleaned over the years from therapeutically parenting children with attachment issues have also, strangely, transformed the way I understand prayer and my relationship with God.

There are a number of problems and paradoxes that we commonly experience when it comes to prayer. Why, despite an intrinsic desire to pray, do we still find it so difficult? Why do we feel so isolated when God doesn't seem to answer? Why can prayer sometimes bring us great peace, and at other times cause great frustration? Why does it feel like prayer doesn't work most of the time? Doesn't God care about what we want? Or is he just too busy to involve himself in our lives? Is it because my requests are too trivial, or too complex, that God doesn't immediately intervene? Is it because of something I've done, or something I've not done? Is my faith too weak, or my words too few, or my attitudes too unholy?

I believe that our adoption into God's family can be the secret to unlocking not only the untold mystery of prayer but also its untold majesty. Adoption gives us a frame of reference which helps us understand the significance and the struggles of prayer, particularly in a context of relationships that are both fractured and restored, temporary and permanent, stressful and secure. Until we have understood our adoption we will never really make sense of prayer, and until we have understood prayer, we will never really make sense of who we are as adopted children of God. There is a sacred synergy between our prayer life and our adoption.

A new hope

Prayer is one of God's primary mechanisms for deepening and exploring our relationship with him. Prayer is the way that we spend time together, converse together, find comfort, guidance, reassurance. It is the means by which we build trust, intimacy and depth in the strange new relationship in which we find ourselves. It is the safe place, the secure base where our broken attachment with God, together with all of its knock-on effects, can get reordered and repaired.

A powerful starting point given to us by God when it comes to seeing prayer as a way of repairing our attachment to him is the Lord's Prayer. This scripted prayer is difficult for some of us. Perhaps we have recited it so often that it has lost its meaning. It might be that the terminology used does not seem to connect with our own struggles. But when we view it not as a spell, a ritual or a formality, but as a reframing tool given to us by God for our flourishing, perhaps we can access some of its life-changing power. The Lord's Prayer was never supposed to restrict our relationship, it was given to help restore it. Like a parent helping a child find the words to express their deepest feelings, so God here graciously encourages and enables us to begin talking to him about the stuff that really matters – our relationships, our fears, our daily struggles, our temptations, our longings, our future, our identity:

This, then, is how you should pray:
'Our Father in heaven,
hallowed be your name,
your kingdom come,
your will be done,
*   on earth as it is in heaven.*
Give us today our daily bread.
And forgive us our debts,
*   as we also have forgiven our debtors.*
And lead us not into temptation,
but deliver us from the evil one.'

(Matthew 6:9–13)

These words can reshape, reboot and refocus our prayers, offering a rhythm for expressing our own hurts and needs, setting a pace that is neither arduous nor mindless. In the context of the religious teaching of the day, which said prayers had to be showy and wordy, this short and simple example gave hope to those who prayed in secret,[3] who prayed on their knees, who didn't know where to start or what to say. Jesus saw right through the sham and pretence of many religious leaders and offered a model of authenticity and hope for everyone.

There are three main sections to the Lord's Prayer, and each is given a powerful new perspective when we factor in our adoption into God's family. First comes our ability to call God 'Father' and learn where we belong; second is the implication of our new identity and learning how we are accepted; and, third comes the resources we can rely on as we learn when to trust our Father's provision.

A new bond

I will never forget one little boy who turned up on my doorstep wearing his school uniform and carrying just his lunch box and his swimming kit in his hands. He was so full of rage that his face was permanently red and it looked like every muscle in his body was tight and constricted. All he wanted was to be able to go home. But he never did. I found him once on a laptop zooming in on Google Earth desperately trying to find his house. My heart went out to him. He felt so betrayed, displaced. Nine months later, I drove that little boy to a new family who had promised to care for him for the rest of his life. It was a journey we had made frequently over the previous weeks as they had got to know each other. This time would be the last, and now he had significantly more than his swimming kit with him. Surrounded by suitcases full of clothes, a bike, and toys and mementos of his time with us, he was excited and nervous. After a while, having been unusually quiet, he asked me if I thought it would be okay if he called this new family 'Mum and Dad'. That question broke me, especially knowing how much he had longed to go home. We had to drive a bit slower after that, as the road was blurring through my tears.

Helping a child become ready to call someone else Mum and Dad is one of a foster parent's greatest ambitions. For those children who can't go home again, this is the next best thing. To see them overcome the broken attachments in their life so that they are ready to commit and trust again is a major therapeutic goal. The apostle Paul understood something of this. In both of his clearest expositions of the doctrine of adoption he talks about the Holy Spirit's work in preparing us to call God 'Father'. We have already looked at the occasion in Romans when Paul says it is because of the Spirit of adoption that we cry '*Abba*, Father'.[4] Similarly, in Galatians he says it is the Spirit of adoption whom God sent 'into our hearts, the Spirit who calls out, "Abba, Father."'[5] It is no wonder that Jesus begins the Lord's Prayer by encouraging us to address God as our 'Father'.

There are many other names that God uses throughout the Bible as he helps us know him. Jesus could have taught us to address God as Lord, Yahweh, the Almighty, the Most High, the Everlasting One, the great I AM. Compared with the thousands of times God is introduced with these names in the Old Testament, he is referred to as 'Father' only fourteen times.[6] The great patriarchs and prophets Abraham, Moses, Isaiah and David didn't dare to call God

'Father'. But in the New Testament, Jesus commands his disciples to call God this most intimate of all his names. Paul drives home that sense of intimacy with the word 'Abba', which was Jesus' unique, affectionate way of addressing God. Incredibly, Jesus and the Holy Spirit encourage us to share that privilege – because of our adoption. And because of our adoption, we are to share that privilege with others – we address him not as *my* Father but as *our* Father, affirming our attachment both to God and to one another. Because of our adoption we recognise that God is the ultimate standard of fatherhood – he is *our Father in heaven* – far removed from the deficiencies of our earthly parents and far exceeding the beauty of our earthly parents.

A new acceptance

Immediately following the pronouncement in court that I was now a father to the little girl in my arms, I was given a form to fill in. I had filled in many, many forms over the course of becoming an adopter, but this one seemed momentous. There was a small box where I wrote in her new surname. With that I became her father. And she took on the name 'Kandiah'.

Whenever I read or say the Lord's Prayer now, I am reminded of that life-changing little box as I notice the same link: 'Our *Father* in heaven, hallowed be your *name*'. When we get to call God 'Father', his name becomes our name. His honour becomes our honour. This is a momentous truth that deserves more than a moment's reflection.

I remember going on a primary school trip to France. It was only a short trip across the Channel, but it felt like we were going to the ends of the earth. As we sat on the coach dressed in our simple school uniform, bubbling with excitement, our teachers told us that the reputation of our school rested on our behaviour. This was underlined by the fact that our school sweatshirts carrying the insignia 'Fairlight First School' were visible for all to see. The school uniform helped me to feel safe – even in a new country with a strange language I could spot my party and know where I belonged. It helped me to feel proud – I was representing my school on this important occasion. And it helped me behave as I sought to live up to the expectations of the teachers. As the adopted children of God, everywhere we go, we carry our Father's name and reputation. This should give us first of all security, self-esteem and a sense of belonging; and second, it gives us an incentive to live to honour him.

Some Christians think that our prayer for God's name to be honoured is simply a reminder not to blaspheme. But the Lord's Prayer links it with two other petitions showing that there is much more at stake. 'Hallowed be your name' is closely followed by

'Your kingdom come' and 'Your will be done, on earth as it is in heaven.' God's name will be honoured when his will is done. God's kingdom comes as his will is done on earth as it is in heaven. God's will is done when we live mindful of the name and reputation of God that we carry with us.

This connection is corroborated in the rest of the Bible. Each occasion when God explains that his name has been dishonoured clearly stems from the way his people have failed to offer justice and grace to those around them. Here are two examples from Jeremiah and Amos:

> *But now you have turned around and profaned my name; each of you has taken back the male and female slaves you had set free to go where they wished. You have forced them to become your slaves again.*
>
> *(Jeremiah 34:16)*

> *They trample on the heads of the poor*
> *as on the dust of the ground*
> *and deny justice to the oppressed.*
> *Father and son use the same girl*
> *and so profane my holy name.*
>
> *(Amos 2:7)*

It is as we seek justice, help the poor, and stand up to abuse that we honour God's name, do God's will and usher in God's kingdom. This is our privilege and our responsibility.

But what happens when we don't?

There have been many times when my children have acted in small ways that undermine the reputation of my name. I remember one of them having a tantrum at a church picnic at the age of three. Another was caught, aged five, carving his name onto his school desk while bored in a lesson. Another got a detention for inappropriate language at the age of twelve. Did any of these incidents ever cause me to retract their name? Of course not. I try to love my children unconditionally, which means that although they experienced unenjoyable consequences for their choices, their place in the family, their name, was never in question.

We are accepted by God unconditionally. God loves us when we honour him. He loves us when we fail him. The prophets Amos and Jeremiah were sent to God's people not to disinherit them of his name, but rather to give them a chance to change, to repent and reconcile with God, to remind them to live up to the name they had been given. Similarly, the Lord's Prayer is not teaching us that we must earn our salvation; rather, Jesus is acknowledging that honouring God's name is not always easy, and we need God's help and grace, and the help and grace of our brothers and sisters. Paul leads by example when he writes this to the church in Thessalonica:

With this in mind, we constantly pray for you, that our God may make you worthy of his calling, and that by his power he may bring to fruition your every desire for goodness and your every deed prompted by faith. We pray this so that the name of our Lord Jesus may be glorified in you, and you in him, according to the grace of our God and the Lord Jesus Christ.

(2 Thessalonians 1:11–12)

A new provision

One boy who came into my care always made us smile at mealtimes. Before the rest of the family had gathered at the table, he would run to his place and heap the lion's share of food onto his plate. I used to tell him: 'Trust me – take your time – there's plenty to go round,' but he just couldn't get past the years of feeling hungry and unprovided for before he came into care. And so he always ate like it was his first-ever meal and, at the same time, could be his last.

Sometimes I see myself in that lad when it comes to my prayer life with God. I want it now. I want it all. I'm not really considerate of everyone else's needs. I don't really trust that God has plenty to go around. I don't really learn from experience that God will provide for me tomorrow, just as he did today and yesterday. I need to hear a kind, gentle voice reassuring me that I can trust God to provide for everything, every day.

The final section of the Lord's Prayer is that voice. It whispers a reminder that our heavenly Father cares for us and will provide for all our needs, for always. All we have to do is ask. Not in a wordy way as though we can verbally bully God into submission.[7] Not in a showy way as though we can manipulate God into thinking we somehow have earned his grace.[8] Not in a spooky way, as though we were uttering a magical spell to force a distant deity to intervene in a world he doesn't care about or know. Not in a desperate way, as though we were fighting a losing cause. Prayer is simply like a child talking to his father. And our Father, who knows our history and our hurts and our hang-ups, graciously listens and graciously provides.

In this final phrase there are four petitions:

Give us today our daily bread.
And forgive us our debts,
   as we also have forgiven our debtors.
And lead us not into temptation,
   But deliver us from the evil one.

                              (Matthew 6:11–13)

Here we see Jesus putting words to our most basic needs: our physical needs, our relational needs, our ethical needs, our spiritual needs. When a child comes into care with an attachment disorder, they require exactly the same things. They need help learning to trust that we will provide for them physically, that we will support them as they work out their relationships, that we will offer them wisdom in their decision-making, and that we will support their spiritual development too. We don't expect them to tell us to do these things, we just do them anyway. But as they put into words their wants and needs, as they accept, and as they seek out our input, this builds a deepening trust over time.

Another child we cared for used to hide in the furthest corner of the house. When we would go and sit with him he would relocate to a different isolated spot. His experience of adults had taught him to avoid them at all costs. One day the little boy appeared in the kitchen. The vehicle he had been playing with had broken. I fixed it for him and off he went. Five minutes later he returned and held up the vehicle again for me to fix. This happened about ten times before a guest in the house got a little exasperated and suggested that I should throw it away and give him a different toy. I smiled and explained with a tear in my eye that the broken car may just have been the best gift he could hope for. Every time he asked for help, it reinforced that here was an adult whom he could trust, who would welcome him, listen to him and help him as best he could.

When we put ourselves in the shoes of an adopted child learning to trust a good father who is desperate to provide the world for them, we see that prayer is not just a task to be done or an order to be obeyed, it is a lifeline to the most safe and permanent relationship we could ever wish for. Communication with God, even of the most repetitive sort, can help begin to rewire our brain, overcome the hurts of the past and build an intimacy into the future.

I prayed a lot for that little girl who sat expressionless on my lap, her eyes glazed over, silent and apparently lost. She is a teenager now. She is bubbly and outgoing, and when she walks into any room she is very happy to be the centre of attention. Because of her history there are ongoing challenges in her life, things that she struggles to grasp about who she is, behaviour that she struggles to manage. And so, even though she has come so far, I continue to pray for her to become a confident young woman, make her mark on the world and know her Father God's comfort, challenge and compassion. Every time I pray for her I am challenged to remember my Father's listening ear when we pray, his attentiveness to our cries and his awareness of our longings.

The Spirit of adoption can do that for you. He can burst your prayer life out of the formalities. He can ground your prayer life in the reality of all your needs and all your weaknesses. He can fuel your prayer life as your eyes are opened to the needs of those around you. He can shift your prayer life gradually so that you start to seek God's glory and his kingdom rather than your own comfort and agenda. And he can bond you with the Father who loves you, helping you know his security, compassion and provision. As the Spirit of adoption changes your prayer life, you may just find that he changes you and those you love too.

~

Questions for reflection

1. What difficulties relating to attachment have you experienced, and how may those impact your relationship with your Father God?

2. Which of the three fostered children described in this chapter do you relate to most spiritually – the one who had to come to terms with a new 'dad', the one who was learning to trust he would be provided for physically, or the one for whom broken things led to a closer bond with the one who could fix things? How could prayer help you to trust that God will provide for your spiritual, physical and relational needs?

3. How could listening to the Spirit of adoption transform your prayer life?

Chapter 5

The secret that changes everything about mission

The missionary myth –
and where we go from here.

Since the age of fifteen, when I became a Christian, I wanted to become a missionary. I had a world map on my wall and at night would dream about where God would send me. As I got older, I would spend Saturdays combing the shelves of my local Christian bookshop and devouring compelling stories of missionaries such as Jim Elliot in Ecuador, Hudson Taylor in China and Amy Carmichael in India. That was until I managed to secure a Saturday job opening envelopes for American Express, which then gave me the opportunity to help raise funds to go on short-term mission trips in my summer holidays. By the time I had my sixth-form meeting with the school careers advisor my CV was ready: I could now finalise steps to become a lifelong missionary.

A few months later I went to a Christian missions conference and everything changed. The room was packed full of eager young women and men who wanted to serve God across the planet. The keynote speaker launched into the grand finale of the conference and asked us to stand up if we met any of the following criteria:

Number one: can you speak a foreign language fluently? I guessed my GCSE French and the random Tamil slang words my cousins had taught me didn't count. I stayed in my seat.

Number two: can you repair a car? I was surprised by how many other people stood up at this point. My own engineering skills were exhausted by opening the bonnet of the car and breathing in deeply through my teeth.

Number three: are you good with children? Well, I had been one for most of my life, but I didn't think that was what they were looking for. I didn't move.

Number four: do you have IT skills? I was pretty nifty with a Word document and not bad at Microsoft Paint. But building IT infrastructure, networking, programming, not so much. Still sat down.

Number five: are you great at administration? Seriously? My ability to administrate my life was limited: it was a miracle when I made it to lectures and submitted my coursework on time. I was always running out of milk and clean socks. I didn't think my 'administration skills' were something the mission field would appreciate. Never mind. I had one more chance.

And finally – can you drive a car? Er, no. Driving lessons were an expensive luxury that was out of reach for my family.

Everyone in the room had stood up. Except me. Everyone in the room was then prayed for as they anticipated their exciting futures as missionaries. Except me. Everyone went home from the conference buzzing. Except me.

My friends back on my university campus thought I had had a lucky escape. They seemed to imagine God as a reality TV show producer recruiting cross-cultural missionaries and subjecting them to maximum discomfort and embarrassment. In their eyes God seemed to deliberately send people to inhospitable places and get them to eat foods that would make them retch purely for his own personal entertainment. They thought they could hang out with me more now that they weren't always expecting me to start preaching to every stranger I met and manipulating conversations towards a 'Jesus punchline'.

My romantic bubble of missionary dreams had been well and truly burst, and I was left wondering not only what I would do with my life but also what I would do with my faith. It wasn't until years later that I finally realised that the missions conference keynote speaker had got mission pretty wrong. By then I had also understood that many other Christians get mission all wrong too. Some seem to think mission is only mission if you live in a hut in Africa. Others think mission is only mission if you have to go round asking for financial support and giving out prayer letters. Some of us seem to live with a continual sense of panic that the fate of the world rests on our shoulders, while others of us are so relaxed with the idea that God will do everything himself that we just get on pursuing the same dreams and ambitions we had before we became Christians.

My mildly traumatic experience at that student missions conference may have been one of the reasons I ended up investing ten years of my life in academic study and teaching in the area of missiology. But, like so much in the Christian life, it turns out that our understanding of mission might be given a significant head start by tuning into the Spirit of adoption.

The beginning of mission

As a young person, I was taught that the first mention of mission in the Bible comes in the Great Commission at the end of Matthew's Gospel, when Jesus tells his disciples to go to the ends of the earth and make more disciples. For a long time, it was not only my starting point for understanding mission

– it was my entire understanding of mission. Then I heard a sermon suggesting that mission in the Bible began a lot earlier – way back in the opening chapter of Genesis. That's when the penny dropped. The whole Bible is the story of the mission of God,[1] what he is doing in the universe. Mission is not what we do *for* God, it is what we do *with* God. (As, by the way, the Great Commission confirms, on closer inspection.)

A simple way to break down what God is doing in the universe is by seeing it in terms of four relationships:[2]

1. **The *us-and-God* relationship**: God created human beings in his image so that we would reflect his character to a watching universe.
2. **The *us-and-others* relationship**: God created human beings with an inbuilt need for one another so that together we might build families, communities, nations, companies and systems that would honour him by caring for one another.
3. **The *us-and-our-world* relationship**: God created a place for human beings to explore, nurture and cultivate together.
4. **The *us-and-ourselves* relationship**: God created human beings to be reflective and self-aware and able to cultivate an inner life that could honour him too.

We can find all these relationships perfectly in sync in Genesis 1 and 2, and all these relationships severely fractured by the fall in Genesis 3. The rest of the Bible tells the story of God's mission to restore and reconcile all of these fractured relationships and of how God is superintending history so that, one day, they will all be repaired and renewed. The end of the book of Revelation shows us a beautiful picture of the four restored relationships – *us-and-our-world, us-and-God, us-and-others* and *us-and-ourselves*:

Then I saw 'a new heaven and a new earth,' for the first heaven and the first earth had passed away, and there was no longer any sea. I saw the Holy City, the new Jerusalem, coming down out of heaven from God, prepared as a bride beautifully dressed for her husband. And I heard a loud voice from the throne saying, 'Look! God's dwelling place is now among the people, and he will dwell with them. They will be his people, and God himself will be with them and be their God. "He will wipe every tear from their eyes. There will be no more death" or mourning or crying or pain, for the old order of things has passed away.'

He who was seated on the throne said, 'I am making everything new!' Then he said, 'Write this down, for these words are trustworthy and true.'

He said to me: 'It is done. I am the Alpha and the Omega, the Beginning and the End. To the thirsty I will

*give water without cost from the spring of the water of
life. Those who are victorious will inherit all this, and I
will be their God and they will be my children.'*

(Revelation 21:1–7)

God's mission is to repair all four of the fractured
relationships, and here in Revelation he paints this
majestic picture of his end goal that culminates in his
intention to live as an adopted family: *they will be my
children.* In other words, if the whole story of the Bible
can be summarised by this journey to restore relationships from the original family to God's ultimate family,
then understanding the goal of adoption and the lens
of adoption should help us enormously as we seek to
serve God in the world today.

Us-and-God: adoption of humanity

When my wife and I understood the need our foster
daughter was in, there was no doubt or hesitation in
our minds that adoption was the best thing we could
give her. Adoption was the way we could commit to
taking full account of her needs in a lifelong intimate
and loving relationship where she would be safe to
grow and flourish. She didn't just need money and
food and education and opportunity – she needed us.
In one sense we were the best gift we could give to
her. When God sees humanity's need he recognises

that *he* is the best thing that he could give to us. God expresses this in all sorts of ways in the grand Bible narrative. God comes to Moses and, before he commissions him, he wants him to know who *he* is, revealing himself at the burning bush as 'I am'. God could easily have led his people to the Promised Land in a few days, but he eked it out over a few decades, because the most important thing was to build that bond with him – *he* would protect and provide for his vulnerable children. *He* was there in the fire, the cloud, the water, the rock. He wanted them to rely on *his* provision of food in the desert so that they would know we don't live by bread alone but by the promised provision of God.[3] God could have sent Jesus on a much shorter-term mission to die for the sins of the world, but first he sent Jesus to live with us, because being with God is the whole point of our salvation. God wants us to know that *he* is the best thing he could give to us. That Father–child relationship is the root of his mission, just like Christ is the root of Christianity. We are doing mission when we recognise that it is all about who he is, how we are with him and how we point others to him.

Us-and-others: adoption into a family

I have lost count of the number of times people have asked me what impact each adoption has had on my other children. This question quite rightly stems from the recognition that adoption changes every relationship within the family. If you don't think about it before you adopt a child, you will certainly think about it afterwards. Every day involves guiding each of our children through the positive and challenging interactions with one another. In the same way, God's mission in adopting humanity necessarily involves creating a family, with all the complex relationships with one another that entails. I love that the Bible shows this so honestly. From Adam and Eve struggling to parent two very different children, to Noah's dysfunctional family, to Abraham being tempted to idolise his long-awaited child and disinherit his surrogate child, to Jacob's complex family dynamics with children from different mothers. I could go on through most of the families of the Old Testament. In the New Testament, church families are presented as being equally challenging, with jealousy, arguments, idolatry and affairs. God knows that it is difficult for us to get on with one another, but it is his mission to guide us through our relationships because he is committed to building his family: a family that will be so diverse it could be compared to a great city, and yet be so integrated and unified that it displays the beauty befitting the perfect bride of Christ.

God's mission is our mission when we are adopted into his family and are working out the adopting grace and love of God in our relationships with others. Whether it is the way we treat our neighbours and our politicians, our colleagues and our teammates, friends and family, strangers and enemies, as Christians we are called to be part of God's irresistible revolution of love and to treat everyone as though they are, or one day may be, our brothers and sisters. We are doing mission when we are learning to love our neighbours as ourselves, sharing our food with those who are hungry, seeking the welfare of the city, speaking up on behalf of vulnerable people, patiently supporting dysfunctional families, building just and equitable systems, institutions and companies[4] infused with grace and mercy, and loving one another as Christ has loved us.

Us-and-our-world: adoption and a home for good

When we were first turned down for adoption it was because the social worker who answered the phone to our initial inquiry thought we did not have enough space in our home. We argued that it did not matter if we did not have much space in our home, because the important thing was that a child had space in our hearts, but she was having none of it. So we moved house. Now there was space – a whole extra bedroom. It ticked a box for a social worker. But that space gave me an idea. This would not just be any old space. I put up a cot. I hung a mobile, I chose soft furnishings. I filled the wardrobes with clothes, the shelves with books, and boxes with toys. This was not just a tick box for a social worker – it was a beautiful environment that would make any child smile. And it was not just any old beautiful environment – it was to be *my daughter's* beautiful environment – *her* world, *her* home. The provision of this 'space' and these things was a mark of our love for her before we even met her. As we created her room, we envisioned her enjoying it all, interacting with the different elements, and even adding to it – photos that we would take of her, paintings that she would make, Lego structures she would build, the odd handprint she would add to the paintwork.

God's nursery for humanity was far grander. He painted the walls with trees and flowers and chose ambient lighting that could appear in all different colours. He hung stars in the sky, and he hid gold in the mountains and onyx in the rivers. He brought us real live animals to pet and nurture. God gave us this environment – our world, our home – so that we could enjoy it and flourish in it, and he commanded us to take care of it and make something wonderful out of it. Even though the effects of the fall mean that the world is broken and damaged, the cultural mandate still stands: 'fill the earth and subdue it. Rule over the fish in the sea and the birds in the sky and over every living creature that moves on the ground.'[5] We are called to 'make something of the world'[6] that God has given us stewardship over. In other words, God's mission to restore the world is our mission too.

Personally, I found that when I adopted my daughter and rediscovered my relationship as an adopted child of God, the world looked different. When I saw what a difference I could make to one child, I also saw the huge need for the hundreds of other children in the care system lacking not only a family where they belonged, but a place they could call home. The Spirit of adoption kept putting this need on my heart, and it eventually led to the founding of the adoption and fostering charity 'Home for Good'.[7] But it didn't end there either. Although we are working closely with churches and local authorities to find homes for all the children in the UK who need one, what about the children in other countries in the world? What about children in orphanages, where nobody is even trying to find homes for them? I am a man with a mission as I seek to play a small part in making the world a better place.

Us-and-ourselves: the adoption condition

Stuck to my daughter's mirror is a Bible text that she chose to buy at a Christian festival. It quotes the words from Psalm 139: 'fearfully and wonderfully made'. It is a message I want her to take to heart in a culture that says that unless you look a certain way and dress a certain way, you have little or no value. It is a message I want her to remember when her so-called friends tell her she is too tall, too fat, too loud. When they tell her she is a waste of space, I want her to know that she has inherent dignity and worth. When they tell her that her adoption means that she was unwanted and unloved, I tell her that her adoption means precisely the opposite: she has twice as many parents as her peers have, and two of them chose her specifically.

Thank goodness for the Holy Spirit, who can do a much better job than me at comforting her and confirming to her that her adoption is not a dirty secret to be ashamed of, but a powerful visual aid to the meaning of the universe. Her life path is planned, her forgiveness effective, her status in God's sight secure. Thank goodness for the Bible that shows us that, because of the fall, it is normal for us to feel insecure about our bodies, to feel miserable when people put us down, to feel broken and frustrated when we do things wrong.

Thank goodness for the affirming truths of the Bible, too. God loves us – even when we fail. God wants us even when nobody else does. God can renew our hearts and our minds and one day will renew our bodies too. God's mission to speak truth, to comfort, to affirm our secure adoption is our mission too.

The problem is that those promises in the Bible are sometimes difficult for us to hear and grasp. Sometimes we are so desperate to know them for ourselves that we keep them to ourselves. Sometimes we are far more comfortable applying biblical blessings to ourselves and biblical curses to others. Yet, think of the difference it would make to our world if it were no secret that we are each fearfully and wonderfully made. I meet people every day who have grown up being told the opposite – that they are worthless and useless, that they are a waste of space and a drain on society. Too many people grow up feeling that they are unloved and unwanted, treated as though they were unworthy of even basic care and attention. From what I have learned about therapeutic parenting, I know the messages of love and acceptance and affirmation are not just something adopted children need to hear. An essential component of God's mission – and therefore our mission – is to let the world know that he loved us enough to send his son to die in our place so that we can be called children of God.

We don't need to be able to drive to be able to guide people to a life-changing relationship with God who wants to be their Father. We don't need to be able to fix a car to be able to fix relationships, look out for our neighbours and forgive our enemies – and our friends. We don't need to have good computer skills to get involved in programmes that will make the world a better place. And we certainly don't need a foreign language to speak grace and dignity into the lives of people we meet. Wherever we are, wherever we go, whatever we do, we can join in with God's mission to let everyone know the secret that changes everything – God is in the business of restoring relationships and preparing the world for the ultimate adoption celebration.

~

Questions for reflection

1. Recall the four dimensions of mission. How do they help us to understand our calling as Christian disciples?

2. To what extent are we already involved in mission according to this framework of understanding?

3. What else could we do to help those around us see, know and understand God's plan for the universe? Pray that the Spirit of adoption would speak to you now.

Questions for reflection

Chapter 6

The secret that changes everything about the Bible

The greatest story never told –
and how to be part of the happily ever after.

Perhaps you know the story of a little boy and his sister who are removed from their parents because of domestic violence and, eventually, adopted. But not together. Like so many children in care, they have to be separated because very few adopters are willing to take a sibling group. The little girl is raised in a well-to-do family, while her brother finds himself in the middle of nowhere in the back of beyond. When she grows up, the girl enters public service as she wants to give something back to society. The boy ends up, as is so often the case for care leavers, in the military – a place of structure, belonging and clear-cut social rules. One day they will be reunited. And one day the boy will end up saving not just himself, but his whole squadron. He will be recognised not just as a national hero, but as a global one.

This all took place a long time ago in a galaxy far, far away . . . to a boy called Luke Skywalker.

I have always loved films and like to think of myself as a bit of a film buff. I am a regular at my local cinema half-price-Tuesday-night showings, and it has been known for me, on occasion, to watch three films in one day. But when I adopted my daughter everything changed. I don't mean it curtailed my hobby – in fact, she gave me a fresh excuse to watch old movies again and new Disney movies as they were released. No, everything changed because suddenly I saw themes around adoption cropping up all over the place. This opened up a whole new world of cinematographic engagement.

My blog at the time began filling up with reviews of films and explanations of how, as a Christian and an adoptive father, they helped my understanding of adoption practice and theology, and how, as a charity founder, they helped me promote adoption. A film critic friend of mine, Martin Saunders, used to tell me off. He thought I was seeing things, twisting things, reading my agenda into the narratives. Then, after seeing *The Lego Batman Movie*, the penny dropped for him too and he published a very public apology to me, stating: 'Well, it turns out Krish was right. There is a huge concentration of cinematic story time being given over to one idea: the theme of adoption.'[1]

A eureka moment

Think about it next time you go to watch a film. Chances are if there are children (or young animals or fish) featured, one of them has lost their family or will find a new one – think about Snow White, Bambi, Simba, Tarzan, Anna and Elsa, Nemo, and the protagonists in almost every other Disney film you can think of. Chances are if there are flawed heroes involved, their backstory involves them having lost or gained significant family members. Let's take the major movie franchises of recent decades: Luke and Leia Skywalker were adopted, as we have seen. Superman was adopted. Spiderman was brought up by his aunt. Frodo Baggins was an orphan and brought up by his uncle. Harry Potter was fostered (terribly) by the Dursleys. Paddington lived in supported lodging. James Bond was adopted. Batman was orphaned and brought up by his butler. The list goes on and on.

You see, our screenwriters, authors, playwrights and television producers know that the secret to a good story is a good adoption journey. They know that children who have had the most unimaginably difficult starts in life are the very ones who can develop and portray the resilience and skills they need to make unimaginable successes of life. They know that our families can, paradoxically, cause the deepest of wounds and bring the deepest healing. They know that someone's history does not dictate their destiny. And they know that this storyline seems to connect universally with viewers at a profound, perhaps even spiritual, level.

When I became an adoptive father, I had a eureka moment. I had been let in on entertainment's greatest secret that meant no film would ever be the same again. I had exactly the same experience at the same time in the same way with the Bible. Suddenly I was seeing adoption all over the place. At first, like my friend Martin, I was sceptical. Was I just seeing and twisting things? Was I just projecting my own agenda on to the texts? I decided to delve a bit deeper. But then something happened to me. It's an occupational hazard for every Christian: God spoke to me through his Word. I realised that adoption themes are not simply strewn throughout the Bible – adoption lies at the heart of everything.

A central storyline

At first it was the obvious parts. The three times that Paul describes our adoption into God's family he portrays it as the highest privilege of our salvation, involving all three members of the Trinity in a divine, cosmic, eternal plan. He begins his letter to the Ephesians, for example, with the declaration:

> *Praise be to the God and Father of our Lord Jesus Christ, who has blessed us in the heavenly realms with every spiritual blessing in Christ. For he chose us in him before the creation of the world to be holy and blameless in his sight. In love he predestined us for adoption to sonship through Jesus Christ, in accordance with his pleasure and will – to the praise of his glorious grace, which he has freely given us in the One he loves.*
>
> *(Ephesians 1:3–6)*

This was a major clue as to the absolute importance of adoption to the central storyline of the Bible. But why, if this was the ultimate plan for us, stemming back to before the creation of the world, is it hardly mentioned in the Old Testament?

Just because a term is not used widely in the Bible, it does not mean the theme is not present all the way through. For example, the word 'Trinity' does not appear at all in the Bible, and yet once you have read the New Testament description of God the Father, God the Son and God the Holy Spirit it is virtually impossible to read any part of the Bible without seeing hints of the Trinity. The same is true with adoption. The term is not used in the Old Testament and yet the theme is latent throughout the whole storyline.

The Bible begins with God's corporate family decision to 'make mankind in our image, in our likeness'.[2] Then we read on, seeing God's Spirit at work, foundations being laid that point to Jesus and his mission, and the overarching sovereignty and protection of God the Father. Three mysterious visitors call on Abraham, wisdom is strangely personified in the book of Proverbs, and David glimpses a conversation between his Lord and the Lord.[3] God is a family. God creates a family. And God intervenes to care for dysfunctional families, orphans and widows, ultimately bringing it all together with the adoption into his ultimate family.

Like a melody resonating throughout a symphony, once we begin to understand adoption as the goal towards which God is orchestrating the universe, we should not be surprised to find the theme recurring throughout the Bible in all sorts of different ways.

An orphan turnaround

Perhaps the best place to start is the adoption of the Hebrew child Moses by the daughter of Israel's most feared and oppressive enemy. Moses should have been terminated at birth in Pharaoh's cull, but instead he becomes the greatest human hero in the Old Testament. Moses, the Jews' Jew, the national treasure, was not raised by his birth parents Jochebed and Amram, not because of any fault or deficiency in them, but due to the brutal slavery, oppression and attempted genocide brought about by the Egyptian regime. I love this story and tell it to my daughter often. I find great hope that God can take someone with a traumatic childhood and turn them into a liberator of his people. God saw the child relinquished by his birth mother and hidden in bulrushes and offered him unsurpassed face-to-face access to himself such that the boy's face shone with the reflected Shekinah glory of God. God chose the rescued child to be the one to rescue God's children from captivity. God commissioned the 'orphan' whom the Egyptian princess had found crying to take his law to his people – a law that includes the command:

Do not take advantage of the widow or the fatherless. If you do and they cry out to me, I will certainly hear their cry.

(Exodus 22:22–3)

There are over forty occasions where the Bible refers specifically to God's concern for orphans or the 'fatherless'. That's more than the number of times Scripture talks about tithing or taking communion. God makes it clear throughout the Bible that he is particularly interested in the care of vulnerable children. Over and over in the Law revealed through Moses, God reiterates his concern for those who are vulnerable and marginalised:

> *For the Lord your God is God of gods and Lord of*
> *lords, the great God, mighty and awesome, who shows*
> *no partiality and accepts no bribes. He defends the*
> *cause of the fatherless and the widow, and loves the*
> *foreigner residing among you, giving them food and*
> *clothing.*
>
> (Deuteronomy 10:17–18)

> *Do not deprive the foreigner or the fatherless of justice,*
> *or take the cloak of the widow as a pledge.*
>
> (Deuteronomy 24:17)

> *Cursed is anyone who withholds justice from the foreigner,*
> *the fatherless or the widow.*
>
> (Deuteronomy 27:19)

A Father to the fatherless

It is not just in the Old Testament Law that God shows his concern for vulnerable children. It is visible throughout the prophets, in the book of Job and in the Psalms. On one occasion King David is inspired to write:

> *A father to the fatherless, a defender of widows,*
> *   is God in his holy dwelling.*
> *God sets the lonely in families,*
> *   he leads out the prisoners with singing.*
>
> (Psalm 68:5–6)

How does someone become a father to someone else's child? How does God set the lonely in families? Surely David is talking about adoption. And David knew a bit about that. He had come from a large family with six older brothers and two sisters. We are given a clue that things were not always easy in this family when the prophet Samuel comes to visit David's father Jesse to anoint one of his sons. Like Cinderella, not considered worthy enough to be summoned from the cellar when the prince is searching for the belle of the ball, David is not considered important enough to be brought in from the fields. When David was sixteen years old, he had to leave his family behind to begin his new job singing and fighting for King Saul. He struck up a friendship with Saul's son Jonathan, but this relationship was to be wrenched away from him too. Intensely jealous of David, King Saul banished him. David then spent around fifteen years in exile, and many of the psalms are heartfelt cries of loneliness and distress from this period of his life. But God had not forgotten David – eventually he did become king and have his own family. But David never forgot the truth that God sets the lonely in families. He had experienced it for himself; now he felt it was his turn to pass on the blessing.

Remembering his valued friendship with Jonathan, David asked around about what happened to his family after Jonathan had been killed in battle, and when he found out that there was one dependent son left, he effectively adopted him. Mephibosheth had been orphaned and crippled at the age of five, but his emotional scars and permanent physical disabilities were no obstacle to David's love. He provided for him not only financially, but treated him like a son, ensuring that he always joined him at mealtimes. A mighty king using his power and influence to set the lonely in families – this was what David knew about God and what David loved about God, what filled David's lyrics and what filled David's home.

It is argued that because of the complexity of land inheritance rights in Jewish law, there is no legal provision for adoption in the Old Testament.[4] But David finds a way around this when he commands that Saul's land be restored to Mephibosheth, and that Saul's servants are to farm it and bring in the crops. On top of that he gives Mephibosheth a permanent place at his table – a fact that is mentioned four times in seven verses. As this was a privilege usually reserved for the king's sons, it seems that this was the clearest way that David could announce publicly that this boy was to be forever considered family.

An adoption relationship

Just as the two greatest Old Testament heroes – Moses and David – have their adoption journeys, so God also gave the two greatest heroines in the Old

Testament – Esther and Ruth – an understanding of what it meant to be adopted.

The relationship between Esther and Mordecai is one of the most beautiful in Scripture and one that I aspire to in my relationship with my adopted daughter. Mordecai is the model of faithful resistance willing to face death for his love for God, his people and his adopted daughter. Esther is a model of faithful resistance too, willing to risk death for her love for God, his people and her adoptive father. Together they spur each other on to courageous and patient endurance and become the means through which the Jews are saved from genocide.

The book of Ruth is infused with adoption themes. There is the moment when Ruth vows lifelong commitment to Naomi. And Naomi is also presented as a kind of orphan, having lost all her family members, and is then set by God in a family. Boaz goes to court to prove his intention to be the kinsman-redeemer for Ruth. And later, when Ruth and Boaz present their son to Naomi, she prays a blessing over the child that is reminiscent of adoption promises.[5]

When I was younger I read the Bible through from cover to cover in a year by reading three chapters of the Old Testament and a chapter of the New Testament each day. I did this several times, but somehow even then I didn't pick up on God's concern for or prioritisation of the vulnerable. I think I had subtly assumed a filter and subconsciously screened out the parts of the Bible that I didn't think were relevant. Once that filter was lifted, the whole Bible suddenly looked very different.

In Romans 9, Paul describes the whole history of the Israelite nation – in other words, the majority of the Old Testament – as an adoption story:

> *For I could wish that I myself were cursed and cut off from Christ for the sake of my people, those of my own race, the people of Israel. Theirs is the adoption to sonship; theirs the divine glory, the covenants, the receiving of the law, the temple worship and the promises.*
>
> *(Romans 9:3–4)*

Paul explains that the only way the chosen people of God can claim to be God's children is through adoption. He then shows how all of God's people are part of that story (the New Testament part) through God's mercy. Paul quotes Hosea, who argues:

> *Yet the Israelites will be like the sand on the seashore, which cannot be measured or counted. In the place where it was said to them, 'You are not my people,' they will be called 'children of the living God.'*
>
> *(Hosea 1:10)*

This is an adoption pronouncement. It is only because of adoption that anyone can be 'called' or counted as somebody else's child. John entreats us to grasp the incredible significance of this when he writes:

> *See what great love the Father has lavished on us, that we should be called children of God! And that is what we are!*
>
> *(1 John 3:1)*

I could give you many, many other examples of how, throughout the Bible, God calls us his children, shows himself to be a Father to the fatherless, sets the lonely in families and includes people who were not his people into his family.[6] But I think it is better that I leave them hidden in the Bible for you to discover for yourself. As you discover the secret that the Bible can be seen as a collection of adoption stories that point to The Great Adoption Story, I hope that you will hear the melody in the symphony of your own Bible study.

A Hollywood ending?

There is an occupational hazard that comes with reading the Bible. It might change us. Eugene H. Peterson, the esteemed theologian and author of the best-selling translation of the Bible into contemporary language, *The Message*,[7] explained why he was so committed to the teaching and explanation of Scripture when he wrote:

Christians don't simply learn or study or use Scripture;
we assimilate it, take it into our lives in such a way that
it gets metabolized into acts of love, cups of cold water,
missions into all the world, healing, evangelism and justice
in Jesus' name, hands raised in adoration of the Father,
feet washed in company with the Son.[8]

When you read, discover and assimilate the biblical threads of God's plan for adoption, God's heart for adoption and God's Spirit of adoption, they might just be metabolised into an adoption story of your own. They might lead you, like David or Mordecai, to reach out to adopt someone into your family.

Adoption of vulnerable children does not come with a promise of a happily ever after ending, despite what the entertainment industry would have us believe. There isn't always a big show-stopping song-and-dance routine as the looked-after child gets adopted by a billionaire, like Annie in the musical named after her. There isn't a guaranteed international showdown as three orphaned girls manage to turn super-villains, like Felonius Gru in *Despicable Me*, into model fathers. Children who have been placed in families by social services may be more likely to find themselves in Her Majesty's Prison Service[9] than in Her Majesty's Secret Service like James Bond. Neither does the Bible promise that our adoption into God's family will be a rose-tinted fairy tale where we become heroes riding off into a Disneyesque sunset. But when we read the biblical accounts of both earthly and heavenly adoption we are given something much more substantial, much more audacious – and much more wonderful.

The same Jesus who promised we would not be left as orphans, but would one day be brought safely to his Father's many-roomed house, also warned us of the troubles we would face in this world.[10] The same Jesus who warned us against misunderstanding our salvation at the final judgment also urges us to pass on God's compassionate grace to the most vulnerable in our communities.[11] The Bible is full of hope and realism, beauty and brokenness, mourning and dancing, comfort and challenge, transformation and frustration, trauma and triumph. Just as we know the reality of that in our own experience of being Christians, adopted into God's family, so too we see that in the adoption of children into our earthly families. And for those of us fortunate enough to experience the two stories side by side, we learn that, as each one informs, impacts and inspires the other, we are helped to live and share our ultimate hope of the truly happily forever after ending the Bible promises.

~

Questions for reflection

1. Think of the last five films you have seen or novels you have read. What adoption themes have they included?

2. 'The Bible can be seen as a collection of adoption stories that point to The Great Adoption Story.' Which passages of Scripture are most radically reframed for you by the adoption plot line of the Bible?

3. What difference could it make in the world if the Church assimilated something of God's plan for adoption, God's heart for adoption and God's Spirit of adoption?

Chapter 7

The secret that changes everything about worship

*Doing right things wrong –
and putting wrong things right.*

My daughter has a rebellious streak. When I ask her to walk, she runs. When I ask her to run, she walks. When I ask her to be quiet, all sorts of information bursts out of her. When I ask her to talk to me, her mind suddenly goes blank and she has nothing to say. On a good day, I admire her confidence, her guts to do things her own way: it might help her make her unique mark on the world. On a bad day, I worry that it might end her up in a lot of trouble – and I think I might explode with frustration. It is very often the case that the latter reaction is provoked when my camera is involved. You see, my daughter is beautiful – she has long curly hair, sparkling eyes, and a smile that lights up a room. People stop me in the street to tell me how stunning she is. Her phone full of selfies tells me she knows exactly how to pose for a picture. But when *my* camera comes out and I ask her to stand still and smile, she does the exact opposite. It is hard enough trying to get family photographs with seven children facing the same direction. But when one of them is constantly squirming and scowling, it makes the already difficult task virtually impossible. The frustration rises up within me.

Ironically, I can be just like my daughter. Not when it comes to cameras, but at church services. Sometimes if a worship leader stands at the front of the church and tells me to stand, smile and sing, or kneel, confess and pray, or even greet my neighbour with a handshake, something inside me just wants to rebel and do the exact opposite. Telling me how to join in corporate worship for some reason can be as counter-productive as shouting at my daughter to look happy and 'say cheese'.

But the rebellion doesn't stop there. On the way home from church I find that I just have to express my pent-up frustration that they sang that awful song again, that they shouted down the microphone again, that the computer operator couldn't keep up with the PowerPoint slides again, that the preacher ran over time again. Don't get me wrong. I love church. I love the people in my church. I also love singing and praying and preaching. At least I love them most of the time. I think.

I have it on good authority that I am not alone in having these rebellious trains of thought. I understand that many of us have similar after-service conversations on our Sunday journeys home. We analyse our 'worship' experience based on how moved we were, how bored we were, whether the music was up to spec or the preacher was on point. Even when we know better, we struggle to factor in that the only person qualified to rate our worship is the one to whom our worship is directed: God himself.

What would God say?

When I began reading the Bible through the lens of adoption, I became highly sensitised to the Bible's emphasis on care for vulnerable children. It reframed my understanding of who God is, who I am, what I was supposed to be doing with my life, how I was supposed to see my church family, and how that impacted my prayer life. In other words, it began to change the way I worshipped God, how I related to him in every part of life. But I still felt no less rebellious and critical when I went to church. Was there something wrong with me? Then I discovered something that would significantly challenge and change my view of worship.

One of the chapters in the Bible where God talks about the 'fatherless' is Isaiah 1. The book of Isaiah is full of awe-inspiring pointers to Jesus and the wonderful comfort, redemption and salvation that he would bring. It also contains the most excoriating review of corporate worship ever written, and it comes right in the first chapter. It makes those post-church-worship autopsy conversations seem quite tame. God begins by likening his people to the notorious cities of Sodom and Gomorrah, famous for their immorality and wickedness and prime examples of God's terrible judgement. If this makes for uncomfortable reading, it is only going to get worse:

> 'The multitude of your sacrifices—
>   what are they to me?' says the Lord.
> 'I have more than enough of burnt offerings,
>   of rams and the fat of fattened animals;
> I have no pleasure
>   in the blood of bulls and lambs and goats.
> When you come to appear before me,
>   who has asked this of you,
>   this trampling of my courts?
> Stop bringing meaningless offerings!
>   Your incense is detestable to me.
> New Moons, Sabbaths and convocations—
>   I cannot bear your worthless assemblies.
> Your New Moon feasts and your appointed festivals
>   I hate with all my being.
> They have become a burden to me;

I am weary of bearing them.
When you spread out your hands in prayer,
    I hide my eyes from you;
even if you offer many prayers,
    I am not listening.
Your hands are full of blood!
Wash and make yourselves clean.
    Take your evil deeds out of my sight;
    stop doing wrong.
Learn to do right . . .'

(Isaiah 1:11–17)

Why so passionate?

These verses are so brutal that it is perhaps little wonder that we hear them read out in church so infrequently. These words are not going to translate well into a praise song. No amount of drum rhythms or 'ambient worship pads' are going to be able to disguise the disgust God has for his people's corporate worship. God decries the sacrifices and festivals. Even turning up at the Temple is considered 'trampling' God's courts. And he will not even listen to their prayers. But surely this is wrong – doesn't God command us to worship him through gathering together, offering sacrifices, celebrating, praying and singing? Why does he command us here to stop and shut up?

My daughter's rebellious streak can help us. The first chapter of Isaiah says that our corporate worship can be an act of rebellion against God not because of *what* we are doing, but because of *when* we are doing it. And more importantly, this rebellion is deeply frustrating to God not because of what we *are* doing, but because of what we *are not* doing.

Isaiah is clear that what God's people have left undone is the essence of their true worship. The way we treat and defend those who are fatherless, widowed and oppressed is the worship offering God really cares about. Immediately after the passage quoted above, he reminds us to 'seek justice. Defend the oppressed. Take up the cause of the fatherless; plead the case of the widow' (Isaiah 1:17).

Understanding this vital introduction to the prophecy of Isaiah can shape the way we read the whole book, indeed the whole Bible. Grasping what God's passion really is and what lies at the heart of God's anger and behind all his warnings of judgement reframes the way we can appreciate our salvation and all the beautiful promises God offers us through Isaiah and beyond. It changes the way we appreciate worship, because it changes the way we appreciate God.

Imagine that one of my children cycles past your house each day to get to school. One morning he takes the corner too quickly and goes flying across the tarmac, skinning his arms and his legs. Luckily, he knows you live just there, and elbows his way to your door. He puts his mouth next to your conveniently located floor-level letter box and cries out for help. You recognise his voice and welcome him into your home. You bandage his wounds, you give him a hot mug of cocoa and then (with another responsible adult present so that you don't break any child-protection protocols), you put him in your car and drive him to my house. If we were acquaintances before, we are friends for life now.

But what if the scenario was slightly altered. My son comes flying off his bike near your house. He makes his way to your front door and cries for help. You recognise his voice at the letter box, but this time it reminds you of a book you are currently reading, as it happens to have been written by me. You decide it is time to thank the author. So you fire up your computer and drop me a line on social media, where in the most eloquent and articulate words possible you make known your exceeding gratitude to me. I am delighted by such an encouraging message. But later that evening, I find out that you did this instead of helping my son. You left him at the doorstep bleeding while you took the time to write to me. That encouraging message you sent me has turned into an insult. Your praise of my book only serves to remind me more forcibly of your neglect of my son in his hour of great need.

Too often it is a lot easier to substitute choruses for

caring, songs for service, piety for personal sacrifice, words for actions. This seems to be God's issue with the Israelites. They have offered God the ritual of worship but have neglected the heart of it. They have not cared for those whom God cares for. They have people on their doorsteps who are fatherless, widowed, and oppressed and in great need, but neglected them while they busied themselves with praise services and festivals, with gatherings and sacrifices. God says stop. He can't stand it any longer.

True signs of spirituality

Reading Isaiah 1 showed me that I was guilty of rebellion in my worship to God. Not because I didn't always stand and sing when I was told to by the worship leader, but because my passions and concerns didn't always match God's passions and concerns. This, I realised, was not just something God wanted me to hear from Isaiah 1. It was a theme that spilled over into the New Testament.

I noticed it in Jesus' criticisms of the ritualistic observances of the Pharisees and the teachers of the Law who tithed their herb gardens but 'neglect[ed] justice and the love of God', or who loaded people down with burdens while they themselves 'will not lift one finger to help them'.[1]

I noticed it in Jesus' life. When it came to a choice

between going to the Temple and healing a lame man,[2] he chose the latter. When it came to a choice between spending time on his own praying or attending to the needs of the crowd, again he chose the latter.[3]

I noticed it in Jesus' teaching. The parable of the sheep and the goats divides those who appeared to worship God on the basis of whether or not they fed the hungry, clothed the naked, welcomed the outcast and visited the imprisoned.[4]

I noticed it in Paul's teaching. In that masterpiece chapter on worship, 1 Corinthians 13, he notes that the outward manifestations that we might have pointed to as evidence of the Holy Spirit being present in our worship – speaking in tongues and prophecy – are nothing without the presence of the love of God. On their own they are not signs of spiritual activity but actually empty clanging carnality. Similarly, according to Paul, being able to fathom great theological and expository mysteries is nothing without love. Even sacrificial giving to the poor and facing persecution are nothing without love. Paul exhorts us to a genuine loving relationship with God that spills over into genuine practical love for our neighbour.

I noticed it in the epistle of James. He writes: 'Religion that God our Father accepts as pure and faultless is this: . . .'[5] I wonder what you would expect the punchline to be here? The term 'religion' is an unusual one in the New Testament. In the original Greek the word used here only occurs twice more, both times being used to describe veneration and worship.[6] Here, however, James is describing worship directed at God and affirming that what matters most is not that it is acceptable to us, but that it is acceptable to God. James recognises that in order for God to be able to receive our worship it needs to be 'pure and faultless', which is a phrase taken from the impeccable standards of Old Testament Temple worship.[7] Having used all the devices and language he could muster to help us frame the importance, purity and quality of worship that God is looking for, James goes on to define religion that is acceptable to God as being:

> *to look after orphans and widows in their distress and to*
> *keep oneself from being polluted by the world.*
>
> *(James 1:27)*

I have spent so much of my life as a church leader focusing my attention on the experience of the gathered worshippers, making sure that everyone in the church is happy with the volume, the style, the variety of the music, sweating over the expository clarity of the sermon and the rigour of the theology of what I was preaching. Though these things are important, it turns out that, in God's eyes, they are all irrelevant and, indeed, irreverent if they are not coupled with a concern for those in need. In James, God gives us his wish list for our worship, and at the top of it is caring for vulnerable, traumatised children.

This makes most sense when we see that at the heart of the gospel, the heart of God's mission in the universe, is our adoption and the reconciliation of all things. This makes most sense when we understand that the Spirit of adoption is the same Spirit that prompts and enables us to worship in spirit and in truth. He is the same Spirit who produces the character of Christ in us, enabling us to grow in love, joy, peace, forbearance, kindness, goodness, faithfulness, gentleness and self-control. Why? Because these are exactly the characteristics needed to care for the vulnerable and oppressed and to be united as one adopted family.

Isaiah leaves us with a challenge here. He expects us to rebel against our corporate worship. Not by being complainers or critics but by cutting through any hypocrisy in our own lives. Why aren't we doing something to stand up for the needy today? Why can't we make it part of our daily rhythm to show care for widows and orphans in whatever way we can, reflecting something of the heart God has for the vulnerable? This is the way we transform worship, the way we transcend the ritualistic habits, the way we translate God's passion into our own lives.

~

Questions for reflection

1. What do you find yourself critiquing most in the worship gatherings of your church?

2. How does Isaiah 1 challenge the way that you view worship?

3. What are God's priorities for worship? (See James 1:27 or Matthew 25:31–46 or Isaiah 1 or 1 Corinthians 13.) What most surprises you? What may need to change in your life? What difference could this make to the Church?

Chapter 8

The secret that changes everything about justice

*When it's just not fair —
and it's right under our nose.*

As any parent who has more than one child will tell you, one of the most frequent complaints heard in the home is: 'It's not fair!' It's a criticism I feel keenly whenever those words are addressed to me. I love my children equally and am desperate for them to know that they have equal value, and equal access to my love and care. But when they see me giving out different amounts of pocket money, working my way through staggered bedtimes and installing or deleting different social media applications on their various mobile phone devices, often my actions are interpreted as unjust, provoking those dreaded words.

Recently that complaint was addressed to me in my local play area. Not from any of my children this time, but from another parent. We were the only two families there, and after twenty minutes the woman marched over to me, loudly complaining that my child had monopolised the swing for the entire time. Rather taken aback by her aggressive approach, as politely as I could, I muttered something about not knowing she was wanting a turn, and had she asked earlier of course I would gladly have moved my child on. Inside I was seething. I looked at her son in his private-school uniform skipping happily around the playground and stopped myself shouting back at her, 'You think that's not fair? Shall I tell you what's not fair? It's not fair that my son had no permanent family until he was four years old. It's not fair that he is so traumatised from abuse in the past that he can't enjoy most of the equipment in the play area. It's not fair that because of his hidden disabilities he finds the predictable rocking motion of a swing soothing. It's not fair that because of government cuts he is unlikely to enjoy an education system that caters for his learning needs. It's not fair that you shouted at me for no good reason and it's not fair that I am far too well mannered to shout back at you!'

The more children I foster, the more injustices I come across. And I don't just mean the ones in my home or in my local park. There are deeply ingrained injustices in our education system, in our mental health care services, in our political system, in the biases regarding race and disabilities and religion. I have encountered injustices in social services, in passport offices, in the benefits system and even in the legal system. And the more injustices I come across, the angrier I become. I agree with my children: it's just not fair!

It's just not fair

It turns out that quite a lot of people in the Bible express their frustration that life isn't fair. Cain thought it unfair of God not to accept his offering but to accept his brother Abel's. Moses argued with God for picking him to speak to Pharaoh when his brother Aaron was the eloquent one. Jonah sulked at the injustice of God saying he was going to punish Nineveh and then having mercy on the city after all. Habakkuk complained that good things happened to bad people and bad things happened to good people. Jeremiah thought it was unfair that he was persecuted just for delivering God's message. Many of the psalmists composed laments to voice their frustrations when life just wasn't fair. I have derived great comfort from the way the Bible, by including these complaints, permits me to voice my anger towards God at the injustices I encounter.

The Bible challenges me not only to call out the injustices before God but also to speak them out in the public square. For example, we are commanded to:

Speak up for those who cannot speak for themselves,
for the rights of all who are destitute.

(Proverbs 31:8)

It is not right that children who have had the toughest starts in life are left waiting for permanent loving homes. It is not right that too many children too often 'pinball'[1] around the care system in multiple foster placements. It is not right that children with disabilities cannot access the services they need. It is not right that children caught up in war and violence have to risk their lives again by making perilous journeys trying to find refuge, only to be stranded and ignored far from home in dangerous camps. Never mind manners – I can't keep quiet about these things. After all, as I reread my Bible through the lens of adoption, I saw in Moses and the Law, and in Isaiah and the prophets, and in the Gospels and Jesus' concern for the poor, that God spoke out when things weren't fair. God spoke up for the voiceless to make sure that those who were vulnerable were protected and provided for, and he expects us to do the same.

I would never have imagined back when I adopted my daughter that it would lead to me becoming so passionate and vocal about all sorts of justice issues. But adoption, I discovered, is the secret that changes everything about justice.

Justice everywhere

I used to think justice was a dirty word. In my younger years as a Christian, many of my mentors seemed to think social justice was somehow related to the social gospel. At its worst, the social gospel movement was an attempt to spread the values of the kingdom of God on earth without necessarily recognising God as King.[2] Those who would write about and preach social restoration at the time did not seem to have much interest in spiritual renewal. And so I was taught to filter out God's care for physical needs in the Bible and see only God's interest in our spiritual needs. I became an evangelist, and at the time I understood that the extent of my responsibility was simply to pass on the good news of our salvation in terms of speaking out the message of our forgiveness, justification and redemption – an individual gospel of reconciliation with God.

Adoption changed all that for me. Our adoption into God's family does not just mean that he cares for our spiritual needs. He also cares for our social needs – welcoming us into a church family of brothers, sisters, fathers and mothers. God cares for our physical needs – he tells us that we can rely on him as our heavenly Father to provide the food for our stomachs and the clothes for our backs. God also is committed to helping us with our emotional and pastoral needs, sending the Spirit of adoption to comfort us and confirm that we have the right to call him Abba, Father. God's provision is total, you might even say holistic.

Jesus did not only speak the gospel of the kingdom with passion and clarity, he also demonstrated the kingdom of the gospel through serving the poor and standing up for the oppressed. Jesus did not have to choose between the two greatest commandments – to love God and to love our neighbour: he did both. We don't have to choose between the social gospel – caring for the needy without helping people discover a relationship with God – and the selfish gospel – offering people right standing with God without showing compassion to those around us. We are called to pass on the whole gospel, not an emaciated,[3] dualistic, edited version of the gospel, but the whole counsel of God. That means we all have some responsibility to pass on in both word and deed the good news of the availability of our full and complete salvation. Because of the Spirit of adoption, I seek to preach justification *and* practise justice; I seek to preach compassion *and* practise redemption.

The word *mišpāt* occurs in its various forms more than 200 times in the Hebrew Old Testament. Its most basic meaning is to treat people equitably. A second similar word, *tzadeqah*, refers to a life of right relationships . . . it refers to day-to-day living in which a person conducts all relationships in family and society with fairness,[4] generosity and equity. These two words are brought together scores of times in the Bible to explain the idea of justice. In a simple but telling note in the *New Dictionary of Theology*, we find that under the entry for justice it simply says 'see righteousness'.[5] Righteousness and justice in the Bible are interchangeable; they are intertwined, interconnected and indistinguishable. They are not only integral to our understanding of *who God is* as the Righteous One, the Judge of all the earth, they are also integral to our understanding of *how God acts*; he is righteous and just in all his ways. Furthermore, this is consistently shown to be *what God wants* of his people: that we seek righteousness and justice. Trying to take justice out of the Bible is like trying to take the heat out of the sun, or the university out of Oxford.

I love visiting Oxford. I have spent many hours taking my children for walks through the historic and picturesque streets, strolling through the meadows, taking photographs of the architecture, and even punting on the river. I love the multicultural feel, the connection with centuries of education, the cultural grandeur of the place. On more than one occasion I have been stopped by a tourist and asked for directions to the university. This always made me laugh in a rather bemused way. The problem is that the oldest university in the English-speaking world is not housed in a single building, nor is it even located on a campus;

its thirty-eight colleges and six permanent private halls are liberally dispersed all over the compact city. The university was literally all around those tourists as they looked for it. In it, they lived and moved and had their being. Justice is like that in the Bible. Some people can't see it there at all. But when you do see it, suddenly it is everywhere. Its architecture holds the landscape of the Bible together. Its themes fill every page. Its pursuit is woven into the very purpose of the Bible's existence. Its rhythm ripples out all around the world.

Justice for everyone

Because justice is the essence of the character of God and the heartbeat of the Bible, it is no surprise that seeking justice is also the call of every Christian. All of us who wish to walk humbly with our God should mirror God's character and obey God's command by loving mercy and acting justly. Not just as an add-on tacked on to our faith, but as an integral part of our work life, our home life and our social life, so that in it we live and move and have our being.

I have had the privilege of visiting many hundreds of churches around the world and I have been pleased to notice that it is increasingly difficult to find churches that are only concerned with meeting the needs of Christians. Most are also doing something to offer loving, practical service to their communities. Whether it is by running food banks or debt counselling services, helping elderly people or supporting refuges for abused women, providing staff to work with children and young people, resettling refugees or assisting ex-convicts to reintegrate into the community, the local church is at the forefront. The Church is waking up to the God of justice that Scripture reveals and is actively pursuing his purposes in the world.

But in many of these churches there is a disconnect between the programmes and the congregation. This works at two levels. First, fewer church members are now available to help run these events as more people work full time, so programmes are often run by paid staff. Second, those people who attend the language classes or financial support groups rarely turn up to our worship services. If they did, would we even know what to do with them? And so, for all our justice programmes, there is still the justice challenge of relational integration.

Building relational bridges between congregation and community is difficult. Many people commute to church and so have very little relational connection to the neighbourhood where the church is. Some people are busy at work and prefer to give money instead of time to help the needy – and they really don't expect to have much to do with them apart from that. Church leaders often feel the pressure of providing the kind of church experience that is expected by those who faithfully attend, and financially support, their churches. Our regular punters want excellent children's ministry, high-quality music and engaging biblical preaching, but our visiting community members may have different criteria. Some churches solve the 'problem' by running alternative services for those who come from difficult backgrounds. And still the relational gap persists.

Justice in everything

Bryan Stevenson, the American civil rights campaigner, argues that justice has to be more than something we do from a distance. When he visited black prisoners in jails in America, he began to grasp just how difficult their circumstances were, and how unjust the system was that led to one out of every three black American males spending some time in prison. Getting up from his desk in his law office and accompanying his clients into the challenging and dark places not only transformed his understanding of inequality, but also ignited his passion to change the system. He said:

> When you get proximate to the excluded and the disfavored, you learn things that you need to understand if we're going to change the world . . . Our understanding of how we change things comes in proximity to inequality, to injustice.[6]

If those we seek to help are kept at a relational arm's length, they remain projects to us rather than people. If we are happy to welcome people into church buildings and community centres but not into our homes, then we have dehumanised them. Keeping people at arm's length, at a safe distance, in detached objectivity does not accurately reflect the kind of love that God has shown us. The Spirit of adoption shows us that relational proximity changes your commitment to justice twenty-four seven.

God the Father delights in welcoming us into the same relational intimacy that he enjoys with Jesus and the Holy Spirit, and when we draw alongside others in the same way, learning their names, seeing their faces, dressing their wounds, holding them in our arms, we cannot but want to change the world for them and with them.

How many hours a week was Jesus seeking justice? How many days a month? The question is ludicrous. Jesus commanded us to be continually seeking first the kingdom of God and his righteousness–justice that that entails.[7] Justice is not just to be our hobby, or even our passion, it is to be our ontology – our way of being. Justice should be the dialect of our language, the flavour of our work assignments, the colour of our home lives, the rhythm of our footsteps.

To my surprise, adoption brought justice issues into the heart of my home. Because of the journey I have been on with my fostered and adopted children, I have fought for things I would not even have thought about before. It doesn't really matter whether a Nigerian boy has a passport or not – until he is a member of your family and you can't imagine going on holiday without him. It doesn't really matter whether the disability benefit system is fair – until you have two children with the same needs getting different amounts of support. It doesn't matter how the local government spends my income tax – until they are closing down services you know can make a world of difference to your daughter. Suddenly I am reading policy documents and writing campaign letters late at night and collaring my MP and signing petitions. Suddenly it doesn't matter whether my politics are red, blue, green or gold – or whether the budget will make me better or worse off. Those children in my home who are already massively disadvantaged need someone to fight for them, and as the dad in their lives, I will be their champion whatever it takes.

Jesus knew that parenting changes us, and that it can offer powerful insights into our relationship with God the Father. He said:

Which of you, if your son asks for bread, will give him a stone? Or if he asks for a fish, will give him a snake? If you, then, though you are evil, know how to give good gifts to your children, how much more will your Father in heaven give good gifts to those who ask him! So in

*everything, do to others what you would have them do
to you, for this sums up the Law and the Prophets.*

(Matthew 7:9–12)

Whatever I do for my children pales into insignificance compared with God's great and generous love and provision for us. I can bask in that wonderful promise for a long time. But that was never meant to be the end of the story. It's not an excuse to sit back, it's a motivation to step forward. The Law and the prophets are full of stories and injunctions and commands to treat people generously and fairly. Jesus notes this and raises the bar, as he does throughout the Sermon on the Mount. He says that the way we have experienced God's father–child provision and advocacy is the model for the way we are to champion justice for others. The Spirit of adoption changes everything about justice. And justice can be as close as our kitchen table.

~

Questions for reflection

1. Why do you think Christians often divide up the good news of the gospel and the good deeds of the gospel? How does remembering our adoption into God's family help to keep these things together?

2. How do we avoid our involvement with justice being

limited to tokenism, hobbies, fads, programmes or rotas? What would it take to stop seeing justice as an add-on, and to begin to bring justice into the heart of everything we are and do?

3. What practical steps can you make today to speak about and demonstrate our heavenly Father's love for the world?

Chapter 9

The secret that changes everything about suffering

*When we can't resolve the problems —
and we can embrace the suffering.*

I don't like suffering. I'm bad enough when I've got a cold or the flu. I feel so sorry for myself sometimes I curl up and plan my own funeral. Take your vitamins, my mum used to say. Keep fit and healthy. Look after number one. Don't mix with the wrong crowd. Walk away from trouble, she told me. And so I tried to steer well clear of suffering at all costs, just like she said. Then I became a Christian. That's when I discovered that Jesus was not like my mum. Instead of avoiding suffering, Christians, it appears, are supposed to search it out.

Blessed are you when people insult you, persecute you and falsely say all kinds of evil against you because of me. Rejoice and be glad, because great is your reward in heaven, for in the same way they persecuted the prophets who were before you.

(Matthew 5:11–12)

But before all this, they will seize you and persecute you. They will hand you over to synagogues and put you in prison, and you will be brought before kings and governors, and all on account of my name. And so you will bear testimony to me.

(Luke 21:12–13)

Remember what I told you: 'A servant is not greater than his master.' If they persecuted me, they will persecute you also.

(John 15:20)

For it has been granted to you on behalf of Christ not only to believe in him, but also to suffer for him.

(Philippians 1:29)

But rejoice inasmuch as you participate in the sufferings of Christ, so that you may be overjoyed when his glory is revealed.

(1 Peter 4:13)

The promise of suffering

It has to be said that none of these verses were pointed out to me before I became a Christian. It is one of those cover-ups that most of us discover after conversion. Like the small print on the contract of a mobile phone, you only really read the true ongoing costs for that incredible bargain that seemed too good to be true when something goes wrong with your device. The suffering clause is not advertised as one of Christianity's key features, but as soon as trouble hits, you are also hit with the hard truth that this was always part of the deal.

Jesus, Peter and Paul did not shy away from being honest and upfront about suffering for the sake of Christ being part and parcel of the normal Christian calling. Moreover, they specifically highlighted the part we often prefer to leave in the small print, by explaining suffering in terms of a promise, a privilege and even a pleasure! What was their secret for having such a transformed perspective on suffering? Can the Spirit of adoption help us in any way to dovetail our own attitudes with that of the Bible?

The paradox of suffering

Ironically, it was my own aversion to suffering that motivated me to begin my adoption journey. Living and travelling in Eastern Europe in the 1980s and 90s, my wife and I came across many of the orphanages where children were caged up like animals, shaved like criminals and quarantined from human interaction like viruses. When the media began highlighting these terrible practices, one of the consequences was that more children appeared on the streets. Everywhere we went we saw the terrible need, but could do nothing, as any attempts to help were seen as further judgement and interference. When we returned to the UK, we saw that we could alleviate something of the global suffering of children separated from their families by using the 'starfish' principle. This idea stems from the oft-told story of the boy walking along a beach who comes across a thousand dying starfish left stranded by the tide. He has just thrown one back in the sea when an old man passes by and asks him why he bothers – he can't make a difference to such a massive problem. The boy astutely replies that it had made a difference to that one, now safely back in the sea. Faced with the huge global crisis of children growing up without families, perhaps we could make a difference for that one, out of many millions in need, growing up in our home.

When we adopted our daughter, we realised that although we had set out to alleviate suffering, something more profound had happened. The traumatic family background from which she had come, the cycle of neglect and abuse that had caused chaos through generations, was not a story that had now been resolved by us

– rather, it was a story that now involved us. It was still part of *her* story and it had now become part of *our* story. We had somehow become united with her in the suffering.

This shed new light on Paul's teaching about our spiritual adoption:

> the Spirit you received brought about your adoption to
> sonship . . . Now if we are children, then we are heirs
> – heirs of God and co-heirs with Christ, if indeed we
> share in his sufferings in order that we may also share
> in his glory.
>
> (Romans 8:15, 17)

When Jesus set out on his mission to save his people for adoption into his family, he saw our suffering and became part of it. He suffered in every way, was tempted and was tortured physically, emotionally, socially and spiritually. He shared our darkest paths. Our story became his story. And when Jesus suffered and died on the cross to redeem us and justify us and adopt us, he called us to share in his sufferings too. He told us to take up our cross and follow him. His story became our story.

Dietrich Bonhoeffer recognised that the cross unites us with Christ not only through the once-for-all sacrifice made, but also through the ongoing suffering shared:

> The cross is laid on every Christian. As we embark upon
> discipleship we surrender ourselves to Christ in union

with his death – we give over our lives to death. Thus it begins; the cross is not the terrible end to an otherwise god-fearing and happy life, but it meets us at the beginning of our communion with Christ. When Christ calls a man, he bids him come and die.[1]

The circumstances that led to my daughter being adopted were in one sense a terrible ending, and in another sense a wonderful beginning. The cross plays this pivotal role in our lives as Christians. Suffering marks the birth of our adoption story, and it also marks the path of our adoption journey. There is a paradox here. God, our heavenly Father, who has paid the great cost, who is committed to our well-being, who promises to meet every need we have, also provides us with a lifetime of hardship. Can you imagine what a social worker would do if I welcomed a child into my care by offering to carry their burdens, and then promising to weigh them down with a few burdens of mine in return? I would fail the assessment forthwith. How can it be okay for God to promise us suffering when he also promised to protect us, have compassion on us, never forget us and graciously give us all things? What kind of father would do that?

This paradox is one that the book of Job wrestles with, and it is worth exploring because there is a surprising connection here between suffering and adoption that can help us.

The purpose of suffering

I have always been challenged by the story of Job because here is someone who experiences the most unbearable and extreme suffering and yet still remains faithful to God. I have also been troubled by the story of Job because the Bible makes it very clear that the terrible things that happen to him are not a series of unfortunate events but an orchestration of extreme suffering that is specifically permissioned by God himself.

The narrative[2] introduces a man of unblemished character who was revered in the region. Then it peels back a layer to reveal what effect Job's life and character has in the heavenly realm. What we find is a form of divine courtroom where Satan is some kind of (un-)angelic prosecutor, laying down his challenge to God. Satan argues that Job's devotion to God is based purely on the fact that life has been good to him, and if all of the blessings were stripped away, he, like anyone else, would surely renounce his love for God. In response to this challenge a deal is struck: God agrees that Job will be a test case. Despite the blatant challenge to his authority and the attack on his character, God permits Satan to bring suffering into Job's life. The essential question that runs through the rest of the book is whether Job will still honour God when all of his prosperity is taken from him, or whether he will 'curse [God] to [his] face'.[3]

Sometimes it seems that our loving heavenly Father may allow us to suffer because there are other factors in play that we cannot see or understand from where we are. God is willing to let Job suffer because of a wider cosmic conflict that needed to be resolved. We see this again in the suffering of Jesus. God the Father loves his Son, but for the sake of the salvation of humanity and the restoration of all things, God allows Jesus to suffer. When I see the terrible suffering around me and it feels like such a waste, I cannot imagine how God could either orchestrate it for a greater good or even weave it into something vaguely okay. Nevertheless, the sufferings of Job and Jesus give me a glimmer of hope that suffering may lead to more positive outcomes than it may appear to.

I hope that my daughter will one day understand something of the redemptive logic of suffering. When she was adopted into our family, one thing that happened immediately was that she changed from being a fostered child to being a fostering child in a fostering family. This has resulted in her being exposed to some of the terrible stories and distresses of those children that have come through our family from the care system, some with backgrounds similar to her own. She has made sacrifices without question over the years, and the care and compassion she has shown her foster siblings has helped them to experience love and mercy.

Watching her and my other children suffer for the sake of others in the home has sometimes made my heart ache in pain for them, and sometimes made it swell with pride in them. Sometimes watching them suffer for the sake of others has made me want to quit being a foster carer. They would have had so much more space and attention and freedom without foster children around, and I long to give them those things in abundance. But suffering does not always make you resentful, as Job shows us. Watching my children grow in kindness and empathy and generosity not just despite their sacrifices, but because of them has helped me understand something of God's promise to work all things for good for the sake of those who love him.

When someone tells me that they have adopted a child, it fills me with joy and admiration. I congratulate them profusely, and love to share with them the incredible privileges of being an adoptive father. But I know also that for that adoption to have taken place there must have been extreme suffering. Separation from their birth family is no small thing, no matter what age the child is at the time. Any history of neglect, abuse, violence, poverty and displacement leaves psychological scars on even the tiniest of babies. And the suffering of the child is only part of the bigger story. Behind every child in care is a grieving, sick or damaged parent. Sometimes two. Often grandparents and siblings and aunts and uncles are affected too as they watch their family torn apart. Then the suffering is taken on not only by adoptive parents, but by adoptive grandparents, aunts, uncles and siblings.

Adoptive mum, author and youth activist Rachel Gardner put it like this:

> Sometimes we feel overwhelmed by the fact that our two children, born to other people, call us 'Mumma' and 'Dada'. It carries with it feelings of unspeakable joy and deep sadness at the same time. Even as we seek to be the parents to our children God calls us to be, it breaks our hearts that there are birth families out there who don't get to be with the children they brought into the world. I know we're not the only ones who know what it is to hold the joy and the sorrow in tension.[4]

There is no adoption without suffering. They usually arrive hand in hand. They usually go through life hand in hand. Adoption cannot simply be seen as a rags-to-riches story. The rags and riches weave together. There is dust and there are sparkles of diamond. Beauty and ashes, joy and sorrow. If, as the Bible says, adoption is the ultimate purpose of the universe, then suffering must have a purpose too. Even Job's unhelpful friends knew that. They were just looking for it in the wrong place.

The power of suffering

There have always been narrow-minded, theologically naive and downright unhelpful believers far too willing to force their opinions on others in their times of weakness. Job's counsellors prove themselves to be ignorant, not only of their God, but of their friend too. They present Job with a litany of accusations that make him look back and check not only his actions but his motives too. In his reflection, he offers a most remarkable picture of his life:

> If I have denied justice to any of my servants,
>   whether male or female,
>   when they had a grievance against me,
> what will I do when God confronts me?
>   What will I answer when called to account?
> Did not he who made me in the womb make them?
>   Did not the same one form us both within our
> mothers?
> If I have denied the desires of the poor
>   or let the eyes of the widow grow weary,
> If I have kept my bread to myself,
>   not sharing it with the fatherless—
> but from my youth I reared them as a father would,
>   and from my birth I guided the widow—
> if I have seen anyone perishing for lack of clothing,
>   or the needy without garments,

and their hearts did not bless me
  for warming them with the fleece from my sheep,
if I have raised my hand against the fatherless,
  knowing that I had influence in court,
then let my arm fall from the shoulder,
  let it be broken off at the joint.
For I dreaded destruction from God,
  and for fear of his splendour I could not do such
  things.

(Job 31:13–23)

Job presents here a radical understanding of human life. In cultures where people would have assumed that wealth and heritage made some people more important or more valuable than others, he presents an understanding of human value and dignity that shines with the noblest aspects of politics, equality and human rights, thousands of years before such ideas were normalised in theory at least. His motivation was his righteous respect for our common creator, and his godly fear of our common judge. Because we all share the same origin story and we all have to give an account of ourselves before God, Job believed that everyone should be treated with equity and righteousness.

This was not just doctrine for Job. This was worked out in the way he cared for the needy and vulnerable and, particularly, the fatherless. His description reminds me of the work of foster carers and adopters with vulnerable children. He mentions the practical assistance of providing food and clothing. He mentions the emotional proximity that comes with child-rearing and offering guidance. He mentions the relational privileges of blessing and being blessed. And he mentions the professional advocacy of using his power and influence for the sake of the fatherless, actively seeking their welfare, not only avoiding doing them harm. When he speaks of 'raising a hand against the fatherless', he may be referring to a miscarriage of justice, a dodgy business deal or physical abuse:[5] Job claims innocence on all three counts, citing his ultimate respect for the glory and judgement of God.

When others suffered, Job reached out to them and stood up for them. And when Job himself suffered, those selfless actions enabled him to face down his critics and maintain perspective. At this stage in the book Job's suffering has been going on a while, and yet he can still claim to be innocent of ignoring or exploiting the needy. Even in the middle of his own suffering Job continued to care for those around him in need. This seems to suggest that the power of suffering to shake or disrupt our faith may be offset to some degree by our power in alleviating the suffering of others.

This is not to say that caring for the vulnerable insulates you from difficulties. Job continues to suffer terribly, even though he is just and righteous and committed to the welfare of the needy. I meet many people who make incredible sacrifices for the sake of others, and yet also face incredible challenges of their own. Sometimes we receive suffering not only *as* we relieve suffering in others, but *because* we relieve suffering in others. Job, in his own wrestling with the cause-and-effect questions of his suffering, at least had one thing to hold on to: his understanding of who God is compelled him to help others in need, and the more involved he got, the more he understood God. His sufferings were terribly hard, but he would endure them. His faith would be shaken, but it would also be strengthened.

The pursuit of suffering

Christians are as likely to face suffering as firefighters are to face burning buildings and lifeboat volunteers to face rough seas. A doctor running away at the sight of blood, a zookeeper who can't stand being around snakes, and a pilot terrified of flying would have major problems in their chosen vocations. A Christian who isn't willing to endure suffering is in the same category. As Paul writes, 'everyone who wants to live a godly life in Christ Jesus will be persecuted'.[6]

In the previous verses, Paul had referred to some of his persecutions and sufferings, and said that they had not detracted from his teaching, way of life, purpose, faith, patience, love and endurance. I cannot read these lines without thinking of stories I have heard of Christians around the world in extreme situations. I think of Perpetua, a young woman in Roman times who refused to renounce her love for Christ even though she knew it would cost her her life and she would not be able to bring up the baby she had just given birth to. I think of Christians in Burundi and Rwanda who, because they refused to participate in racial discrimination practices, were butchered by machetes. I have met Christians from Syria, from the former Soviet Union, from North Korea, whose terrible sufferings make any difficulties I have faced seem relatively insignificant. Their endurance, like Job's, deeply challenges me when I am tempted to say that life is hard or when I feel unwilling to make sacrifices for the sake of others.

Job embraced those who were suffering around him, and pursued justice for them, because he understood God's heart for those who suffer. This legacy, particularly in regard to caring for the fatherless,[7] helped him when he found himself in the middle of troubles of his own, with his own family stripped from him. It did not take away the pain and the questions and the struggles, as the forty chapters of the book attest, but it did help him to trust God when things happened that he could not understand and when people accused him of things that were not true. It enabled him to persevere to the end and not lose his faith.

When I found myself struggling in a pointless and hopeless situation, it happened to coincide with my discovery of the biblical thread of caring for the fatherless. I could relate to Job a little in my care for my adopted child. My colleagues – sometimes my accusers, sometimes my comforters – made me question my life, my ministry and my motives. Unlike Job, I found a lot of faults and failings that I had to hold my hand up to. However, also unlike Job, I had the whole of the Bible to help me. I understood much more of the spiritual battle than he could see. I understood much more of the spiritual victory than he could know. I read Jesus' promise not to leave us as orphans,[8] but to give us the Holy Spirit. I began to learn that because of the Spirit of adoption, there is an antidote to fear, to hopelessness, to self-destructive thoughts. In suffering there is comfort, there is a Father to whom we can cry, there is a future, there is hope, there is glory.

Dr Tim Keller, in his reflection on Romans 8, puts it like this:

Our adoption means we are loved like Christ is loved. We are honoured like he is honoured – every one of us – no matter what. Your circumstances cannot hinder or threaten that promise. In fact, your bad circumstances will only help you understand and even claim the beauty of that promise. The more you live out who you are in

Christ, the more you become like him in actuality. Paul is not promising you better life circumstances; he is promising you a far better life. He's promising you a life of greatness. He is promising you a life of joy. He's promising you a life of humility. He's promising you a life of nobility. He's promising you a life that goes on forever.[9]

~

Questions for reflection

1. What are the ways you have had to suffer as a Christian? To what extent did you see your difficulties as sharing in Christ's suffering?

2. Think of all the ways that adoption and suffering go hand in hand. How could this give us hope, endurance, purpose and comfort?

3. Read again Job's defence in chapter 31 quoted above. How does the 'fear of [God's] splendour' compel you to live differently from those around you?

Chapter 10

The secret that changes everything about holiness

*Conforming to the family likeness –
and daring to be different.*

She is tall, I am short. She has big, beautiful, curly blonde hair. I have a diminishing amount of black hair. She has ancestry from one side of the globe, and I, well, it's complicated, but basically mine is from the opposite side of the globe. My adopted daughter has no biological connection with my ancestry. And yet strangers often remark how alike we are. It happened so often it got me wondering. What on earth were people seeing? I asked around a bit and this is what people told me. We both have eyes that sparkle. We both smile a lot. We are both energetic and bubbly. We both talk constantly. We love being out and about and meeting people. We remember faces. We love music. We relish joking around and winding up other members of the family. We can both eat crisps until they are coming out of our ears. The list went on. It turns out that even though there is little similarity physically, people nevertheless see a similarity because of behaviour and personality. Nurture has trumped nature.

This little insight helped me a lot when it came to understanding holiness – first, because becoming like God and like Jesus may be a slow-developing process of relational osmosis, however differently you start out. Second, because sometimes others can see this more in you than you can notice yourself. And third, because when adoption is involved the shared traits of family likeness can be both more surprising and more significant than we might imagine.

It was time to take a closer look at the Bible to see if viewing it through this lens of adoption could help me understand holiness better.

Be conformed

My starting point was the extraordinarily challenging verse in 1 Peter:

> *As obedient children, do not conform to the evil desires you had when you lived in ignorance. But just as he who called you is holy, so be holy in all you do; for it is written: 'Be holy, because I am holy.'*
>
> *(1 Peter 1:14–16)*

Peter clearly notes our status as God's children, and the link between nature and nurture, being and behaving. We are to *be* holy, and to *do* holy. Holiness is to mark who we are *and* what we do. But how does that work out in practice? What does it look like? My youth group leader always talked about holiness as things we did *not* do: excessive drinking, taking drugs, shoplifting, rock music, tattoos. It was sometimes hard to work out which of these were sins in the eyes of God and which were sins in the eyes of the youth leader. Peter, too, at first sight seems to present holiness in this negative way, telling us not to conform to the evil desires. It took me a while to understand this in the wider context of Peter's letter, where he describes other positive family traits that come from being like Jesus.

Peter's idea of holiness as a process of conforming brought me back to Romans 8, that great chapter that centres on the Spirit of adoption. Later in the chapter Paul writes this:

And we know that in all things God works for the good of those who love him, who have been called according to his purpose. For those God foreknew he also predestined to be conformed to the image of his Son, that he might be the firstborn among many brothers and sisters. And those he predestined, he also called; those he called, he also justified; those he justified, he also glorified.

(Romans 8:28–30)

God has a purpose for our lives. In all things, even in the mess and chaos, even with the abuse and violence and suffering we see around us, God is working something good out. This is not to say God is the author of evil (even in the book of Job, God does not directly cause the suffering to Job, but allows Satan some degree of influence over him). Rather, God can take the bad in our lives and in the world and somehow redemptively weave them into something good. Like a tattoo fixer who can design a new intricately designed tattoo using the lines of a bad one, God can turn ugly into beautiful, shameful into admirable, mistakes into masterpieces. In fact, the creativity and ingenuity of a tattoo fixer is best demonstrated by the more disastrous tattoos they have to try and rework. In the same way, when God makes all things work together for good, he takes the broken pieces of our lives, the tragedies of our story, the disasters of our history, and creates them into something more wonderful and incredible than we could imagine.

It is God's work to make us beautiful, good and holy. It is his purpose not just to brush us up a little, but to conform us to the image or likeness of Jesus. The Greek word for likeness, *eikon*, is the root of our word 'icon'. These days the word 'icon' usually conjures up in our minds the little images used to represent apps and computer programs. One click on the icon and the full program is launched. But this is a great illustration of our role in the world. We are to be God's icons,[1] representing him in the world so that people can look at us and see the likeness, the link to God himself. Jesus is the perfect icon of God in this respect. Not only that, Jesus is the perfect icon for us as the eldest brother among many sisters and brothers. Paul here is reminding us of the picture of adoption he painted earlier. The purpose of God from creation to new creation[2] is the formation of a new family through adoption. And now we find out that this new family is to resemble the Son of God, and that God is doing this holiness work in us.

One little boy who came into our family at the age of seven was physically stronger than me. He had been known to throw chairs through double-glazed windows. The teachers at school could not restrain him when he had a meltdown, even two or three staff together. We were not told this when we were asked to take him in, but we soon learned just how strong he was. The slightest anxiety would cause him to run into roads, slam his fist into walls and lash out at those who were trying to protect him. How was this placement ever going to work? How could he fit into family life when he was a danger to himself and others? It was no good telling him to behave, to conform, to change his ways. The damage that others had caused him over the years had created such an extreme fight-or-flight mentality that his panicked reactions had become ingrained. It was not his responsibility to manage that at the age of seven. It was mine. Because he was part of my family, I had to provide him, as best I could, with a calm environment, a predictable environment, a fun environment, a loving, safe home with clear and consistent boundaries and lots of lovely things to look forward to. My eldest sons became role-model foster brothers for him, channelling energy into sports and aggression into an Xbox controller. Gradually the triggers subsided and the reactions became less extreme. A transformation began.

What a powerful picture that is of God's work in us. We were out of control, damaged by the sinful environment that we grew up in. God knew we could not change by ourselves. So he stepped in to adopt us, to bring us home, to give us positive relationships, different expectations, a perfect role model. Gradually, because of God's work in our lives, we are conformed to the image of our elder brother, Jesus. There will be a family likeness. There will be transformation.

Be different

I once knew a boy who was adopted into a family that already had a child the same age as him. Before long, I noticed that the parents started dressing the adopted child like his brother, giving him the same haircut, the same school bags. Was this their way of treating them equally? Or was this their way of making sure he conformed to their idea of a son? I feared that his uniqueness was being squeezed out by controlling parents who had an idealised picture in their head of who their adopted son should be. Sometimes, when it comes to holiness, I worry that God may be like that too. Does he have an unrealistic picture of who we should be? Does he not accept us the way we are? Is he forcing me into a mould that I don't fit? Are we always going to be compared with the perfect older brother and be found wanting?

To find the answer to this, we need to work out what it means to be conformed to the image of Jesus. Jesus has many incredible attributes to which we are to aspire. He is compassionate, faithful, just, righteous, loving, gentle, strong, courageous and much, much more. He also has some attributes that we can never achieve. In the verses from Romans above, Paul makes this distinction by calling him the 'firstborn'. Of course he was not literally born – he is the eternal son of God. He is 'firstborn' in the sense that he has priority over us. He is the Word of God incarnate. He is the resurrected King before whom every knee will bow. He is omnipotent, omniscient, omnipresent. Because of our adoption we are somehow given the same intimacy and welcome that Jesus has to God the Father. But we are not, and never will be, the same as Jesus.

I have enjoyed watching the Netflix series *The Crown* as it tries to reconstruct what might have happened behind the closed doors of Buckingham Palace during the reign of Queen Elizabeth II. Sometimes it feels almost sacrilegious to wonder how the Queen fell in love and what it was like for her struggling to handle the pressure of national and familial crises. But, for me, one of the most interesting relationships is the one between the Queen and her sister, Princess Margaret. The two sisters are the same in so many ways, and yet one became queen and sovereign, while the other remained a princess and a subject, which brings all sorts of complications into their relationship. In a royal family your sister can be your queen; in the same way, in our spiritual family, as the adopted children of the King of the Universe, our older brother is also our Lord.

When we are adopted into God's family we can recognise that there are unique things about Jesus but there are also unique things about us, too. God has made each of us distinct and special, and at the end of time, he pictures beauty in the diversity that he sees. In the book of Revelation, we are told that all the nations will gather to sing praise to Jesus, as a great crowd made up of people from every tribe and language.[3] So even though we are conformed to the likeness of the Son, God relates to us individually; he gives us different gifts, skills, experiences, personalities, so that as a rich, diverse family we together reflect the wonders of the grace and glory of God. There is a family likeness, yet we are all still very different.

To be able to understand holiness we need to grasp both our common goal and our unique call. Yes, we are being conformed to the likeness of Jesus. But we will still be different from each other. And we are certainly different from the world. My daughter may resemble me, she may reflect something of me, but she is not me. I want my daughter to blend into my family well, to know she is one of us, but I also want her (just as I do my other children) to stand out, to find her niche, make her mark and be extraordinary. At school, while her friends and her teachers are often preaching conformation, I am daring her to be different. Different from the world. And different for God.

Be distinct

I remember waiting on the red carpet, loitering with intent. I had somehow managed to blag tickets for the world premiere of a film in London's Leicester Square. I had borrowed a tuxedo from a teenage member of our church and was as smart as I could make myself. We were supposed to go into the cinema ahead of the major celebrities and then patiently watch their arrival on the big screen. I had other plans. I wanted to meet the stars, to shake hands with the director. And because it was a royal premiere, perhaps catch a glimpse of the Queen herself, wearing 3D glasses for the first time. But the longer I waited and loitered, the more the security men with their dark glasses and earpieces made sure I kept well back. They were on a mission to make sure people like me didn't get near Her Majesty. And so I gave up. I obviously wasn't special enough, smart enough, famous enough to be anywhere near the Queen.

Some of us are like this when it comes to holiness. It seems like we have tickets to access God, but we end up just waiting around, too far away to get a close look, until eventually we give up even trying to enjoy being in the presence of our King. God is too difficult to access. He is holy. And we are not. Nothing we can do will ever bridge the immense gap between us.

The Old Testament reinforces this idea of separation. The Temple system separates off the Holy of Holies. It is strictly off limits except to a small number of very special people under very special ceremonial circumstances. And then God gave laws to help his people distinguish between the clean and the unclean, the holy and the common. Even the days of the week were separated, so that one day was set apart to be 'holy'.[4] But the New Testament seems to present a new way. The curtain around the Holy of Holies is ripped in two. Jesus walks around with no red carpet in sight. He spends his time with the lowest of the low. He blesses the children that nobody else wanted him to see, he heals the sick who had no hope even on the seventh day of the week, he hangs out with the sinners and tax collectors. It was no wonder the religious elites were outraged. If Jesus were the Messiah, God's holy servant, the undefiled High Priest, then why would he allow himself to be tainted by being in the presence of the undeserving? It was a scandal.[5] What Jesus surely needed was some security men with dark glasses and earpieces to keep the riff-raff away.

The Bible presents us with this conundrum regarding holiness. On the one hand, holiness demands separation. But on the other hand, holiness also demands hospitality. The Pharisees could not resolve the paradox. Even today Christians tend to polarise towards one camp or the other. But true holiness is embracing both tenets. It is hating the sin and loving the sinner. It is truth and grace. It is a pure heart and an open spirit. For Jesus, holiness was never compromised. He did not distance himself, but drew near. He embraced the prodigals and forgave the profligate, offered grace to the prostitutes and touched the lepers. He lived a perfect life and then he died the perfect death so that the stain of sin could be removed and we could freely access the Holy of Holies.

Unfortunately, many of us compromise holiness on both counts. Instead of hating the sin in our lives, we choose just to dislike it, to avoid it if we have to, to excuse it when we can, to learn to live with it. And instead of loving the sinner, we prefer to socialise with the acceptable, the religious, the fit and healthy.

The Spirit of adoption challenges us. God chose us to be welcomed into his family even when we were unacceptable, sacrilegious, sick, broken. We who were far away have been brought near.[6] We who were unclean and contaminated have not just been cleansed, we have been welcomed into the family of God, redeemed, restored, forgiven, purified and adopted. We have received radical hospitality from the most holy God who is committed to conforming us to the likeness of Christ, and to celebrating our uniqueness and diversity. Now that we are different, distinct and set apart for God's purposes, will we mirror that Spirit of adoption in our lives, compelled by the Holy Spirit to seek out the needy, the lost, the sinful, the broken and the displaced? Just like Jesus did.

But isn't that dangerous? Won't that just bring trouble and hardship into our lives? Won't we be accused of compromising our faith? Won't that cause us to suffer and tempt us to sin? Won't we wind up losing our access to God? The rest of Romans 8 addresses these questions. The answers are yes, yes, yes, yes, and definitively no. Paul concludes:

For I am convinced that neither death nor life, neither angels nor demons, neither the present nor the future, nor any powers, neither height nor depth, nor anything else in all creation, will be able to separate us from the love of God that is in Christ Jesus our Lord.

(Romans 8:38–9)

When I adopted my daughter I asked the social worker questions. Can this be undone? Could a birth relative turn up and claim rights over her? Is there a legal loophole that I need to be aware of? What if my circumstances changed? What if I moved to a different country? I was told definitively no, an adoption order cannot be revoked. Nothing can separate us legally as father and daughter. It is an irreversible decision. For those of us worried that our connection to God seems flimsy and fragile or temporary and insecure, that our faith wavers with our circumstances, that it fades with distance, or that it will fail under pressure, God wants us to know that our adoption is absolute. God calls us to be separate from the world, but the world cannot separate us from his love. He calls us to be the best we can be, while accepting us just the way we are. He is conforming us to the likeness of Jesus, and is conferring on us equal rights, even though we would never be holy and blameless without his grace. We cannot separate holiness from hospitality when it comes to the way God has accepted and adopted us. Perhaps holiness and hospitality should always go together in our lives too.

Questions for reflection

1. In what ways do you resemble your earthly family? In what ways do you resemble your heavenly family?

2. Reflect on the theme of separation in the Bible. You can find it in Genesis 1, Leviticus 20:22–6, Isaiah 59, Matthew 25, Romans 8. How does this theme point towards the holiness of God?

3. Why was Jesus criticised for his hospitality? How can our hospitality demonstrate the holiness of God?

Epilogue

A letter

To my dear daughter,

I remember the moment you first arrived. A tiny, beautiful, sleepy newborn baby placed in my arms, while your brothers and sister danced around the room, pausing only occasionally to creep close and gaze into your eyes. I laid you in the Moses basket, remembering that Moses was the first fostered child and first adopted child in the Bible and, with God's help, went on to change the world. I knew you were our first fostered child, but I did not know then that you would be our first adopted child too. I knew I had changed your world, but I did not know then that you would change my world too.

There were lots of things I did not know. I did not know your future. I did not know your history. But I did know that the nine months of assessments, of waiting, had all been worth it. There was mystery, and there was you, real and helpless, tiny and momentous. I was in no doubt that you were absolutely precious, perfectly unique and already deeply treasured. I wondered how it was possible to feel so fiercely protective over someone with no biological connection to myself, someone I had only just met. Well, you brought joy and wonder into our family from the moment you arrived, and you still do today.

As your little personality grew and developed and got stronger despite the legal wrestling in the background, I faced problems of my own. They were such heavy burdens, I thought I might collapse under the weight of them. Your smile, and the way your brothers and sisters elicited it, kept me going hour by hour. And when the moment came that we finally legally adopted you, I realised things would never be the same again. The celebration at the ice-cream parlour gave me a taste of what heaven will be like – the joy of becoming a forever family after so many obstacles and difficulties.

I had thought that by adopting you I was rescuing you, providing you with a home and a hope for the future, passing on to you all the wisdom I had gleaned in life. But it wasn't long before I realised that you were teaching me, helping me, showing me more profound truths than I had learned in any Bible college. In the midst of chaos and despair, there can be hope. Despite trouble and hardship, there can be resilience. If I could care for you so deeply and fight for you so determinedly, then God, whose love is infinite, must feel even more passionately about you – and about me. He is our Father.

It has been one of my life's ambitions to be the best dad I can be to you. I want my fatherhood to point you to your heavenly Father. I know I get it wrong a lot. I often miscommunicate, misunderstand, and I make many mistakes. Maybe this, too, points to God – you and I together need a Father who is perfect in all of his ways. He is there when I fail. He can turn all things to good.

You make mistakes sometimes too. You get frustrated and angry with yourself, and with me. You dislike yourself occasionally and think you don't deserve my love, or God's. It breaks my heart – not because I am disappointed in you, but because I am desperate for you to know that, in God's eyes and in mine, you are perfect. You have been fearfully and wonderfully made and God doesn't make mistakes. When things go wrong, my love for you doesn't stop. Even my discipline is an expression of my protective love for you. I'm not trying to make you the same as your brothers and sisters, I am trying to help you become the unique you God made you to be.

One of my biggest fears is that you will misinterpret my love. That when I am angry with something you have done, you may imagine I am angry with you. That you might see my hopes for you as expectations, my care for you as duty, my discipline of you as dissatisfaction with you. I imagine that you might imagine that I stole you from your birth family, adopted you for my own ends, and that now I resent being stuck with you. Nothing is further from the truth. Whatever you feel, I can assure you my love for you is real, unconditional and everlasting. Not perfect, but as close as I can get.

There is a story in the Bible that plays on my fears. It's one I have told you many times. It's about a father whose son walks away from the family. He turns his back on the ones who have cared for him his whole life, with no intention of ever seeing them again. He thinks he would be better off without them, and gets as far away as he can go. Jesus said that that father was like God. If a child can walk away from a perfect father, then I sometimes wonder what hope *I* have – what right do I have to hold on to you?

I have never met a teenager who doesn't go through questions about their identity. I have never met a teenager who doesn't struggle a bit with their relationship with their parents. It is natural for young adults to dream about leaving home. But for adopted children, sometimes those years can have an extra dimension of complexity. Perhaps they think the grass could be greener somewhere else. Perhaps they believe the films that romanticise a renewed acquaintance with the birth family. One day you will leave home, and I hope it will be something we plan together and enjoy together. I really hope so. It could be a lot of fun. You have so much to offer the world, and I would love to be a part of it. But maybe it won't happen quite like that.

The boy in the story takes his share of the inheritance prematurely and leaves home on his own terms, breaking the heart of his father. Because he has money to spend, he also has lots of friends and, for a while, life is good. But when the money runs out, his friends run out too. He tries to get work, but the only job he can get is the one nobody else wants to stoop to. He is in a bad place. That's when he realises that home, for all its frustrations, was not so bad after all. He rehearses an apology and heads back to ask for a lifeline – it's his only hope.

You know what happens next. The story zooms in to the father, waiting and waiting for his child to come back. Everyone tells him not to bother. The child wouldn't dare come back. He is probably dead. But the father waits anyway. And one day he sees someone coming down the road towards him. It looks remarkably like the boy he last saw walking in the opposite direction. The pace is slower, the mood is more solemn, but he would recognise that gait anywhere – he was the one who had taught the boy to walk in the first place. And just like that time when, as a baby, his son had taken his first steps, the father opens out his arms in encouragement and welcome and embrace. It is a momentous occasion.

In that embrace is one of the most amazing pictures of God's love for us. The lad is filthy, covered in dust, mud and unmentionably worse, but the father embraces him anyway. The lad says something about not deserving anything – and he doesn't – but the father embraces him anyway. The boy doesn't even have to mention the obvious thing – that all the money is gone – the father continues to embrace him anyway. The neighbours laugh at the indignity, and the older brother is indignant, but the father embraces the boy anyway. He gives him new clothes and prepares a celebration feast. His son, who had, by claiming his inheritance prematurely, permanently and officially removed himself from the family, is now, as signalled by the ring on his finger, officially adopted back into the family, fully reinstated as a son.

I love this story. You might think that I, as your dad, relate mainly to the adopting father. But to be honest, I relate more closely to the adopted child. I spent many years turning my back on God, living for myself, doing what my 'friends' told me to do, pursuing my destiny on my terms. I did not deserve God's welcome home. I did not expect his embrace, or his joy on my return. But there he was, ready and waiting to adopt me back into the family. You remind me of that arms-outstretched, joyful adoption moment. I hope you have felt it from me too.

This book is written for you. I could have filled

many more pages with all you have taught me about what it means to be an adopted child of God. I dearly hope that the words written here reflect to you not only the wonderful mystery of belonging to God's family, but something of my incredible love for you. I hope all my readers find delight and challenge and fresh insights and renewed grace and strength from grasping the miracle of their adoption, but I especially pray that you, with your backstage pass to the story behind the book, will recognise yourself on the pages, and see that you – just by being the wonderful you that you are – are making your indelible mark on the world.

Here's to the ongoing adoption adventure!

Your dad

Endnotes

Chapter One

1 See *The Lego Batman Movie*, Warner Bros., directed by Chris McKay, 2017.

2 Romans 8:1.

3 Romans 8:39.

4 Romans 8:28.

5 T.J. Burke, *Adopted into God's Family: Exploring Pauline Metaphor* (InterVarsity Press, 2006), p. 62. Octavian Augustus (27BC – AD14); Tiberius (AD14–37), Gaius Caligula (AD 37–41), Claudius (AD41–54) and Nero (AD54–68). '[A]doption was a means by which succession to power was brought about . . . successive Roman emperors adopted men not related to them by blood with the intention that the adoptee should succeed the emperor in the principate.'

Chapter Two

1 C. Hamilton, *Growth Fetish* (Allen & Unwin, 2003).

2 See J. Haidt, *The Coddling of the American Mind: How Good Intentions and Bad Ideas Are Setting Up a Generation for Failure* (Penguin, 2018).

3 Revelation 21:26 speaks about the glory of the nations being brought into the New Jerusalem, and the prophecy is full of references to every language being used to praise Christ.

4 See K. Kandiah, *God is Stranger* (Hodder & Stoughton, 2017).

5 F.F. Bruce, *Romans: An Introduction and Commentary*, vol. 6 (1985), p. 161. Biblical scholar F.F. Bruce explains that the word for condemnation is *katakrima*, and it carries the meaning of 'the punishment following sentence', or, in other words, penal servitude.

6 J.I. Packer, *Knowing God* (Hodder and Stoughton, 2005), pp. 206–7.

7 *The Princess Diaries*, (2001) Directed by Gary Marshall

8 Dietrich Bonhoeffer, *Letters and Papers from Prison* (Fontana, 1959), p. 173.

Chapter Three

1 Philip Melanchthon, 1531.

2 John 13:34–5.

3 Galatians 6:2.

4 Hebrews 10:25.

5 Hebrews 10:24.

6 John 19:26–8.

7 Matthew 15:3–4.

8 1 Timothy 5:1–2.

9 Romans 16:1,13.

Chapter Four

1 See M.D.S. Ainsworth & J. Bowlby, 'An Ethological Approach to Personality Development', *American Psychologist*, 46, 1991, pp. 331–41. https://fosteringandadoption.rip.org.uk/topics/attachment-theory-research, accessed June 2019.

2 See http://www.mbird.com/2016/10/attach-ment-theory-and-your-relationship-with-god, accessed June 2019.

3 Matthew 6:5–6.

4 Romans 8:15.

5 Galatians 4:6.

6 J. Jeremias, 'The Key to Pauline Theology' (1964), p. 18, quoted in D. Bosch, *Witness to the World: The Christian Mission in Theological Perspective* (John Knox Press, 1980), p. 9.

7 See Matthew 6:7.

8 See Matthew 6:5.

Chapter Five

1 See C. Wright, *The Mission of God: Unlocking the Bible's Grand Narrative* (InterVarsity Press, 2007).

2 See K. Kandiah, *Destiny: What's Life All About?*

187

(Monarch, 2006); and also L. Newbigin, *Sin and Salvation* (SPCK, 1954).

3 Numbers 14:34 provides another perspective that the desert wandering was also punishment for their rebellion.

4 See A. Crouch, *Culture Making: Recovering Our Creative Calling* (InterVarsity Press, 2008).

5 Genesis 1:28.

6 Crouch, *Culture Making*, p. 23, citing cultural commentator Ken Myers.

7 For more information, visit www.homeforgood.org.uk

Chapter 6

1 M. Saunders (2017) 'There's a Single Christian Theme Running through Modern Cinema. Is God Speaking through Hollywood?' https://www.christiantoday.com/article/theres-a-single-christian-theme-running-through-modern-cinema-is-god-speaking-through-holly-wood/104819.htm, accessed June 2019.

2 Genesis 1:26.

3 Psalm 110:1.

4 *Huiothesia* is the Greek term for adoption that Paul uses regularly in the New Testament. 'There are no biblical laws in the Old Testament governing the practice of huiothesia' (Burke, *Adopted into God's Family*, p. 47).

5 See Kandiah, *God is Stranger*, pp. 115–41.

6 See K. Kandiah, *Home for Good: Making a Difference for Vulnerable Children* (revised edition) (Hodder & Stoughton, 2019).

7 Eugene H. Peterson, *The Message: The Bible in Contemporary Language* (NavPress, 2002).

8 E. Peterson, *Eat This Book* (Hodder & Stoughton, 2006), p. 18.

9 Fifty per cent of male prisoners under 25 years old have experience of being in care (National Audit Office, 'Care Leavers' Transition to Adulthood', 2015, p. 5).

10 Luke 10, John 16.

11 Matthew 25.

Chapter 7

1 Luke 11:42, 46.

2 Luke 5:17–26.

3 Matthew 14:13–21.

4 Matthew 25:31–46.

5 James 1:27.

6 'The other NT references are in Acts 26:5, which employs it of Jewish worship and practice, and Col 2:18, where it is said to characterize a veneration devoted to or practiced by angels in the Colossian philosophy' (R.P. Martin, *Word Biblical Commentary*, Vol. 48 on James (Thomas Nelson, 1988), p. 52.

7 'Her priests do violence to my law and profane my holy things; they do not distinguish between the holy and the common; they teach that there is no difference between the unclean and the clean; and they shut their eyes to the keeping of my Sabbaths, so that I am profaned among them' (Ezekiel 22:26).

Chapter 8

1 Anne Longfield, the UK's Children's Commissioner, https://www.bbc.co.uk/news/education-44289645, accessed June 2019.

2 Sadly there are still those who make some unhelpful and dualistic assumptions about the gospel: see 'The Statement on Social Justice & the Gospel' by John MacArthur et al. https://statementonsocialjustice.com, accessed June 2019.

3 D. Bosch, *Witness to the World: The Christian Mission in Theological Perspective* (John Knox Press, 1980).

4 J.B. Payne, 'Justice'. In D.R.W. Wood, I.H. Marshall, A.R. Millard, J.I. Packer & D.J. Wiseman (Eds), *New Bible Dictionary* (3rd ed.) (InterVarsity Press, 1996), p. 634.

5 S.B. Ferguson & J.I. Packer, 'Justice'. In *New Dictionary of Theology* (electronic ed.) (InterVarsity Press, 2000), p. 359.

6 Quoted from HTB Leadership Conference 2018,

but see also B. Stevenson *Just Mercy: A Story of Justice and Redemption* (Scribe, 2015).

7 Matthew 6:33.

Chapter 9

1 D. Bonhoeffer, *The Cost of Discipleship* (SCM, 1996; German original 1937), p. 79.

2 Job 1–2 and 42.

3 Job 1:11.

4 Facebook post, 29/11/18 (used with permission).

5 F.I. Andersen, *Job: An Introduction and Commentary*, vol. 14 (InterVarsity Press, 1959), p. 262.

6 2 Timothy 3:12.

7 Job 31:16–23.

8 John 14:18.

9 T. Keller, 'The Christian's Happiness' https://www.monergism.com/christian's-happiness-romans-828-30.

Chapter 10

1 For more on this theme, see S. McKnight, *The Jesus Creed: Loving God, Loving Others* (Paraclete Press, 2009).

2 Romans 8: 22–4.

3 Revelation 7:9–10.

4 Exodus 20:8.

5 Luke 15:1–2.

6 Ephesians 2:13.